FEMINIST
PERSPECTIVES
ON
WIFE ABUSE

OTHER RECENT VOLUMES IN THE
SAGE FOCUS EDITIONS

FEMINIST PERSPECTIVES ON WIFE ABUSE

Edited by
Kersti Yllö
Michele Bograd

SAGE PUBLICATIONS
The International Professional Publishers
Newbury Park   London   New Delhi

For information address:

SAGE Publications, Inc.
2455 Teller Road
Newbury Park, California 91320

SAGE Publications Ltd.
6 Bonhill Street
London EC2A 4PU
United Kingdom

SAGE Publications India Pvt. Ltd.
M-32 Market
Greater Kailash I
New Delhi 110 048 India

Printed in the United States of America

Library of Congress Cataloging-in-Publication Data
Main entry under title:

Feminist perspectives on wife abuse / edited by Kersti Ylló and
   Michele Bograd.
         p.   cm.
      Bibliography: p.
      ISBN 0-8039-3052-6   ISBN 0-8039-3053-4 (pbk.)
      1. Wife abuse. 2. Feminism. I. Yllo, Kersti. II. Bograd,
   Michele Louise, 1952-
   HV6626.F46 1988   87-18762
   362.8'2--dc19   CIP

92 93 94 10 9 8 7 6

Contents

Foreword

It has been just over a decade since the publication of Del Martin's *Battered Wives* (1976)—the first feminist book on wife abuse to be published in this country. *Feminist Perspectives on Wife Abuse* shows the considerable progress that has been made in feminist research and thinking in the intervening years. When feminists write chapters in nonfeminist books or articles for nonfeminist journals, we often have to tone down our language and analysis. In his personal note in this volume on publishing feminist research, Lee Bowker carefully substantiates his conclusion that explicitly feminist articles on wife abuse are much more likely to be rejected than nonfeminist articles. I have often suspected as much, but never thought I'd see it so cleverly documented. It is thrilling to be able to read so many excellent and overtly feminist pieces between the covers of one book.

There are some excellent articles on feminist methodology in Kersti Yllö and Michele Bograd's anthology, and I am happy to see that they have gone beyond the oversimplistic but commonly held view of a few years ago that quantitative research is by definition nonfeminist. There are also several thoughtful discussions on the impossibility of doing research that is free of bias or value judgement. It is ironic that feminists are among the first to acknowledge this, and yet our commitment to try to do nonsexist research and theorizing surely causes us to be less biased than nonfeminist social scientists. Ignoring the relevance of gender, which nonfeminist social scientists do, can lead to distorted or downright erroneous theories and analyses. For example, the oft stated view that battered children become spouse batterers in adulthood ignores the fact that few women batter their husbands. Yet feminists are the ones who are usually considered biased while most nonfeminist social scientists continue to think of themselves as unbiased and objective.

One of the most noteworthy events in the short history of our movement against wife abuse is the emergence in 1980 of a sudden preoccupation with battered husbands. Several authors in *Feminist Perspectives on Wife Abuse* address this phenomenon and its source. Kersti Yllö, Daniel Saunders, and Rebecca and Russell Dobash are among the contributors who critique the methodology and conclusions of Murray Straus, Richard Gelles, and Suzanne Steinmetz in *Behind Closed Doors* (1980), and deservedly so. In their national survey of U.S. families, Straus and his colleagues applied a measure of violence (the Conflict Tactics Scale) that resulted in their finding that severe husband abuse is a more prevalent problem than severe wife abuse. Since this finding contradicts all previous research, clinical experience, and gender sensitive theories of violence, one would expect these researchers to question the validity of their scale (for example, that it doesn't distinguish between offensive and defensive violence). However, despite ten years of debate and criticism, Straus and Gelles once again applied their Conflict Tactics Scale in a new survey and reported the same conclusions.Their refusal to listen and learn from the dialogue is distressing, since in many ways they have been pioneers in the field of wife abuse research.

It becomes clear that just as the problem of battered wives cannot be eradicated as long as men have the power in the family and in society, so the problem of patriarchal research on "family violence" will not easily be transformed by feminist critiques. We should not be surprised that it is feminists whose views are considered distorted, not the mainstream researchers. This is not to say that we should stop what we are doing any more than that battered women should give up their struggle to be free of violence. But we do need to confront our predicament. This volume represents an important effort to do so by bringing feminist research to the mainstream.

Anthologies seem to have gotten a bad name in the publishing world. This anthology shows how good they can be. It would be very unusual for one or two authors to be able to offer the variety in research projects and stimulating changes in focus evident in *Feminist Perspectives on Wife Abuse*. Several of the authors report on provocative new research, and the overall quality of the articles is impressive. It is also a treat to read a number of contributions from men who identify as feminist researchers.

This anthology shows the utility of a femnist theoretical framework for research on wife abuse. I believe we'd be much further along in our understanding of this problem and what to do about it if all research on wife abuse was informed by a feminist perspective. Meanwhile this collection on *Feminist Perspectives on Wife Abuse* certainly takes us several significant steps forward.

—Diana E. H. Russell
Author of
RAPE IN MARRIAGE (1982)

Acknowledgments

It is gratifying to us that this volume is part of a growing collaboration between feminist researchers and feminist activists. A central goal of this book is to make clear the inextricable link between research, politics, and activism; what we do as researchers has broad consequences for which we must be consciously responsible. Our hope is that this volume is one step in the effort to create a united feminist response to violence against women.

We would like to thank Wheaton College, Norton, Massachusetts, for institutional support for this project. We are especially indebted to Nancy Shepardson who was responsible for the word processing and organizing of the innumerable drafts of chapters. Also, we appreciate the efforts of Diane Rowe of the Wheaton Computer Center and Susan Mansfield, research assistant. And finally, thanks to Rick Schwertner for editorial and moral support.

* * * *

This volume is dedicated to the women and men who are putting feminism into practice in the struggle against violence against women.

Feminist Perspectives on Wife Abuse

An Introduction

MICHELE BOGRAD

Wife abuse is part of contemporary family life. This sentence doesn't surprise anyone anymore, but 15 years ago the physical abuse of wives was a hidden phenomenon. Starting at the grass roots level, feminists named its existence with terms such as *battering* and *marital rape* and began to put into place an underground network of shelters and safe houses for women and children. Only then did significant numbers of mental health professionals, social science researchers, police, judges, and policy makers begin to notice and to seriously address the widespread incidence of wife abuse. Since that time, there has been a virtual explosion of information on wife abuse. Newspapers, magazines, and television programs cover the stories of many women, and social science researchers have collected a great deal of empirical data on many dimensions of violence in families. Yet basic differences exist between the variety of people who are dedicated to understanding and stopping woman abuse, depending on whether they identify themselves as feminists or not.

In 1984, the University of New Hampshire sponsored the Second National Conference for Family Violence Researchers. The majority of participants were academicians. Although one or two workshops focused on feminist methodology or feminist approaches to family violence, most presentations did not address feminist issues. A small groups of activists, some of whom were also researchers, organized themselves in order to provide a feminist perspective on family violence at almost every presentation. The resulting dialogue was intense, often heated, and productive. Out of this context, as women voiced interest in developing a forum for the dissemination of ideas that spoke to the tensions that arise as we attempt to integrate political and social scientific concerns, this book was born.

This volume is the first of its kind to bring together academicians and activists from a variety of disciplines who share an explicit commitment to feminist theories and practices. All of us have a special investment in ending wife abuse, although we are also aware that men use a wide variety of physical and nonphysical means of coercively controlling women. To set the stage for this volume, this introduction will first discuss why we focus primarily on wife abuse, in spite of the current trend to study battering as a form of "family violence." The dimensions common to a variety of feminist perspectives will be outlined and clarified through brief critical analysis of mainstream approaches to wife abuse. But feminist perspectives do not have simply theoretical ramifications, they pose complicated and difficult questions about the very process of research, which will also be discussed. Lastly, feminists are committed to social action. Balancing the competing and sometimes conflicting demands of research, academic inquiry, and political activism is a difficult but promising and necessary task.

Why Focus Only on Wife Abuse?

Wife abuse is defined in this volume as the use of physical force by a man against his intimate cohabiting partner. This force can range from pushes and slaps to coerced sex to assaults with deadly weapons. Although many women suffer psychological abuse (such as humiliation and verbal degradation) from their partners, we focus primarily on physical abuse. Violence may qualitatively change the nature of intimate relationships, even if they were characterized previously by the presence of severe psychological abuse. Violence threatens the physical safety and bodily integrity of the woman, and intensifies and changes the meanings of threats and humiliation. Although many women are physically or sexually abused by strangers, we examine violence within intimate relationships. As feminists, we believe that the social institutions of marriage and family are special contexts that may promote, maintain, and even support men's use of physical force against women. For ease of exposition, the term "wife abuse" will be used throughout the volume, although the intimate partners may not be legally married.

Commonly, wife abuse is subsumed under the rubrics of "family violence" or "spouse abuse." These terms collapse the distinctions between husband-to-wife violence, wife-to-husband violence, incest, child abuse, and elder abuse. Feminists argue that such terms obscure the dimensions of gender and power that are fundamental to understanding wife abuse (Breines & Gordon, 1983; McGrath, 1979; Schechter, 1982). Generic terms ignore the context of the violence, its nature, and consequences, the role obligations of each family member and the different mechanisms or transactional sequences that lead to various forms of abuse. When general "neutral" terms mask the dimension of gender, they can lead to biases in how the causes and solutions of wife abuse are conceptualized and treated. For these reasons, this volume presents a variety of feminist perspectives primarily on wife abuse.

What Are Feminist
Perspectives on Wife Abuse?

Given the wide variety of feminist philosophies, there is no unified feminist perspective on wife abuse. But all feminist researchers, clinicians, and activists address a primary question: "Why do men beat their wives?" This specific question directs attention to the physical violence occurring in heterosexual relationships that are structured in certain ways within the institution of marriage or partnership as it is currently culturally defined and socially sustained on material and ideological levels. This approach distinguishes feminists from others who ask: "What psychopathology leads to violence?" or "Why are people involved in violent interactions in families?" or "How is violence in the family related to our violent society?" Furthermore, feminists seek answers to their question at the social or group level. Instead of examining why this particular man beats his particular wife, feminists seek to understand why men in general use physical force against their partners and what functions this serves for a given society in a specific historical context (Chapman & Gates, 1978; Dobash & Dobash, 1979; Martin, 1976; Pagelow, 1981; Russell, 1982; Schechter, 1982; Walker, 1979, 1984).

Four major dimensions are common to all feminist perspectives on wife abuse: (1) the explanatory utility of the constructs of gender and power; (2) the analysis of the family as a historically situated social institution; (3) the crucial importance of understanding and validating women's experiences; (4) employing scholarship *for* women.

Gender and Power

When a husband uses violence against his wife, people often view this as a random, irrational act. In contrast, feminists define wife abuse as a pattern that becomes understandable only through examination of the social context. Our society is structured along the dimension of gender: Men as a class wield power over women. As the dominant class, men have differential access to important material and symbolic resources, while women are devalued as secondary and inferior. Although important social class and race differences exist among men, all men can potentially use violence as a powerful means of subordinating women. Although there are many ways that men as a group maintain women in oppressed social positions, violence is the most overt and effective means of social control. Even if individual men refrain from employing physical force against their partners, men as a class benefit from how women's lives are restricted and limited because of their fear of violence by husbands and lovers as well as by strangers. Wife abuse or battering reinforces women's passivity and dependence as men exert their rights to authority and control. The reality of domination at the social level is the most crucial factor contributing to and maintaining wife abuse at the personal level.

The Family as a Social Institution

The family as a social institution mediates between oppression at the broadest social level and the personal relationships of intimate adult partners. But the family is not a monolithic universal entity. Its functions, structures, and processes must be examined in their current sociohistorical context. Feminists challenge the cultural ideal of the family as a "peaceful haven in a heartless world." Wife abuse is not viewed as a rare and deviant phenomenon that results from the breakdown of family functioning, but as a predictable and common dimension of normal family life as it is currently structured in our society. Feminist theoreticians have cogently argued that wife abuse is closely related to the historical development of the isolated nuclear family in a capitalist society, to division of the public and private/ domestic domains, to specialization of "appropriate" male and female family roles, and to the current position of wives as legally and morally bound to husbands (Breines & Gordon, 1983; Dobash & Dobash, 1979; Martin, 1976; Schechter, 1982). This is not to deny that wife abuse has existed across the centuries in societies of varying political persuasions and structures. But wife abuse cannot be examined out of its particular sociohistorical context, which shapes its dynamics, its social acceptability, and its meaning. Furthermore, as feminists link wife abuse to the structure of current family life, they draw theoretical and empirical links between the personal and the political, which leads to new understandings of battering: Wife abuse is not a private matter but a social one.

Validating Women's Experience

Feminists take as a given that male domination influences everything from brief interpersonal exchanges to the most abstract theories of human nature. Ideology and knowledge are shaped by the interests of the dominant class (Jagger & Struh, 1978; Spender, 1980). When men's lives, values, and attitudes are taken as the norm, the experiences of women are often defined as inferior, distorted, or are rendered invisible. To counteract this, feminists believe that a basic step toward understanding the factors contributing to wife abuse is illuminating the experiences of women from their own frames of reference. Feminists critically analyze current lay and academic theories about wife abuse for biases against women. We are especially concerned with the numerous ways that women are blamed or implicated for the violence. In contrast to dominant views of battered women as helpless victims or as provocative women who ask for the abuse, feminists approach battered women as survivors of harrowing, life-threatening experiences, who have many adaptive capacities and strengths. From this perspective, feminists examine how current theories and interventions may revictimize battered women. Furthermore, biases in theories and practices are linked to systematic patterned beliefs that reflect male-constructed understandings of women, abuse, and intimate relationships.

Scholarship for Women

Because of these concerns, feminist scholarship is not simply about women. Instead, it is dedicated to advocacy *for* women. The goal of research is not merely to incorporate women into preexisting theories but to develop theories and models that more accurately reflect women's experiences. As such, it is woman centered and provides a balance to the majority of theoretical frameworks that exclude or devalue women. This explicit goal is not an end in and of itself, since it is currently reparative. Ultimately, feminist approaches to wife abuse will necessitate the transformation of existing explanatory frameworks to encompass both male and female defined paradigms of human behavior (Eichler, 1983).

Social Scientists and the
Empirical Study of Woman Abuse

Since the recent consciousness raising about wife abuse, most social scientists engaged in the study of woman abuse are explicitly antisexist and dedicated to ending wife battering. How then are we to understand the ongoing debates between feminist and nonfeminist academicians, researchers, clinicians, and activists? We will begin to answer this question here through a brief discussion of popular psychological and sociological explanatory theories about wife abuse, most of which lack a political or feminist perspective. This discussion will highlight major theories, rather than provide a comprehensive review of the literature (for this, see Breines & Gordon, 1983; Dobash & Dobash, 1979; Schechter, 1982). The major conceptual and methodological debates between feminist and nonfeminist researchers and activists are addressed in greater detail in the following chapters.

Psychological Approaches
to Wife Abuse

Psychologists seek to understand wife abuse through examination of characteristics of individual men and women (see, for example, Roy, 1977). Psychodynamic researchers focus on personality traits, internal defense systems, and the presence of mental illness or psychopathology. For example, abusive men have been labeled *passive-dependent, infantile,* or as *lacking impulse control,* while battered women have been defined as *masochistic, paranoid, or depressed.* Social learning theorists study other factors, such as the presence of violence in individuals' families of origin or how battered women presumably learn to be helpless when they perceive lack of control over their environment. Yet, the search for psychological causal factors or distinct personality configurations associated with wife abuse has not proven very useful. Not all abusive men evidence psychopathology and those who do reveal no consistent psychological patterns, while women of all sorts may become victims of their husbands' abuse.

Feminists have offered many cogent criticisms of current psychological approaches to wife abuse (see, for example, Bograd, 1984, 1986; Dobash & Dobash, 1979; Schechter, 1982; Walker, 1979, 1984). The focus on psychopathology suggests that wife abuse results from abnormal behavior. However, the widespread prevalence of wife abuse suggests that it may be more a function of the normal psychological and behavioral patterns of most men than of the aberrant actions of very few husbands. Psychological explanations also can be differentially applied to men and women. In general, trait theories tend to excuse the abusive man through reference to alcohol abuse or poor childhood histories. In contrast, battered women are implicated for their abuse, since many psychological theories suggest they need or tolerate the abuse. Feminists have argued that it is an error to compare battered women to nonbattered women on a variety of psychological variables. The search for differences between these two groups of women rests (usually implicitly) on the assumption that revealed differences are the reasons for the abuse (Wardell, Gillespie, & Leffler, 1983). Most importantly, through a focus on mental illness alone, most psychological theories ignore the question of power. They cannot answer the question of why allegedly mentally ill men beat their wives and not their bosses, nor why impulse ridden, out of control husbands contain their rage until they are in the privacy of their homes, at which time they bruise their wives but less frequently kill them.

Feminist theoreticians do not deny that some wife abuse may be linked to psychopathology in either partner, nor do they dismiss the validity or importance of psychological theories. Instead, we seek to connect our psychological analyses with understandings of the patriarchal social context, of the unequal distribution of power, and of the socially structured and culturally maintained patterns of male/female relations. In this volume, David Adams analyzes sexist biases that exist in popular psychological approaches to why men batter, and offers an alternative feminist perspective that blends psychological, sociological, and political insights. Feminist psychologists also reframe and relabel constellations of emotions and behaviors typical of battered women. Instead of viewing them as preexisting contributing factors to the abuse, they are examined as the consequences of repeated brutalization and potentially life-threatening violence. Rather than drawing on traditional personality theories, feminist theoreticians have begun to make links between the experiences of battered women and other victims of terrorism (Russell, 1982). Dee Graham, Edna Rawlings, and Nelly Rimini's chapter draws on recently developed theories of psychological reactions of hostages to suggest new ways of understanding the typical patterned responses of many battered women. Such feminist perspectives normalize and depathologize the often extreme strategies evidenced by battered women as they struggle to survive and make sense of their victimization by their husbands. As part of this effort, feminist psychologists also carefully examine and reinterpret differences revealed between battered women and presumably nonbattered women on standard psychological tests. In her chapter, Lynne Bravo Rosewater discusses psychological profiles of battered women as measured by a popular psychological instrument, but radically redefines their significance by challenging conventional interpretative frameworks based on models of female psychopathology.

Sociological Approaches
to Wife Abuse

The sheer prevalence of wife abuse as well as the patterned variation in rates among different social groups raises questions about efforts to identify psychological factors as primary causes of battering. Sociologists are not concerned with individual psychopathology or personality traits, but rather assume that social structural factors lead to wife abuse (Finkelhor, Gelles, Hotaling, & Straus, 1983; Gelles, 1979; Russell, 1982; Straus, Gelles, & Steinmetz, 1980; Straus & Hotaling, 1980). The social structure contains two analytically distinct elements: (1) social organization, or the patterns of relationships among groups, and (2) culture, or the norms and values guiding behavior.

Some sociologists focus on empirically observable behavioral regularities or rates of wife abuse and their association with relatively stable, enduring, supraindividual dimensions of society such as class, education, race, and religion. These sociologists generally assume that particular structural arrangements within families produce stress and conflict, that the family system responds to the dynamics and conditions of the larger society, and that, mediated through socialization and learning, violence is one response to structural and situational stimuli. Other sociologists place more causal emphasis on the domain of social meanings—norms and values that specify who can hit whom, how hard, and under what circumstances. These sociologists have linked wife abuse to social norms and cultural values that legitimize the sexist structure of male/female power relations and men's prerogative to use force against their wives. But although many sociologists give credence to some of the variables important to feminist analyses, philosophical differences distinguish mainstream researchers and clinicians from feminist researchers and activists.

Many sociologists tend not to be antifeminist, but "gender-neutral." That is, violence is seen as a problem of both sexes (Gelles, 1972; Straus, Gelles, & Steinmetz, 1980). As sociologists develop systems models of wife abuse, sexual inequality is addressed as simply one factor among many. In this way, sociologists minimize the importance of the dimensions of male domination and power that are critical to feminist analyses. When sociologists examine the family as a social institution, wife battering is often attributed to the breakdown of family functioning, resulting from external stresses or changing cultural norms. In contrast, feminists suggest that stresses are not simply external impositions on the family, but are built into the very nature of contemporary family life because of the way heterosexual intimate relations are structured along lines of gender and power. Husband-to-wife violence is thus conceived, not as an aberrant phenomenon, but as a fundamental dimension in most normally functioning families.

Although sociologists seek to understand links between personality, family life, and the broader social context, their analyses are often so general that they beg the question of why men as a class wield control over women. For example, given that a man is under extreme stress, why does he choose to deal with it in certain ways, and to direct his unhappiness against his wife? From a variety of feminist perspectives, sociologists replicate the same errors at the social level that psychologists make at the individual level: Violence is abstracted from a sociohistorical analysis and attributed to deviant structures that cannot adequately account for the empirical reality that it is women as wives who disproportionately are the targets of physical abuse and coercion.

Thus, although sociologists examine wife abuse at the social level, feminist theoreticians and researchers focus on certain kinds of social structures and processes they believe are critical to understanding wife abuse. For example, when sociologists take as a given that the home is a safe, protective place except in certain deviant or unusual cases, they fail to understand the complexity of violence against women. In her chapter, which provides a critique of criminologists' standard theories of the fear of crime, Elizabeth Stanko challenges the cultural notion of the safe home. By suggesting that a focus on a street crime deflects attention away from domestic violence and reinforces the common belief that women are safer in the home, she also demonstrates how such theories may reinforce women's dependency on intimate partners who supposedly protect them, rather than abuse them.

Feminist researchers also challenge the notion that wife abuse is a concrete easily identifiable phenomenon that can be simply observed, measured, and then treated within traditional care-giving institutions. In their chapter, Demi Kurz and Evan Stark suggest, instead, that labeling and identifying wife abuse is a complex social process that draws on popular cultural stereotypes of battered women. This labeling process interacts with and is influenced by patriarchal social structures, such as medical institutions. This both leads to and perpetuates attitudes about battered women that shape care-givers' responses to them in ways that blame battered women and further victimize them. As feminists describe the complex interplay of social stereotypes, social processes, and larger institutions, they also suggest that these processes and institutions need to be radically modified in order to provide careful identification of and compassionate care for battered women.

Feminist Research
on Wife Abuse

Feminist perspectives do not only inform how we think about the causes and contexts of wife abuse. They also raise important and not easily answered questions about the nature of conventional research in this area (Bowles & Klein, 1983; Roberts, 1981; Stanley & Wise, 1983; Wardell, Gillespie, & Leffler, 1983). These include: (1) the place of values in research, (2) the kinds of questions that are asked in research, (3) methods for collecting data, (4) how the data are employed, and (5) the nature of the researcher/respondent relationship.

Values and research. Most researchers attempt to be "value-free" in their work. But feminists argue that research takes place in a social context that is patriarchal, and therefore characterized by the domination of men over women. In this context, most of our personal and scientific knowledge codifies men's experiences and ways of being in the world: Women's experiences are distorted or rendered invisible. From this perspective, there is no such thing as true neutrality in social science, since we can never function completely independently of dominant ideologies and belief systems. Hiding one's values behind the banner of "objectivity" is not the same thing as being unbiased, as Kersti Yllö and Lee Ann Hoff suggest in their chapters. In fact, the common social science practice of not discussing one's values leads to biases that often go unrecognized or unacknowledged. Yet, because male-defined social knowledge is such a fundamental part of who we are and how we think, it requires careful and deep examination to uncover its biases and our personal values. Because of this, feminists suggest that it is crucial that researchers make explicit the values that guide their work. Paradoxically, as feminists try to acknowledge their own values openly, they are often met with charges by others that they are "biased" or "too political."

A primary value of feminist researchers, theoreticians, and activists is a commitment to elucidating women's experiences from their own perspectives. This entails challenging taken-for-granted conceptual categories and stereotypes. The study of how men understand their use of violence also takes place within this special context. For example, in his chapter, Jim Ptacek takes as a theoretical given that our society provides personal, clinical, and legal explanatory systems for men's use of violence against wives that serve the social functions of neutralizing, excusing, or justifying the abuse. He is explicit about his political values, and about his experiences as a feminist researcher. But, he is also self-aware as a man raised in our society, and how this shapes the research process and his interpretation of the results. This is an example of how our values and goals as feminist theoreticians and researchers lead to "passionate scholarship" (Spender, 1980).

Kinds of questions asked. Given their values, feminists tend to ask different kinds of questions than do mainstream researchers in the field of wife abuse. Our questions are shaped by how we think about women, about intimate relationships, and about violence by men against women. For example, social science researchers have been especially concerned with understanding the often repeated and chronic presence of abuse between intimate partners and "Why do women stay?" Feminists began their inquiry with a different set of questions. In a subtle way, asking "Why do women stay?" blames the woman for her own victimization. Instead, feminists asked "What social factors constrain women from leaving?" or "Why do men use physical force against their wives?" From a feminist perspective, the kinds of questions asked by mainstream researchers are often based on untested cultural stereotypes of women in families. For example, a focus on the battered woman, and what she has done to provoke her husband, perpetuates the myths that a wife is responsible for her husband's behaviors and that he has the right to chastise his wife if he perceives her as having failed in her domestic duties (Breines & Gordon, 1983; Schechter, 1982). Exploring how battered women are different from other, nonbattered women also suggests that something is "wrong" with battered women, which results in violence, rather than trying to understand what all women share in common within the institution of marriage as it is currently constituted (Wardell, Gillespie, & Leffler, 1983). Guided by feminist perspectives, researchers and theoreticians not only pose different kinds of questions within their respective disciplines, but they also challenge current explanatory frameworks about wife abuse. This leads us to expand our theories, seek links across disciplines, and integrate theories from a variety of fields.

Methods for collecting data. In part because feminist researchers ask different kinds of questions, they often (but not always) employ different methods for gathering research. Feminist philosophers of science have suggested that fixed format measures, in which the researchers decide on categories among which respondents can choose answers to questions, can lead to biased or distorted results. Especially in early stages of research, feminist researchers rely on qualitative methods in which a large volume of data is collected through general open-ended questions. After collecting this information, the researcher sifts through the data in an effort to see what categories or factors arise out of the data themselves—rather than by imposing preestablished coding schemes. Instead of trying to fit women's experiences into pre-defined "commonsensical" categories, feminist researchers began to explore what violence means to participants themselves. For example, in her chapter, Liz Kelly is first explicit about her identity as a woman, a researcher, and a political activist, and then discusses how this influenced her choice of qualitative research methodology in her study of how women make sense of, define, and experience a wide variety of acts of physical and sexual force used against them by men.

However, methodological questions are complex, as Kersti Yllö outlines in her chapter. Some feminist researchers also convincingly argue that it is important to use traditional research methods that fulfill conventional canons of strict scientific practice. But it is important to build in variables that account adequately for the context of wife abuse. For example, to examine the previously established empirical findings that men and women use similar kinds of physical force, Dan Saunders, in his research for this volume, used traditional research methodology, but built in a different interpersonal context through exploration of the different reasons why men and women resort to force. While feminist researchers may resolve these methodological dilemmas in a variety of ways, one factor unites us: A feminist researcher maintains a self-critical eye regarding how and why they choose to use a given method and the implications for women of the choices made.

How the data are employed. Although researchers of all political persuasions are dedicated to ending woman abuse, feminist researchers are particularly sensitive to how the data are interpreted and then how they are disseminated to the professional and general populations. All researchers, of necessity, condense their data into numbers or a limited number of categories. But feminists urge caution in how these numbers are interpreted, even when there are significant statistical differences. For example, several studies have shown that there is a correlation between wife abuse and child abuse. In their chapter, Lee Bowker, Richard McFerron, and Michele Arbitell offer a new way of understanding this empirical finding that does not blame the battered woman and places child abuse in the context of wife battering.

While this is not always the case, many traditional social scientists believe that the collection of data and its application are two distinct enterprises. In contrast, feminist researchers collect data with the explicit purpose of improving the lives of battered women and changing the status quo. For this reason, feminist researchers often feel that certain areas of study should take priority over those studied by more conventional researchers. An example of this is the chapter by Ellen Pence and Melanie Shepard. What most distinguishes feminist researchers from more mainstream researchers is the feminist belief that data collection, its interpretation, and its use are all inherently political activities. Lack of awareness of this political dimension of all knowledge by many researchers does not obviate it, but simply renders it invisible.

The researcher/respondent relationship. Given that the examination of the distribution of power is a fundamental aspect of any feminist philosophy, feminist researchers are particularly sensitive to the nature of the researcher/respondent relationship. Traditionally, the researcher is supposed to be a neutral detached observer, who brackets off his or her feelings from the research process, and who takes pains to ensure that his or her personal reactions do not influence or "contaminate" the collection of data. Feminist theoreticians have argued that this position objectifies the respondent and creates a potentially biased hierarchical relationship between researcher and respondent. In its place, feminists have tried to develop more collaborative models of research, characterized by shared power between respondent and researcher. Lee Ann Hoff's chapter is illustrative of this approach. This process is often dialectical. Rather than collecting data that is then analyzed in isolation from the respondents, some feminist researchers have experimented with returning to the respondents with their initial findings to ensure that the researcher's interpretations of the data adequately and sensitively capture the experiences of battered women. Ideally, a spirit of open dialogue replaces that of detached investigation.

As part of this process, feminist researchers believe that it is essential that they understand their role in the research process. As Hoff discusses in her chapter, this entails full exploration and explication of their feelings and values that shape and are shaped by the research process. Again, attention to the humanity of the researcher challenges traditional notions of the researcher as a neutral observer who brackets off his or her feelings. The description of the experience of doing research with battered women and abusive men within the context of a formal research report is a distinguishing characteristic of feminist research and is an important facet of many of the chapters in this volume.

Social Science and Activism

Until recently, social scientists and activists often engaged in heated dialogue because of the different values, goals, and philosophies they brought to their work with battered women. Many of the authors in this book, dedicated both to academic purposes and to political activism, have struggled with how to integrate these roles. Ideally, research and social action need not work at cross purposes. Yet their integration requires careful thought, analyses, and collaboration between individuals of different disciplines and professions. Russell and Rebecca Dobash discuss how certain sociologists address issues of social action, and how the inclusion of the dimension of social action affects theory and research methodologies. Susan Schechter reviews the tensions that often arise between battered women, shelter activists, and professionals, and suggests how professionals can learn from activists and help strengthen their goals and efforts.

In bringing together such a diverse group of activists, academicians, and clinicians, this volume extends the feminist critique of current research on wife abuse to show the rich directions and insights that emerge through collaboration of the wide variety of feminists who are dedicated to understanding and eradicating wife abuse.

REFERENCES

Bograd, M. (1984). Family systems approaches to wife battering: A feminist critique. *American Journal of Orthopsychiatry, 54,* 558-568.

Bograd, M. (1986). A feminist examination of family systems models of violence against women in the family. In M. Ault-Riche (Ed.), *Women and family therapy* (pp. 34-50). Rockville, MD: Aspen Systems Corporation.

Bowles, G., & Klein, R. (1983). *Theories of women's studies.* London: Routledge & Kegan Paul.

Breines, W., & Gordon, L. (1983). The new scholarship on family violence. *Signs: Journal of Women in Culture and Society, 8,* 490-531.

Chapman, J., & Gates, M. (Eds.) (1978). *The victimization of women.* Newbury Park, CA: Sage.

Dobash, R. E., & Dobash, R. (1979). *Violence against wives: A case against the patriarchy.* New York: Free Press.

Eichler, M. (1983, August). *The relationships between sexist, nonsexist, women-centered and feminist research.* Paper presented at the annual meeting of the American Sociological Association, Detroit.

Finkelhor, D., Gelles, R., Hotaling, G., & Straus, M. (Eds.). (1983). *The dark side of families: Current family violence research.* Beverly, Hills, CA: Sage.

Gelles, R. (1972). *The violent home: A study of physical aggression between husbands and wives.* Newbury Park, CA: Sage.

Jagger, A., & Struh, P. (1978). *Feminist frameworks: Alternative theoretical accounts of the relations between women and men.* New York: McGraw-Hill.

Martin, D. (1976). *Battered wives.* New York: Pocket Books.

McGrath, C. (1979). The crisis of domestic order. *Socialist Review, 9,* 11-30.

Pagelow, M. (1981). *Woman-battering: Victims and their experiences.* Newbury Park, CA: Sage.

Roberts, E. (Ed.). (1981). *Doing feminist research.* London: Routledge & Kegan Paul.

Roy, M. (Ed.). (1977). *Battered women: A psychosociological study of domestic violence.* New York: Van Nostrand Reinhold.

Russell, D. (1982). *Rape in marriage.* New York: Macmillan.

Schechter, S. (1982). *Women and male violence: The visions and struggles of the battered women's movement.* Boston: South End.

Spender, D. (1980). *Man made language.* London: Routledge & Kegan Paul.

Stanley, L., & Wise, S. (1983). *Breaking out: Feminist consciousness and feminist research.* London: Routledge & Kegan Paul.

Straus, M., & Hotaling, G. (Eds.). (1980). *The social causes of husband-wife violence.* Minneapolis: University of Minnesota Press.

Straus, M., Gelles, R., & Steinmetz, S. (Eds.) (1980). *Behind closed doors: Violence in the American family.* Garden City, NY: Anchor/Doubleday.

Walker, L. (1979). *The battered woman.* New York: Harper & Row.

Walker, L. (1984). *The battered woman syndrome.* New York: Springer.
Wardell, L., Gillespie, D., & Leffler, A. (1983). Violence against wives. In D. Finkelhor, R. Gelles, G. Hotaling, & M. Straus (Eds.), *The dark side of families: Current family violence research.* Newbury Park, CA: Sage.

PART I

The Politics of Research

1

Political and Methodological Debates in Wife Abuse Research

KERSTI YLLÖ

The physical and sexual abuse of women is one of the most political and emotionally charged topics of study in the social sciences. It is not surprising then, that our progress in understanding wife abuse (which has been impressive) has been marked by numerous controversies. While a great deal of important research has been done by mainstream social scientists, there is probably no area of study in which feminist scholarship has been more important. The issue of wife abuse was brought to public consciousness by the women's movement. The shelter movement has begun to offer women alternatives to violence, and feminist activists and researchers have importantly contributed to our understanding of the problem. Yet, our work has only begun and there are important controversies in the field between feminists and non-feminists, and among feminists.

In the broadest terms, there is a division in the field between those who bring feminist perspectives to bear on the problem of battering and those who do not. As our Introduction pointed out, there are diverse feminist views, yet a consensus that sexism in our society and families is fundamentally linked to violence. This chapter has a narrower focus,

AUTHOR'S NOTE: Thanks to Joe Pleck, David Adams, Michele Bograd, and the Wheaton College Family Studies Group for their comments on an earlier draft of this chapter, which was presented at the 1986 National Council on Family Relations Theory and Methods Workshop in Dearborn, Michigan.

however. My concern here is with methodology: How do we do our research and to what end? As I try to answer this question, it will become clear that it is deeply connected to the overarching feminist analysis.

The tensions between those who regard themselves as family researchers and those who see themselves as feminists (researchers and activists) are longstanding, to a certain extent inevitable, and often useful in the development of the field. However, I believe that the tensions, hostilities, and sometimes open conflicts can also be counter-productive, especially when the many sides stop talking and listening to one another.

Since virtually everyone who studies wife abuse and other violence against women wants to see an end to such abuse, we might regard all of this work as feminist in some sense. However, this is clearly not the case. Leaving aside the openly antiwoman analyses of wife battering (usually provided by psychoanalysts), we see extensive research by nonfeminists (though not necessarily antifeminists), most of whom focus on families and wife abuse as part of that system of interaction. Since much of this work does not take gender or power into account as central factors, the focus is not feminist. Further, the methods used (usually quantitative surveys or psychological tests) have been questioned as patriarchal.

These debates are particularly salient to me, because for the nearly ten years I have studied wife abuse, I have been both a family sociologist and a feminist. As a doctoral student and postdoctoral fellow with Murray Straus at the Family Violence Research Program at the University of New Hampshire, I was well-trained in mainstream methodology and a family focused analysis of wife abuse. As a feminist interested in feminist theory and radical critiques of methodology, as well as the practical consequences of our research for the lives of battered women, I have also stepped outside of family studies. So, the debates in the area of wife abuse are often a dialogue I carry on with myself.

Marcia Westkott (1979) comments on the nature of such debate for feminist scholars.

> These dialogues are not debates between outsiders and insiders; they are, rather, critical confrontations among those who have been educated and trained within particular disciplines. The feminist debate arises because some of these insiders who are women are also outsiders. When women realize that we are simultaneously immersed in and estranged from both our own particular discipline and the Western intellectual tradition generally, a personal tension develops that informs the critical dialogue.... In some fundamental way, we as critics oppose ourselves. (p. 422)

The purpose of this chapter is to explore the methodological debates between mainstream and feminist researchers and activists; to identify major points of contention; and to consider possible resolutions or, at least, ways to continue the dialogue more productively.

Two Studies of Wife Abuse

In discussing these issues, I will make reference to two research projects regarding wife abuse that I have undertaken. In many ways, these two studies represent the quantitative and qualitative approaches, which are often regarded as opposed. The first, a quantitative analysis of secondary data on family violence, has been criticized as patriarchal in its methodology. The second, involving in-depth interviews with women who were victims of physical abuse and rape in their marriages, is regarded as a more feminist approach. As I will try to make clear, I believe that the labeling of these two studies as "nonfeminist" versus "feminist" in method is counterproductive. We need not create a simple dichotomy where a complex distinction exists. The deeper issues of epistemology, that is, how we know what we know, need to be explored in order to understand these debates more fully. I refer to these two studies because, as Feyerabend (1978) has argued, "to discuss methodology apart from concrete research is like discussing the role of keys without careful attention to the nature of locks" (p. 42).

The Status of Women and Wife Beating

My first major research project, my dissertation, was a study of how women's status in society affects levels of violence within the family. I had grown frustrated by the proliferation of studies that focused only on individual psychology or marital dyads: So much of the research regarded marriage within a social vacuum, ignoring the patriarchal structure of society. My feminist perspective led me to explore the structure of male power. A real problem for me was how to operationalize gender inequality at the societal as well as at the individual level.

My approach to this feminist question was quantitative and methodologically mainstream. Using census and other data, I constructed a Status of Women Index by which I ranked American states regarding the economic, political, educational, and legal status of women. A typical item in the index was "proportion of women in technical/ managerial occupations." I correlated the index with state rates of wife beating drawn from the nationally representative survey on family violence conducted by Straus, Gelles, and Steinmetz (1980).

My central finding was that inequality within the social context did indeed affect rates of battering, but not in the linear way I had hypothesized. Wife abuse did not simply decline as women's status improved. Rather, the relationship was curvilinear. Wife battering was high in low status states and declined as women's status improved. However, rates of abuse increased in those states in which women's status was highest relative to men's (see Yllö, 1983, 1984a, 1984b for fuller discussion of these findings). The evidence seems to indicate that rapid change toward equality may bring a violent backlash by husbands. The implication that I drew from this is not that we slow the pace of change, but that we need to direct our attention and resources to those who are paying most dearly the price of the change.

I was stunned when my paper reporting these findings was rejected from a respected feminist journal. The problem was not with the nature of my concerns or conclusions, but with my methodology, which, I was told, was "inherently patriarchal." Quantitative studies could contribute no feminist insights, the editor wrote. At that point, I began to explore feminist critiques of science and methodology.

Rape in Marriage

As a postdoctoral fellow I began to work with David Finkelhor on the issue of marital rape. As we explored the intersection of my work on wife battering and his on child sexual abuse, we discovered an enormous gap in the research. Marital rape was legally nonexistent and virtually absent in all of the work on family violence, sexuality, and rape.

As we began our research into the experiences of women who had been raped, Diana Russell conducted her landmark survey on sexual assault, including wife rape (see Russell, *Rape in Marriage,* 1982 for a discussion of the most thorough survey to date). David and I decided to focus our study on describing the experience of rape in marriage. We were concerned with the stereotypes of marital rape (the best known being Rhett Butler carrying Scarlett up the stairs, with Scarlett beaming happily the next morning). We were concerned that journalists and legislators asserted that wife rape was simply not very serious. "But if you can't rape your wife, who can you rape?" asked State Senator Bob

Wilson in the debate about criminalizing marital rape in California.

We decided to interview women who had been raped by their husbands and find out what happened and what impact it had on them. Through family planning agencies, feminist health centers, and battered women's shelters, we contacted women who had indicated in intake interviews that a partner had used force or threat of force to try to have sex with them. I conducted most of the 50 unstructured, in-depth interviews with women ranging in age from 17 to 60. These 50 case studies were the qualitative data base for this study. We chose to talk to women about their experiences because of the exploratory nature of the research. While it is true that an inductive, experiential approach is often equated with a feminist approach, we did not initially choose our methods for those reasons.

The findings of this research are detailed in Finkelhor and Yllö's *License to Rape: Sexual Abuse of Wives* (1985). By listening to the women's experiences we discovered three basic types of rape in marriage. The first, which we call battering rape, occurs in marriages in which there is a high overall level of violence. The women are battered and the rapes are an additional element of the beatings and humiliation. The second type, force-only rape, occurs in marriages that are otherwise nonviolent. The husband's desire for control seems to lead him to use sexual coercion. He uses only as much force as necessary to coerce his wife to comply. Power rather than anger appears to be central to force-only rapes. The third type, obsessive rape, is most openly sadistic. Sexual violence is central to the husband's arousal. The husband is not a batterer who adds rape to the assault, but rather, he is obsessed with sex, usually uses violent pornography, and inflicts pain as part of sex. While these husbands can be termed sadists, it is important to note that the wives were not masochists.

Although the women's experiences with marital rape varied greatly in terms of physical pain and injury, all of the women reported being greatly traumatized. While the impact is different from stranger-rape, it is not less serious (as Russell (1982) has shown statistically). The violation of trust was the most profound psychological consequence. These women spent much time, often many years, in trying to escape their marriages and then let themselves trust and develop intimate relationships with men once more (though many have not gotten to that point and don't believe that they ever will).

In this study (in comparison to the first), I heard the voices of the women themselves. What they told me was a sort of data that was quite different from the data on my computer printouts and I will explore the differences in a later section. Let me turn now to the issue of feminist critiques of methodology, which I will discuss in relation to my two studies and the research of many others.

Feminist Critiques of Methodology

Critiques of
"Sex Bias" in Our Methods

Criticisms of social and natural science methods have been of two major sorts. The first is a critique of "sex bias" in our research. Efforts have been made to correct the blatant biases of mainstream research (e.g., topic selection that leaves women's lives invisible or confined to family; studying male samples and drawing conclusions about all humans; and the development of indices and psychological tests based on male values and characteristics, and so on). Although they have been quite valuable, these critiques are technical and reformist rather than epistemological. They do not question positivism or the scientific method itself. Kathleen Grady (1981), for example, approaches "sex fair" research methods in terms of a "more meticulous application of scientific method" (p. 628). In the same vein, the American Sociological Association (1980) published a list of examples of sex bias in methods in all phases of research several years ago.

Most mainstream researchers in the area of domestic violence are far ahead of their social science colleagues on such matters. My study of the status of women and wife abuse has not been criticized as "sex biased," for example. Most of these problems of bias are technical and fairly easy to resolve given the commitment to do so. For example, Straus and his colleagues were appalled when the contracted research agency took the liberty of printing in the sex of the head of household (M, of course) on the questionnaires for the first national survey. Great effort was made at the last minute to ensure that interviewers allowed the respondents to indicate household membership as they themselves perceived it.

Quantitative Versus
Qualitative Approaches

Problems of sex bias in research can be resolved without questioning the nature of quantitative research. The emphasis on "scientific objectivity," on variables, and the stripping of context that characterizes the experimental paradigm and much of survey research has come under serious questioning by those who take a more radical view of methods.

It appears to some critics that social scientists are suffering from "physics envy," and therefore try to be as methodologically hard as their brothers in the natural sciences in an attempt to prove that they, too, are objective scientists. The distancing of the researcher from the objects of study is being questioned. The reliance on computers, statistics, "hard" data, that so predominate in social science in general, and family studies in particular, is increasingly being criticized.

The simplistic alternative to the "hard/masculinist" approach is to pose a "soft/feminist" paradigm. At numerous methodological discussions at the National Women's Studies Association and in at least one feminist journal, quantitative research has been juxtaposed with qualitative research. Statistical studies are set in opposition to field studies or in-depth interviews, which are regarded as more feminist.

In this view, the marital rape study employed feminist methodology, whereas the status of women and wife beating study did not. The quantitative study involved a secondary analysis of data. I had no contact with the abused women, nor did anyone else who worked on the national survey analysis. All of the interviews were conducted by paid, trained, professional interviewers. Indeed, I sat in front of a computer terminal for over a year constructing indices and running statistical analyses. The lives of the abused women were numerically coded and it was easy for me to think of wife battering as a score on "XC12WS," the index measuring severe violence against wives.

On the other hand, the marital rape study was qualitative and depended on in-depth, in-person discussions with women about their lives and the very brutal attacks they had experienced. Since the interviews were not rigidly structured, the women were able to bring in information and analysis that they thought was helpful in making sense of what had happened. We were not limited to our preconceived hypotheses about marital rape.

There is no question that I learned a great deal about wife abuse from those 50 women that the quantitative data on over 2,000 couples could not begin to reveal. My talks with battered women made clear to me that I am a part of what I am studying. As a woman in this society, I am vulnerable to such violence. Being aware of this makes a difference in how I understand the problem. This research was far more emotional and painful than my previous research. It had more impact on my personal life and my own relationships. The connection I felt to the women could not be simulated by the computer. Moreover, this subjective understanding was not an impediment to my work; rather, it was an important component of my analysis.

I could end this story easily at this point by saying that I had discovered "real" feminist methodology and now see the folly of my former ways (which can always be excused by saying graduate students do what they must to get through). However, this story does not have a simple, happy ending. While this qualitative method may well be feminist, we did not choose it just for that reason. As I mentioned earlier, we decided to conduct interviews because of the exploratory nature of the research. We wanted to expand rather than limit our inquiry and go where the women led us. We learned a great deal through our qualitative approach, but I would not want to be limited to qualitative methods. Our exploratory research generated questions that cannot be answered through further qualitative research. For example, we found that a large portion of the marital rape victims had also been sexually abused as children. We cannot discover the extent of the relationship between child sexual abuse and marital rape unless we construct a controlled study using a representative sample. It may be that child sexual abuse is no more common among marital rape victims than among other women. But, only by comparing marital rape victims with nonvictims could we come to any adequate conclusions.

There is no denying that there are serious problems with quantitative research (not the least of which is its inordinate status in the discipline). However, the creation of a simple quantitative/qualitative dichotomy (especially when posed in patriarchal versus feminist terms) is less than useful. It creates divisions and silences rather than dialogue. Further-more, it stops short of the epistemological discussion that is needed. In the next section I attempt to outline some of the central feminist critiques of social sciences methods, and the norm of objectivity. In the following section these issues are discussed with more specific reference to the political and methodological debates in the study of wife abuse.

Radical Feminist Critiques

Radical critiques of social science methods go far beyond concerns about "sex-bias" or simple quantitative/qualitative dichotomies. They are radical in the sense that they go to the very root of the scientific enterprise to question the basic assumptions of the positivist paradigm, which are largely taken for granted by practicing social scientists.

It is beyond the scope of this chapter to review the massive literature on the critiques of positivism and the scientific method. There have been extensive discussions, for example, of the relationship between science and capitalism. Marxists have long argued that science developed more in the service of industry than in the search for truth. Probably the most influential critique of science is Thomas Kuhn's *The Structure of Scientific Revolution* (1962), which argues that social and historical forces are of central importance in scientific paradigm shifts. Yet, most of this literature has been produced by philosophers of science who were as oblivious to issues of gender and feminism as the scientists they critique. This is not to deny the importance of their contributions, which inform feminist analysis of methodology. However, for the purposes of this chapter, I will focus on the specifically feminist critiques that have been formulated by women scholars who found themselves at odds with their own training—who, as critics, oppose themselves. I will also try to limit myself to those critiques that are most pertinent to the controversies in the study of wife abuse.

My central focus is on objectivity, the hallmark of positivism and the scientific method. In the positivist paradigm, abstract concepts and theories are seen as separate and, in some sense, floating above the empirical world. The deductive testing of competing theories, then, requires the separation of subject from object and thought from sensation or feeling. The strict adherence to precise methodological techniques is regarded as the means to achieve, or at least approach, objectivity. In social science, double blind, controlled experiments, representative-sample surveys, careful measurement of variables, and powerful statistical techniques are all important components of this process.

The assumption that observation and data can be divorced from theory (and values), and that the natural and (even more problematic) the social world can be objectively studied, is at the core of the debate. In order to better understand why this is such an issue for feminists let me review some of the critiques in more detail. They all, in varying ways, support Adrienne Rich's (1979) contention that objectivity is the name men have given to their own subjectivity.

Science, Objectivity, and Masculinity

Evelyn Fox Keller, a highly respected scientist and a leading critic of traditional science, argues that there is a powerful social belief that equates science with masculinity. Science demands rational, unemotional detachment to achieve "objectivity." Keller (1978) points out that "the complement of the scientific mind is, of course, nature viewed so ubiquitously as female. 'Let us establish a chaste and lawful marriage between Mind and Nature,' wrote Bacon" (p. 413). Thus, mind and nature, knower and known, are assigned gender and a particular, gender-based relationship. "The relation between knower and known is one of distance and separation," says Keller (1978, p. 414). Social science is heir to the natural science view that the scientist's goal is to control or master the separate object of knowledge.

Keller extends her analysis by exploring the development of the capacity for objectivity in humans. Freud and Piaget both showed us that the capacity for delineating subject from object is learned, rather than innate, and is closely connected to our separation from our mothers (the almost universal care givers). Feminists such as Nancy Chodorow (1978) have argued that this experience of separation is profoundly different for boys and girls in patriarchal society. In establishing their masculinity, boys are greatly concerned with separating and distancing themselves from their mothers (their first objects). Since fathers are largely absent in child rearing, boys have no close models. Girls, on the other hand, identify closely with their mothers and never make such a drastic break; they remain more relationship-bound.

In pointing to the greater male proclivity toward delineation and objectification and the meaning of such separation for science, Keller emphasizes that these relations are not inevitable. The capacity to objectify, as it develops in childhood, as well as the nature of the subject/object split in science, are socially constructed and changeable. Nor does it mean that we must wait for nonsexist child rearing before science can change. Keller's point is that

> linking scientific and objective with masculine brings in its wake a host of secondary consequences. . . . Not only does our characterization of science thereby become colored by the biases of patriarchy and sexism, but simultaneously our evaluation of masculine and feminine becomes affected by the prestige of science. A circular process of mutual reinforcement is established in which what is called scientific receives extra validation from the cultural preference for what is masculine, and conversely, what is called feminine—be it a branch of knowledge, a way of thinking, or a woman herself—becomes further devalued by its exclusion from the special social and intellectual value placed on science and the model science provides for all intellectual endeavours. (Keller, 1978, p. 430)

The Meanings of Objectivity

Keller's discussion of the connection between scientific objectivity and masculinity gives us a sense of its development and its importance in patriarchal society. Elizabeth Fee (1981), in an article entitled "Is Feminism a Threat to Scientific Objectivity?" delves further into the various meanings of objectivity and the implications of those meanings. Fee writes that "the idea of scientific objectivity is sufficiently vague to carry with it a multitude of meanings; many of these are more closely tied to the ideology of science than to the actual processes of scientific work" (p. 384). One important meaning of the concept, according to Fee, concerns the relation between the production of knowledge and its social uses. The claim of "objectivity" is often the justification for the production of "basic research" without responsibility for its social application. Here, the distance and hierarchy of science become the excuse for political and moral passivity on the part of researchers.

"On a personal level," Fee continues, "the claim of 'objectivity' may be taken as requiring a divorce between scientific rationality and any emotional or social commitment" (p. 385). In this context the concept of objectivity may be used to devalue any positions expressed with emotional intensity or conviction (p. 385). It is easy to see the coupling of objectivity and masculinity when heartfelt feminist critiques of traditional research are dismissed as simply "subjective."

A further consequence of the separation of thought from feeling, and their equation with masculine and feminine, concerns the relationship between "experts" and "nonexperts." Fee writes that the "power relationship is reproduced on the social scale: the scientific experts are in the male role, while the vast majority of the population is in the female role. . . . Knowledge can, in this system, flow in only one direction: from expert to nonexpert" (p. 385).

Challenges to scientific hegemony are coming not just from the women's movement (including feminist scholars, shelter activists, and the women's health movement), but also from environmental and antinuclear movements. Although fundamentalist religious groups have little else in common with these critics on the political left, they, too, challenge the authority of science. (Of course they would like to return to the patriarchal religious authority that has lost ground to science.) Fee argues that these groups, regardless of political persuasion, see the decision-making process in science as insulated from popular participation and view scientific authority as more a form of power than source of truth (p. 383).

This distance between experts and nonexperts and between thinking and feeling are linked, of course, to the separation between subject and object, knower and known, which was discussed earlier. We are back to a central premise of positivism: that theory and observation are separate and distant.

Sandra Harding (1986) summarizes these issues in *The Science Question in Feminism* as follows:

> The androcentric ideology of contemporary science posits as necessary, and/or as facts, a set of dualisms—culture versus nature; rational mind versus prerational body and irrational emotions and values; objectivity versus subjectivity; public versus private—and then links men and masculinity to the former and women and femininity to the latter in each dichotomy. Feminist critics have argued that such dichotomizing constitutes an ideology in the strong sense of the term: in contrast to merely value-laden false beliefs that have no social power, these beliefs structure the policies and practices of social institutions, including science. (p. 136)

While I have touched on some of the problems with positivism and the norm of objectivity above, I have, to an extent, been discussing the role of keys without adequate attention to the nature of locks, to use Feyerabend's metaphor. As Harding points out, this powerful ideology shapes institutions and practice, and the study of the family is no exception. In the following section I will discuss some of these concerns in terms of the research being conducted on wife abuse. In what ways does the quantitative approach, which holds center stage in family violence research, suffer from its positivist assumptions? In what ways is it inconsistent with the tenets of objectivity? What are the main objections of the feminist critics? And, what alternatives are there?

Controversies in the Study of Wife Abuse

The field of family violence, and more specifically wife abuse, is still a very young one. It was not until the early 1970s that shelters began to be established in the United States, that feminists began to expose the issue, and that family sociologists began to study the topic. In an emerging field, where research has such political and personal consequences, it is no wonder that there have been heated debates. Early on, activists and family sociologists took on the psychopathological model of wife abuse, challenging the notion that battering was an individual rather than social problem (Schechter, 1982; Straus, 1974). The sociological analysis of private troubles as public issues and the feminist insight that the personal is political came together in critiquing the practice of viewing abuse as mental illness, which could be treated only on an individual basis.

Despite this commonality, important differences have emerged. Family sociologists study wife abuse as a family issue while feminists regard it as a gender issue. My concern here is not so much with these differences in theoretical perspective, rather, it is with the method-ological controversies that have developed in this context. It could be argued that the disagreements about method are just skirmishes between two theoretical factions; and perhaps there is some truth to that. However, I believe that the methodological debates are not just a consequence of different perspectives on wife abuse. Rather, they are at the core of much of the debate in the field. So let's consider some of the feminist critiques of methodology, and especially the concept of scientific objectivity, as they pertain to wife abuse research. I believe that we can come to a better understanding of some of the problems that have emerged around prestige, funding, findings, and feelings if we look at them in light of methodology.

The Status of Quantitative Methods

First, the quantitative approach that is at the core of the positivist paradigm carries the greatest prestige and respect in the area of family violence, as in all of social science. A great deal of this status can be traced to the privileged position of science and masculinity in our culture. As Keller (1978) shows, science, objectivity, and masculinity are closely linked. Research that appears to be the most rational and objective and provides "hard" data is the most highly regarded in an intellectual tradition and society in which anything linked to the feminine is devalued.

Consequently, statistical data generated by the Conflict Tactics Scale (CTS), developed by Murray Straus and his colleagues (Straus, Gelles, & Steinmetz, 1980), and now widely used, are taken most seriously. The CTS measures abuse by counting up individual acts of violence by husbands and wives without regard to the severity of injury, or the issue of self defense. Undoubtedly, the most controversial finding produced in this way is that "1. 8 million wives are physically abused by their husbands each year (3.8%) while the nearly two million husbands are physically abused by their wives (4.6%)" (Gelles & Straus, 1979, p. 26).

Straus et al. were surprised by these results and have spent many years explaining that they did not consider the context of the violent acts; that most of the women's violence was certainly in self-defense; that they did not measure the consequences of the acts, which surely resulted in greater injury to the women; and so on. Though they have stated that wife abuse, not husband abuse, is the pressing problem, the damage was done. Those few simple numbers and the notion of the "battered husband syndrome" (Steinmetz, 1978) have been a powerful influence on policymakers and the public.

What is most disturbing is that the criticisms of the Conflict Tactics Scale seem to have gone unheeded. Straus and Gelles (1986) recently published the findings of their 10-year follow-up national survey. The CTS was unrevised and the new finding is that "women are about as violent within the family as men. This highly controversial finding from the 1975 study is confirmed by the 1985 study" (p. 470).

The fact that these findings have no relation to the experience of practitioners who are overwhelmed by the needs of abused women makes very little difference. Critiques appear "nonscientific." The fact that most social scientists are men, and that abused wives and their advocates are women, accentuates the divisions and status differences. The challenges offered by feminist researchers, shelter workers, and battered women, themselves, are defined as subjective. Their way of "knowing" about the topic has not been gleaned through the scientific method, which, supposedly, enables an "objective" analysis. Rather, their understanding is grounded in body and feeling as well as mind. The fusion of thought and feeling is regarded as diminishing rather than enhancing knowledge.

While Straus and many other quantitative researchers are critics of the patriarchal institutions that entrap battered women, such as economic discrimination and the criminal justice system (Straus, 1974, 1980), they do not question the patriarchal nature of social science and the status of their methods within it. However, I believe that it is only when we consider these issues at the level of epistemology that the criticisms of the "hard" data become clearer and more substantive. The problem is not just quantification, per se (although the CTS could certainly be made a better measure). It is also in the status of quantitative research as the most objective (i.e. best) way to "know" about a subject.

Objectivity and Social Commitment

A second issue discussed earlier was that scientific objectivity requires a divorce between rationality and research and any emotional or social commitments (Fee, 1981). This is a significant problem when one's topic of study is wife abuse. The majority (if not all) of the researchers who study family violence do not hold to the strictest interpretation of objectivity—that is, that their research is entirely value-free and that they, as researchers, have no social commitments. No, these are people who generally abhor violence and see their work as contributing to the ending of violence. There seems to be little reluctance among these researchers to discuss the policy implications of their work, whether it be before Congressional Committees or at murder trials.

Nevertheless, there are important differences on this question of objectivity and commitment. While mainstream researchers may recognize their own values, they attempt to separate these from the practice of research, which they see themselves as conducting objectively (i.e. by trying to eliminate bias technically). There is certainly something to be said for eliminating technical biases. It is in this area that the critiques of "sex-bias" in methods have been helpful. Yet, there remains a vague and often unarticulated allegiance to the positivist notion of objectivity; that the research simply uncovers what is "out there." In contrast, many feminist researchers regard their work as being not just about women, but for women. The explicit goal is to end violence against women by challenging the patriarchal society of which it is a part. For us, wife abuse is not part of the separate, observable, empirical world "out there." Its existence is intimately connected to our own status as women, whether we have personally been victimized or not. The distance between knower and known diminishes and, in many cases, disappears.

An added aspect of doing research for women involves accountability for how findings are used by others. How data are interpreted, where results are presented and published, and how they may be misused, are all important concerns. Feminists do not release findings into the "marketplace of ideas" assuming that truth will out. They know that the marketplace is not free. Caution must be taken to prevent damaging use of information.

The stated commitment to work for women is another element of the "subjectivity" that is contrasted to the "objectivity" of the empiricists. I have been at a number of national conferences where feminists are labeled "true-believers" or "ideologues," and the work is devalued as a result. Somehow the mainstream researchers' commitments to vague goals such as social justice are not seen as subjective or problematic, whereas feminist goals to end patriarchy are. That the challenge to patriarchy grows out of more radical political theory than the goal of "social justice," which is part of liberal ideology, is the subject of a whole separate paper. The point here is that politics and methods are connected in myriad ways. The evaluation of a particular ideology and its connection to research depends greatly on the prevailing power relations in social science.

"Experts" and "Nonexperts"

A further dimension of the concept of objectivity and empiricism is the distance between "experts" and "nonexperts," reflecting, again, the separation of thought from feeling (and masculine rationality from female emotionality). One of the deepest cleavages in the field is between mainstream researchers and activists in the battered women's movement. I believe that a crucial component of this division lies in the different ways the two groups "know" about abuse and how those different forms of knowledge are evaluated and acknowledged.

The adherence to the scientific method and the claim of objectivity by mainstream researchers sets up a system in which the flow of knowledge is unidirectional. Researchers gather and analyze data and then draw implications for policy and practitioners. While there is nothing wrong with this, per se, the problem is that there is little flow of knowledge in the other direction. The analyses of shelter workers and formerly battered women are often regarded as "nonscientific," subjective, and political. In other words, not comparable to analyses based on "hard" data.

Activists sense a fundamental disrespect for their analyses. Sure, their work "in the trenches" is appreciated and researchers support the development of more shelters. But, the theoretical analyses, which grow inductively from experience, are often regarded with suspicion, if not contempt.

In order to build a better and more productive relationship between researchers and activists, we must challenge positivist assumptions about experts and nonexperts. To regard someone who spends every day working with abused women and helping them negotiate the bureaucracies of welfare, housing, and criminal justice as "nonexpert" is patently wrong. The assignment of that expertise to some lower, "subjective" status robs us of important knowledge.

Efforts are underway to improve the connections between researchers and activists. I believe that these efforts will be most successful if researchers examine their own assumptions about what "counts" as evidence or knowledge. We should involve practitioners in our research, not out of guilt or gratitude for the hard work they do, but out of a recognition that they have important insights to contribute. Further, with their input, more of our research can also be useful to those providing services to abused women.

The Subject/Object Dichotomy

As I discussed earlier in this chapter, the separation between the subject and object of research, between knower and known, is central to positivism and is generally assumed in the social sciences. This distance is regarded as essential for the conduct of "objective" research. Yet, it does not deliver what it promises, because observation is inherently value-laden. The operationalization of concepts and their measurement are not neutral processes. For example, Straus et al. (1980) define violence in terms of the intent to cause harm, yet the CTS does not operationalize the concept to include the dimension of intent. Consequently, it is impossible to distinguish between men's attacks and women's attempts at self-defense, and the numbers show equivalent rates of violence by males and females. Statistical analyses, too, are infused with the researcher's values. The question of which variables to consider and how many controls to introduce are not apolitical decisions. If a result is disturbing to a researcher, he (or she) may well do more or different analyses. This is not evidence of dishonesty, but an example of the impossibility of human objectivity.

The split between subject and object has other implications as well. We have seen that the separation of knower and known through methodological screens does not eliminate the subjectivity of the researcher. But further, this sort of distance results in an objectification of the people we are studying. This is a crucial problem when we are studying women who have been the objects of violence.

Quantitative methods have a special capacity for dehumanizing the people we study. As I mentioned earlier, my research on wife abuse and the status of women was relatively painless for me because the women's suffering had been reduced to a score on an index with the unemotional numerical label. I believe that the disconnection enabled by numbers and computers is problematic, though I do not go as far as some critics of the whole enterprise. Russell and Rebecca Dobash are the most outspoken critics of mainstream violence research. They argue that positivism promised "methodological tickets to scientific respectability but delivered intellectual blinkers and mindless adherence to sterile sophistication" (Dobash & Dobash, 1983, p. 263).

In my experience, shifting from statistical analysis (i.e., "sterile sophistication") to qualitative analysis does not necessarily resolve the problem. Although there was clearly a reduced distance (both cognitively and affectively) between the marital rape victims I interviewed and me, I found that the personal connection did not free me from the problem of objectification. The raw data of taped interviews undergo several transformations before they are published in articles or books. We edit, revise, analyze. We forget the individual women after dozens of interviews that become case studies typed into a computer. The word processor allows us to organize and recombine the women's words to make our points.

I was acutely struck by how words objectify experience when I was editing the third draft of *License to Rape*. The copy editor had picked through the book line by line and I was responding to her inquiries and making needed changes. In the section where some of the most brutal rapes are described, the editor was concerned that we were being redundant. She wanted me to find different ways of saying "he tried to rip out her vagina." I found myself at the thesaurus trying to find substitutes for "rip." How about "yank" or "tear?" At that point I recognized the distance between subject and object and the stripping of context, and realized that avoiding numbers did not avoid the problem. I don't think it is possible to do research and avoid all objectification. As a researcher, I am separate from the women whom I interviewed. I didn't experience their rapes, I can only write about them. I believe that what is important is not the elimination of objectification (which I see as impossible), but a recognition of the problems that it poses.

Where Do We Go From Here?

Throughout this chapter I have tried to clarify the feminist critiques of methodology as they apply to wife abuse research. I think that the problems with unexamined positivism and claims of scientific objectivity are quite clear. What remains murky are the alternatives. Most of the writing on "feminist methodology" is in the form of critiques of mainstream methods. Critics like Westkott (1979) and the Dobashes (1983) make some powerful arguments that puncture aspects of the scientific method. Unfortunately, the alternatives they pose are limited.

Westkott (1979), for example, turns to the interpretive tradition in the social sciences, which has long dissented from positivism. She writes,

> The interpretive approach assumes that . . . historical truths are grasped not by attempting to eliminate subjectivity but through the intersubjectivity of subject and object. . . . The intersubjectivity of meaning takes the form of dialogue from which knowledge is an unpredictable emergent rather than a controlled outcome (p. 426).

Clearly, quantitative analysis is ruled out entirely as a means for gaining knowledge.

The Dobashes (1979, 1983) offer harsh criticisms of positivist approaches. For example, they write of "mindless adherence to a sterile sophistication"; "slums of studies based solely on statistics"; and "manipulat[ion of] abstract theories and abstruse methods that confer status but obscure knowledge about the social world" (Dobash & Dobash, 1983, pp. 263-264). They do elaborate on an alternative methodology called a "context-specific approach," which includes empirical strategy, historical analysis, and theoretical explanation. Their "empirical strategy," which they describe in more detail in the next chapter, involves the examination of historical materials, police and court records, and in-depth interviews with women who had been battered (Dobash & Dobash, 1983, p. 266).

The Dobashes find the subjectivist/interpretive tradition to be limited, however, and pay great attention to the structural and historical context of wife abuse, not just knowledge intersubjectively derived from their interviews. Their thorough and meticulous historical and institutional research is an impressive and valuable framework for explaining the women's experiences. The Dobashes even go so far as to quantify some of their data, however, in a very specific manner. They statistically summarize processes and patterns that they uncover qualitatively. They emphasize that they never use statistics in a reductionist manner to specify the characteristics of individuals (Dobash & Dobash, 1983, p. 269).

The Dobashes' approach grows out of the "realist" tradition, critical of positivism. It is interesting to note that although the Dobashes take a strong feminist position theoretically, their past critiques of methodology have not been framed in feminist terms. They have not cited the feminist literature on methodology, nor have they connected their critiques directly to gender issues. In contrast to many of the current feminist critiques, the Dobashes (1983) write with some sense of closure; that is, that an alternative to positivism and the scientific method has been developed.

Although their "context-specific" approach is valuable, it does not resolve all of the controversies. For example, the Dobashes (1983) argue that "because evidence is theory-dependent, this negates the assumption that we can settle our disputes about competing theories by simply assessing the empirical evidence relative to them" (p. 266). It is not clear to me why a recognition that observation is value-laden necessarily requires us to reject the evaluation of competing theories on the basis of empirical evidence. Perhaps the operative word in their statement is "simply"; we cannot simply assess empirical evidence. Of course, it is important to challenge the positivist assumption that theories do not stand or fall simply on the basis of the accumulated evidence. Wider social and historical forces are clearly influential. Nonetheless, the Dobashes have gathered impressive empirical evidence that challenges antifeminist theories of wife abuse. I am not sure why they so strongly reject other methodological means (specifically much quantitative research) that can contribute evidence to this same end.

In challenging androcentric knowledge, I believe that quantitative studies can and do provide us with valuable knowledge. It is quite possible to recognize the limitations of positivism and quantification, to see oneself as a feminist doing research for women, and still conduct large-scale statistical surveys. In fact, given the power of statistical analysis, I would argue that it is our responsibility as feminists to undertake some of this work. I can think of no better example of feminist quantitative research than Diana Russell's survey on sexual assault (1982, 1984). Her data profoundly question the sexist assumption/theory that rape, both inside and outside the family, is a rare occurrence. She also provides statistical evidence on the impact of rape and shows that marital rape is as traumatic as stranger rape (despite the Rhett and Scarlett stereotype). These are examples of important feminist questions that cannot be answered if we rely only on historical, case study, and interview methodologies.

As Harding (1986) points out, relativist approaches are responding to the use of the claim of "scientific objectivity" as a cover for patriarchal bias. "But," she questions, "does our recognition of the fact that science has always been a social product—that its projects and claims to knowledge bear the fingerprints of its human producers—require the exaltation of relativist subjectivity on the part of feminism?" (p. 137). Fee (1981) reminds us that if we cannot reject theories on the basis of evidence, then creationism is as valid an explanation as evolution is. In the absence of standards for evidence, the decision between patriarchal and feminist explanations of wife abuse would come down to political power (and we know which would win on those terms). Harding (1986) argues that a leap to relativism is not necessary and that it "misgrasps" feminist critiques. Feminist theory and research regard traditional thought as "subjective in its distortion by androcentrism—a claim that feminists are willing to defend on traditional objectivist grounds" (p. 138).

However, at the end of this lengthy discussion of critiques and controversies, I don't want to end with a simple call for the "triangulation of methods" (that is, the use of many different methods to study one issue), a strategy entirely consistent with the positivist paradigm. Instead, I hope that we can work toward an approach to the study of wife abuse that recognizes and challenges the limits of unexamined positivism and the claims of objectivity. At the same time, however, we need to consider what parts of the scientific method are of value. Fee (1981) argues that the idea of creating knowledge through a constant practical interaction with the world and the expectation that all assumptions and findings will be subjected to critical evaluation are aspects of science to be preserved and defended (p. 383). It is not possible, at this point, to envision fully the transformation that science—and social science—might undergo in response to feminist and other radical critiques. Nevertheless, I believe that transformation occurs in small steps. Such work will require more self-reflection and criticism of our assumptions about knowledge, the issue of objectivity, our relations with activists, and our own politics. In trying to meet these challenges, we can do better, less myopic, research on wife abuse. In place of disrespect, distrust, and dissension, I would like to see dialogue—a dialogue that can move us closer to understanding wife abuse and working together to end it.

REFERENCES

American Sociological Association. (1980, January). Sexist bias in sociological research. *ASA Footnotes*, pp. 8-9.
Chodorow, N. (1978). *The reproduction of mothering*. Berkeley: University of California Press.

Dobash, R., & Dobash, R. P. (1979). *Violence against wives: A case against the patriarchy.* New York: Free Press.

Dobash, R., & Dobash, R. P. (1983). The context-specific approach. In D. Finkelhor, R. J. Gelles, G. T. Hotaling, & M. A. Straus (Eds.). *The dark side of families: Current family violence research* (pp. 261-276). Newbury Park, CA: Sage.

Fee, E. (1981). Is feminism a threat to scientific objectivity? *International Journal of Women's Studies, 4,* 378-392.

Feyerabend, P. K. (1978). From incompetent professionalism to professionalized incompetence. *Philosophy of the Social Sciences, 8,* 37-53.

Finkelhor, D., & Yllö, K. (1985). *License to rape: Sexual abuse of wives.* New York: Free Press.

Gelles, R. (1980). Violence in the family: A review of research in the seventies. *Journal of Marriage and the Family, 42,* 873-885.

Gelles, R., & Straus, M. A. (1979). Determinants of violence in the family: Toward a theoretical integration. In W. Burr et al. (Eds.), *Contemporary theories about the family* (Vol. 1, pp. 549-591). New York: Free Press.

Grady, K. (1981). Sex bias in research design. *Psychology of Women Quarterly, 5,* 628-637.

Harding, S. (1986). *The science question in feminism.* Ithaca: Cornell University Press.

Keller, E. F. (1978). Gender and science. *Psychoanalysis and Contemporary Thought, 1,* 409-433.

Kuhn, T. S. (1962). *The structure of scientific revolution.* Chicago: University of Chicago Press.

Martin, D. (1976). *Battered wives.* San Francisco: Glide.

Oakley, A. (1981). Interviewing women: A contradiction in terms. In H. Roberts (Ed.), *Doing feminist research.* London: Routledge & Kegan Paul.

Rich, A. (1979). *On lies, secrets, and silence.* New York: Norton.

Rosewater, L. B., & Walker, L. (Eds.). (1985). *Handbook of feminist therapy.* New York: Springer.

Russell, D. (1982). *Rape in marriage.* New York: Macmillan.

Russell, D. (1984). *Sexual exploitation.* Newbury Park, CA: Sage.

Schechter, S. (1982). *Women and male violence: The visions and struggles of the battered women's movement.* Boston: South End Press.

Stanley, L., & Wise, S. (1983). *Breaking out: Feminist consciousness and feminist research.* London: Routledge & Kegan Paul.

Steinmetz, S. (1978). The battered husband syndrome. *Victimology, 2,* 499-509.

Straus, M. A. (1974). Leveling civility and violence in the family. *Journal of Marriage and the Family, 36,* 13-29.

Straus, M. A. (1980). Sexual inequality and wife-beating. In M. A. Straus & G. Hotaling (Eds.), *The social causes of husband-wife violence* (pp. 86-93). Minneapolis: University of Minnesota Press.

Straus, M. A., & Gelles, R. (1986). Societal change and change in family violence from 1975 to 1985 as revealed by two national surveys. *Journal of Marriage and the Family, 48,* 465-479.

Straus, M. A., Gelles, R., & Steinmetz, S. (1980). *Behind closed doors: Violence in the American family.* New York: Doubleday.

Westkott, M. (1979). Feminist criticism of the social sciences. *Harvard Educational Review, 49,* 422-430.

Yllö, K. (1983). Sexual equality and violence against wives in American states. *Journal of Comparative Family Studies, 1,* 67-86.

Yllö, K. (1984a). The impact of structural inequality and sexist family norms on rates of wife-beating. *Journal of International and Comparative Social Welfare, 1,* 1-29.

Yllö, K. (1984b). The status of women, marital equality, and violence against wives: A contextual analysis. *Journal of Family Issues, 3,* 307-320.

2

Research as Social Action

The Struggle for Battered Women

R. EMERSON DOBASH
RUSSELL P. DOBASH

The question of the relationship between science and social action is relevant to every investigation undertaken, but it is particularly important when the phenomenon under study is a social problem. The facile response to the question is that there is no relationship between science and social action and that there should be none. We argue that a relationship between research, beliefs, values, and social action is inevitable; however, the nature of that relationship is not a straight-forward one. When focused on a social problem, this relationship usually involves, at the very least, the evidence, ideas, explanations, and actions of social scientists as well as those of powerful institutions and struggling grass roots groups. They are intertwined in a dynamic and fluid process that will usually result in some form of development, that will, in turn, move either toward fundamental social change or to the maintenance of the status quo. While this is a general approach that may apply to any social issue from race relations to drug abuse, the present work has been particularly informed by critical and feminist perspectives.

In this chapter, we consider some of the specific issues and problems relating to the relationship between social science and social action as

AUTHORS' NOTE: Portions of this chapter were originally published in the *Journal of Family Issues,* Vol. II, No. 4 (December) 1981, pp. 439-470.

they have developed in the context of our research on violence against wives. After providing a brief history of the rise of this social problem in Britain, the social scientist is placed in this arena. We examine the existing proposals relating to social science research and develop three fundamental aspects of action research: the methodology, the message, and the relationship between social scientists and statutory bodies and community groups. Comparisons will be drawn with traditional approaches not oriented to action research.

Women's Aid and
Violence Against Women

The social problem of wife abuse first came to the attention of the British public in 1972 after being "discovered" by a small group of women working to put the principles of the women's movement into practice. In 1971, this group set up a community meeting and advice center for women in a small derelict house in Chiswick, a London borough. The problem of assaults on women soon became apparent as women began talking about brutal and habitual attacks by their husbands or cohabitants. Although the house was meant to be used during office hours, the women obviously needed a 24-hour refuge where they and their children might escape from violence and the center quickly became a refuge for battered women. This inauspicious beginning was soon to explode into a social movement of national and, later, international proportions with the accompanying struggles for recognition, splits, alliances, and metamorphoses that characterize all dynamic social movements (Charlton, 1972; Pizzey, 1974; Rose, 1978; Sutton, 1977).

Within months, Women's Aid groups were established throughout Britain and they started the arduous campaign to open their own refuges. They pressured reluctant authorities, sought funds, and used the mass media in their campaign to assist battered women. The provision of refuges spread rapidly. Initially, local Women's Aid groups were bound together only by the sense that "they were women working with women for women" (Sutton, 1977, p. 577), and by the limited contact they had traveling across the country to meet and exchange ideas and experiences.

There was a growing awareness that there was also a need for a national campaigning base through which the united voice of local

Women's Aid groups could be heard on issues of legislation, public policy, education, expanding provision of refuges, and more fundamental changes in the status of women. In 1975, dozens of groups met to form a national organization. Based on the principles of the Women's Liberation Movement, the majority wanted to work democratically and cooperatively without hierarchies, authoritarian regimes, or star personalities (Hanmer, 1977; National Women's Aid Federation, 1978; Sutton, 1977, p. 579). An irreparable split occurred between the majority of Women's Aid groups and Chiswick's Women's Aid group, which wished to become the dominant group in the national organization (Rose, 1978, 1985). Despite this opposition, a democratic, feminist organization, National Women's Aid Federation, was formed by 35 of the 39 groups (Dobash & Dobash, 1987, in press). The plight of battered women is now generally recognized as a significant social problem and there have been changes in housing, social services, and legal reforms (Coote, Gill, & Richardson, 1977; Delamont & Ellis, 1979; Pahl, 1985; Parliamentary Select Committee on Violence in Marriage, 1975; Wasoff, Dobash, & Dobash, 1979).

As can be seen from this brief account, both the social movement and the social problem upon which it is focused are dynamic and complex. The social scientists who would do action research enter the arenas of other researchers, grass roots activists, legislators, policy makers, and agency practitioners. To study the social problem and provide a contribution to the changes necessary to develop meaningful proposals for solutions necessitates the entrance of the social scientists into the political world of ongoing social change. Despite all protestation to the contrary, social research and political issues are inevitably related. Yet, social science is largely lacking in models of how to develop scientific work within this context, how to analyze the social and political consequences of the messages inherent in research, and how to participate with community groups and social agencies in the collective creation of social change.

Challenging the Reigning Orthodoxy

We began this process with our research on violence against women. From the onset, we sought to contribute to an explanation and understanding of what was obviously a significant social problem, and contribute to the wider feminist political activity relating to it. This dual intention necessitated a reflexive and introspective process involving a continual examination of the interrelationship among our theoretical position, research methods, the political processes surrounding the problem, and the battered women's movement. There was a paucity of models, explicit examples, or even general discussions in the existing literature about how one might integrate theory, research methods, and social action. This situation prevailed despite the theoretical and methodological developments that had occurred in the social sciences during the preceding two decades.

The 1960s and early 1970s was a period of radical action and rapid social change. Civil rights activists, Vietnam war protests, student revolts, and the women's movement were all challenging the social order and the social and behavioral sciences were not immune to such challenges. Social science research faced a number of formidable critiques of its methodology and theoretical perspectives. In the United States and Europe, the reigning orthodoxy of conservative functional analysis, abstract empiricism (with its emphasis on measurement and questionnaire research), and grand theory (oriented to generalized, ahistorical models of society) were subjected to severe criticism from fundamental inadequacies in the approaches, especially their failure to account for the profound changes occurring in society. The rapid changes and conflicts of this period were impossible to analyze with orthodox conceptions. Existing functional approaches were unable to explain adequately these changes and questionnaires, and statistical analysis seemed too rigid to allow one to grasp the dynamic nature of societies.

As a result of this questioning, new theoretical perspectives and methods emerged to challenge orthodox approaches. In the United States, conflict perspectives (Horowitz, 1964) challenged functionalism, and alternative interpretative epistemologies, such as ethnomethodology and phenomenology, provided explicit alternatives to the method-ological assumptions of empiricism (Cicourel, 1964, 1968). Social scientists proclaimed a new era of social theory and research, one that rejected the supposed value-free stance of the orthodox approach.

Gradually the voices of feminist scholars emerged to challenge the old and the new. Regardless of the epistemological stance or theoretical position, women were generally absent from these analyses. Women's individual and collective struggles were not reflected in the old or the new approaches. They were, as yet, uninteresting and unworthy of carrying the banners of fundamental social change. It was for women themselves to raise the banner, and grass roots activists and feminist scholars did so with considerable effect. The orthodoxies, both old and new, that had routinely excluded women or relegated them to a minor place were criticized (Bart, 1971; Smith, 1974; Rowbotham, 1973) and then supplemented by work that placed women and their concerns in the center of attention. Early works on rape (Brownmiller, 1975), the welfare state (Wilson, 1977), housework (Oakley, 1974), and marriage (Bernard, 1972) contributed to the growing feminist scholarship.

Oddly, when assessing the impact of these approaches today, it is sometimes difficult to observe their effect on the current practice of social science. Certainly, critical perspectives such as feminism have made significant inroads in the new academic scholarship, yet much social science, especially in the United States, proceeds as if nothing has changed. Feminism and critical approaches are ignored or dismissed; interpretative and historical research is denigrated. Survey research continues to be seen as the pinnacle of sociology and an era of neofunctionalism is upon us.

Yet, this picture is too pessimistic. Feminist and critical scholarship continues to grow and some social scientists have taken up the challenge to make their work relevant to social action. Applied sociology flourishes and scholars are attempting to sketch the ways in which social scientists might work with new social movements (Touraine, 1981). Nevertheless, applied sociology as practiced in the United States sometimes refers to clinical work, and an applied approach often involves fulfilling the demands of the state by conducting narrowly defined policy research. Proposals for working with radical community groups are still sketchy or present rather dogmatic blueprints for connecting academic work to social action. We think that much more needs to be done by way of presenting examples and offering suggestions about ways of connecting research and action. The remainder of this chapter is intended to provide a sketch of a number of issues we consider to be important in conducting action research and in forging relationships between social researchers and feminist groups.

Action Research:
The Significance of Methodology

It is often assumed that good intentions are enough to ensure the importance and utility of research. This is, of course, a naïve stance, because research methods and epistemological assumptions are very important in the type of evidence presented, and in the manner in which the research enters the public and political debates regarding a particular social problem and the proposed solutions to it.

In contrast to the empiricists who seek to study social problems as isolated facts and to abstract theorists who rarely confront concrete problems, we developed a form of contextual analysis that establishes the links between contemporary and historical processes, and combines interactional, institutional, and cultural aspects of the problem. This approach has much in common with the general historical methods of Marx (1970) and Weber (1949) and with certain variants of the critical sociology associated with the Frankfurt School (Connerton, 1976). They all rejected the construction of generalized, abstracted, and ahistorical theories of social phenomena and the use of a superficial empiricism that fails to penetrate the most obvious features of the social world (David, 1957; Lukacs, 1971).

Historical and concrete analysis is a necessary aspect of our efforts to explain and understand recurrent social patterns such as violence against wives. Historical analysis must, however, be coupled with a concrete investigation of the everyday context of violence and the meanings and interpretations that women and men attach to these events. In pursuing these general methodological principles we employed various research strategies, including analysis of in-depth interviews with 109 battered women, 34,724 police and court records, historical documents, and media coverage, as well as informal interviews with representatives of social agencies.

In order to learn about the violence in a concrete, meaningful, and sensitive manner we employed a reflexive and contextual form of interviewing (Dobash & Dobash, 1979, 1983). Naturalistic and ethno-graphic researchers have employed this method in various research arenas and found it to provide a more thorough description and understanding of the area under study than can be achieved through survey analysis (Cicourel, 1968; Faulkner, 1973; Toch, 1969; Wegnar, 1975). In deciding to use this approach, we explicitly rejected the use of survey methods employing large probability samples that must invari-ably use superficial questionnaires and interviews based on abstract categories relating to preconceived and, in our view, irrelevant issues. Instead, we developed a technique that enabled us to learn a great deal about the violence itself and about the context in which it occurs. This was achieved by focusing on specific violent events experienced by the women and encouraging them to provide elaborate and detailed accounts of the physical attack, the interaction relating to it, the meanings attached to it, and the immediate and long-term actions of both the woman and the man. We do not, however, see this interpretative approach as a complete methodology, and consider it necessary to locate individual perceptions in the context of a wider cultural and institutional analysis.

Through the use of this methodology and allied research techniques, we were able to gather a wealth of historical and contemporary evidence that pointed to the significance of male dominance in the etiology of violence. Patriarchal concerns and demands were evident in all aspects of the problem. It should not be surprising that violence forms an integral aspect of male dominance, since systems of power and authority are ultimately based on the use or threat of force. On an interactional level, we discovered that it is through taking on the position of wife that women are most likely to become the victims of systematic and severe violence. Although other forms of male violence against women are shaped by patriarchy, it is in the family where men's "right" and privileges are given the most free reign. Once married, women are seen as rightly subject to the control and direction of men who use various methods to achieve these ends, including intimidation, coercion, and violence. Men learn these violent techniques, and the appropriate contexts for their use, through a male culture that condones and encourages violence. In the violent events experienced by the women we studied, violence was used by the men they lived with to silence them, to "win" arguments, to express dissatisfaction, to deter future behavior and to merely demonstrate dominance (Dobash & Dobash, 1979, 1984).

Patriarchal patterns also determine women's predicaments once violence becomes part of the relationship. Women feel guilty and trapped in these relationships. Guilty, because cultural prescriptions make family problems into women's problems regardless of the source. Trapped, because it is considered disloyal to betray patriarchal privacy by seeking help from outsiders and thus expose husbands and the family to potential scrutiny. Women are also trapped by the difficulties associated with living an independent life free from men. Gender stratification keeps women in low paid positions with little possibility of gaining employment that would enable them to live on their own with children.

Women are also faced with the negative responses of the wider society. Our contextual analysis led us to consider the role of outsiders' responses in the perpetuation of violence. We found that relatives and friends often provided support and sometimes material assistance, especially through a supportive female culture. However, women also experienced dismissive responses, and even the helpful ones were usually short-lived. The responses of state agencies were often even less effective. A legacy of patriarchal justice and psychiatric assumptions about women often resulted in less than meaningful responses from the police and social services. The overall effect of these patterns of response leaves women more isolated than they are before they seek help. They also strengthen the position of the husband who gains support for his belief that his behavior is either justified or not truly serious, and who is also strengthened by the certain knowledge that others will not intervene so as to challenge this violent behavior or protect his victim.

In contrast, other researchers studying violence in the home adopted strategies based on the reigning orthodoxy of logical positivism and abstract empiricism, attempting to isolate and abstract the violence out of its wider historical and social contexts. Using the social survey in an attempt to approximate the controls of the experimental method within natural settings, they have tried to isolate the problem under study by using probability sampling, abstract measurement, and statistical manipulation (see Willer & Willer, 1973). While this is a powerful technique when used in the investigation of certain issues, it has inherent limitations when applied to the study of complex phenomena such as violence. Although the method can be used to obtain information pertaining to relatively straightforward sociodemographic character-istics of respondents, it can provide little explanatory information regarding the processes associated with a sensitive problem such as wife beating. These criticisms do not constitute a rejection of the social survey in toto—indeed, we believe it can be employed in feminist-inspired forms of analysis (Yllö, 1983)—but rather an objection to its application to complex problems and to an unflinching reliance on it as a sure route to knowledge.

The research program of Murray Straus and his colleagues Richard Gelles and Suzanne Steinmetz (Straus, Gelles, & Steinmetz, 1980) provides an example of such an approach and illustrates the problems arising from its use on a complex problem such as violence in the home. Their major study was based on a probability sample of over 2,000 families, which revealed fewer than 200 cases of violence, and formed the basis of most of the analysis. The approach is based on simple correlations and ad hoc explanations. As such, many of the findings and conclusions are contradictory, inconsistent, and unwarranted (Dobash & Dobash, 1983; Pagelow, 1986; Pleck, Pleck, & Bart, 1977). The most obvious and contentious example of this comes from the "finding" that there is near "equality between the sexes" in the use of violence between spouses (Straus, 1980, p. 681), that is, "husband beating" and a "battered husband syndrome" are as prevalent as wife beating and battered wives (Steinmetz, 1977; Straus, 1977, p. 447). Furthermore, a 10-year follow-up survey, using the same approach to the measurement of violence, has "found" the same equality between the sexes in the use of violence (Straus & Gelles, 1986).

In fact, such claims cannot be justified given the nature of the research conducted and the results achieved. One of the primary problems with this research is a failure to consider the context of violence and an over-emphasis on abstract measurement such as the Conflict Tactics Scale (CTS) (Straus, 1979). Although abstract scales are not particularly useful in attempts to explain and understand social problems, this is especially the case when they are poorly conceived and constructed. The CTS, for example, suffers from numerous internal faults that call into question many of the results achieved through its use.

Briefly, the scale includes poorly conceived categories of violence (combining threatened, attempted, and actual violence) that are not mutually exclusive (e.g., separate categories of "Kicked, bit, or hit with a fist" and "Beat up the other one," Straus, 1979, p. 88). These inadequacies are compounded in the construction of a Violence Score for each respondent. Having failed to collect any information about injuries actually sustained, the researchers assume that certain acts "carry a high risk of injury" while others do not. Included in the "high-risk" category is "trying to hit with something" and excluded from it is "slapping." Yet, our own research, which does examine injuries sustained from particular attacks, demonstrates that a slap can result in anything from a temporary red mark to a broken nose, tooth, or jaw, and that trying to hit with something never results in an injury unless the blow is actually landed.

These defects, plus the additional failure to develop an overall analysis of specific violent events considered over time, led to fundamental problems in the use of terms such as *wife beating* and *husband beating*. For example, it is possible, and indeed very likely, that a man may have "kicked, hit with a fist" and "beaten up" his wife on numerous occasions injuring her on each, while she may have responded to these attacks by "trying to hit [him] with something" or "threatening [him] with a knife" in order to try to stop him from beating her, but without ever actually hitting or injuring him. By employing the aggregating and dichotomizing techniques used to produce the Violence Scores, it appears that these researchers would describe both husband and wife as "beaten" (Straus, 1979, pp. 77, 80, 88). Given such inadequacies, Straus, Gelles, and Steinmetz have no empirical warrant to employ the terms *battered* or *beaten,* and their results cannot be construed as indicating the existence of "battered husbands" or even "battered wives."

Certainly, there is a vast body of evidence confirming the existence of persistent, systematic, severe, and intimidating force men use against their wives (Dobash & Dobash, 1979, 1984; Gaquin, 1978; Martin, 1976; Pagelow, 1981; Parliamentary Select Committee on Violence in Marriage, 1975; U.S. Commission on Civil Rights, 1979). This evidence does warrant the use of terms such as *wife beating* or *battered women,* but there is no systematic evidence showing a pattern of severe, persistent, and intimidating violence against husbands that would warrant the use of terms such as *beaten* or *battered.* As such, the results of the research of Straus and his colleagues may tell us more about the response of women to their husband's violence (and about the problems of abstract measurement and scaling) than they do about any persistent or severe pattern of husband beating. Indeed, our research and that of virtually everyone else who has actually studied violent events and/or their patterning in a concrete and detailed fashion reveal that when women do use violence against their spouses or cohabitants, it is primarily in self-defense or retaliation, often during an attack by their husbands. On occasions, women may initiate an incident after years of being attacked, but it is extraordinarily rare for women to persistently initiate severe attacks. Although there is no doubt that women do slap and shove their husbands on occasion or throw things at them, one must question any statistical manipulation that defines this, or violence used in self-defense, as husband beating.

Debates about research methods may appear to be purely academic— unrelated to social and political issues. However, this is not the case. For example, the claims made about "battered husbands," although derived from inadequate research, had significant consequences for community groups. After the publication of this research, and its apparent promulgation by the mass media, women's groups in the United States reported greater difficulty in obtaining support for establishing shelters and crisis centers. Some authorities argued that because of the "findings" about battered husbands, battered women did not suffer from a unique problem and as such did not need special resources and assistance (Crowe, 1980; Pagelow, 1986; Pleck et al., 1977). Such misleading findings were easily incorporated within a dominant belief system in which problems of women are either denied, diminished, or blamed on the female victim. The interplay between research findings, whatever their scientific merit, public policy, and popular beliefs and/or prejudice, is all too familiar to grass roots activists and action researchers. The response to feminist scholarship is replete with salutory examples of this process of containment.

The Alternative Message
and Social Change

Inherent in every piece of social research are messages about the nature of the phenomenon and the individuals under study. Some of these messages reiterate and support the status quo while others challenge it and offer alternatives constituting fundamental change. Mathiesen (1974) has argued that social scientists interested in producing research oriented to social action, directed at social change, should offer alternatives, or messages, that not only *contradict* the status quo, but are also taken seriously and therefore *compete* with other proposals for consideration. In order to contradict, the message must differ from the existing ideology (in this case, male domination). Let us use examples from two eras of women's struggles. In order to compete seriously, messages (such as an "end to male domination" or "equal rights") must suggest a myriad of practical solutions. Messages that are fully formed (such as "imprisonment for all abusers" or "votes for women") are finite and cannot lead to other changes or a continuation of a social movement once achieved. Such proposals may also be easily co-opted into the status quo or simply disregarded as irrelevant because they are seen to be clearly outside the established order (Mathiesen, 1974, pp. 11-24).

According to Mathiesen, the potential for change embedded in any social scientific work, social policy, or public demand can be described in terms of four types of messages: the Noncompeting Agreement, the Competing Agreement, the Noncompeting Contradiction and the Competing Contradiction. We will discuss these four types of messages and consider how the arguments and proposals focusing on battered women fit into each category. Of the four types of messages, one represents a clear reiteration of the status quo, two others fail to provide an alternative either because they do not *contradict* the existing order or because they do not *compete* (are not taken seriously) for consideration for future change. Only the message that both contradicts and competes provides a real alternative.[1]

Noncompeting Agreement

The type of message that does not contradict the status quo or compete for consideration, the Noncompeting Agreement, brings nothing new and is simply a restatement of the existing order. There are many such messages concerning wife abuse, and a few examples will suffice here. There are the traditional notions that this is strictly an individual problem, relating simply to personalities, upbringing, or biology (as opposed to being a complex individual, social, institutional, and cultural problem); that the problem can be solved solely through individual therapeutic means; and that patriarchal relations (often disguised by the label "the traditional family") should be maintained in any proposals advanced. The usual messages regarding wife beating have focused primarily on the traits of the victim and sometimes on those of the offender, but rarely on wider social issues. This has largely taken the form of blaming the victim, excusing the violence, and setting limits on when violence is "legitimate" by concentrating on ideas such as female masochism, provocation, nagging, and insubordination.

Such messages fit well with the existing patriarchal system. They require no change and advance no challenges to it. It is not surprising that such arguments appear in some of the early statements on wife beating (Gayford, 1976; Lion, 1977; Schultz, 1960; Snell, Rosenwald, & Roby, 1964; Storr, 1974) and that they have been popularized by the press and entertained by some government bodies. A report in *The Guardian* (1974) illustrated these types of arguments. It quoted two psychiatrists who proclaimed that the perpetrators of such assaults are usually "badly brought up, heavy drinkers, spoilt as a child, and incapable of looking after themselves." A third psychiatrist reported that drink was "a very potent cause of unhappiness" and invoked a strong British prejudice by stating that "a disproportionate number of the women had Irish husbands." In the United States, people of color might be substituted, but the nature of the argument remains the same. Minority groups, deviants and/or the inadequate, are violent. Thus the logic of difference separates them from "us." But the most comforting explanation, for the complacent public and statutory bodies, has been that "the wife often puts herself in a violent situation." Messages of this nature do not compete with the existing views of the problem because the proposals are fully integrated into the established order and reiterate what everyone intuits as the "cause" of the problem. That is, the woman somehow "causes" the man to be violent and is therefore also responsible for the solution to her problem.

Another example of the type of message and action that support the status quo involves the use of the highly dubious idea of the "battered husband" (Steinmetz, 1977; Straus et al, 1980). In its most simple form, the supposed existence of a population of battered husbands has been used to diminish the significance of the very real existence of a population of battered wives. A more convoluted form of reasoning takes place, however, when the violent behavior of one population (i.e., men known to beat their wives persistently and severely) is implicitly compared with an entirely different population (i.e., women who supposedly beat their husbands in the same fashion), and the behavior of each is seen to cancel out that of the other. Since each group of individuals are "equally" culpable, the usual victim, the woman, is guilty and not worthy of support and sympathy. Even more basic is the fact that there is little or no public, governmental, or scientific demand, as there was with wife beating, that we know in great detail the nature, extent, persistence, and injuries involved in this so-called husband battering before it is considered serious. Instead, it has been satisfactory for many simply to accept that those women who have ever hit their husbands or thrown something at them or threatened to hit them have "battered their husbands" (a definition that would never be allowed if the woman were the victim).

Competing Agreement

The second type of message that fails to provide a real alternative is one that competes for attention but does not contradict the status quo. The Competing Agreement is really a "fictitious competition." Examples of this sort of message concerning wife abuse are often complex because they may contain elements that posit an alternative and sometimes include feminist analysis as well as features that reiterate and support the status quo. The work of Lenore Walker (1977) provides an example. She argues from a feminist perspective that the emergence and continuation of wife beating is related to the subordinate position of women, and proposes fundamental social changes in order to make any real impact on the problem itself as well as on the individuals now experiencing it. But in discussing this apparent alternative, Walker focuses almost exclusively on the individual level, concentrating on the characteristics of the victim, and restricting her specific proposals to individual learning and therapy. The wider vision of change is truncated and contradicted by the concept of "learned helplessness" and the implied culpability of women in the so-called "cycle of violence." Concentrating on the female victim and positing that she learns to be helpless and thus contributes to the perpetuation of the violence directed at her is similar in its implications to the old psychiatric notions of masochism and victim-blaming.

Given the congruence of the idea of learned helplessness with the conventional wisdom about wife abuse, it is not surprising that this notion has been widely embraced. It is ironic that the concept of learned helplessness has been adopted by professional and community groups, since the analysis of Walker's own data demonstrates that the explanation of why women remain in a violent relationship lies much more in social and economic circumstances (employment, housing, number of dependent children, and so on) than in individuals' supposed helplessness (Nielson, Eberle, Leidig, & Walker, 1979).

The initial message in Walker's work appeared to offer an alternative to the patriarchal system. It also offered a form of agreement with that old system. The response of the established institutions and some community groups has been to adopt the congruent message.

Additional examples of the Competing Agreement are the arguments of Pizzey and Shapiro relating to "violent-prone women" and proposals for crisis intervention. Pizzey and Shapiro, like Walker, begin by asking why women find it difficult to leave violent relationships. Their answer is that at least one third of battered women are hooked on an adrenalin high associated with violence and simply cannot leave it alone (Bowder, 1979; Pizzey & Shapiro, 1981). Therefore, these "violent-prone women" and their children need to be taken into institutional care in order that they might be cured of this addiction. This argument, which is based on no systematic evidence, is clearly a "fictitious competition." It sounds new but, in fact, nothing new is being proposed. In both in its form and content, it replicates existing myths about masochistic women. Even the question to be answered "why do women stay" is based on traditional assumptions. (Why do we not ask why men use violence to coerce and dominate women?) Ignoring the violent man and wider social issues, these ideas focus on traits of the female victim that supposedly cause her own victimization (see Shainess, 1986 for a similar position; Dobash & Dobash, 1979, for a critical evaluation).

Noncompeting Contradiction

The forces pulling away from the alternative, contradictory, and competing message are many and strong. The forces exerted on the alternative message come through several sources, including language, particularly as it is related to power and the requirements that one use the language of the powerful in order to "define the problems at hand . . . [and] to persuade the powerful that our contradiction is sensible" (Mathiesen, 1974, p. 19). Sometimes, the alternative message is pushed toward the established system or efforts are made to assure the message remains outside of the established system. That is, integrate or be banned. Underlying all this is the issue of revolutionary change versus reform. According to Mathiesen, demands that one must choose one label or the other—rather than remain ambiguous, open, and unfolding in working toward an alternative—are "characteristics of an authoritarian social system . . . intolerant of ambiguity." They are demands that those who propose social change choose a label by which they can be "defined out" as irrelevant or "defined in" as undangerous (Mathiesen, 1974, p. 23).

Putting forth a contradiction of the old system but being defined out as irrelevant, or noncompeting, is the fate of the third type of message, the Noncompeting Contradiction. Critical feminist analysis always runs the risks of being denied, ignored, and rejected. John Stuart Mill recognized the difficulty in putting what we call a Competing Contradiction when he observed: "In every respect the burden is hard on those who attack an almost universal opinion. They must be very fortunate as well as unusually capable if they obtain a hearing at all." Feminist perspectives are often dismissed as one-dimensional, biased, irrelevant, extreme, and unworthy of consideration. The mere label "feminist" carries negative connotations, whereas other perspectives that stress functional, liberal, individual, and even reactionary accounts are all considered worthy of serious consideration.

Competing Contradiction

Finally, we reach the message that offers an alternative because it both contradicts the premises of the old system and competes for consideration: the Competing Contradiction. The foreign message that is suggestive, rather than fully formed, competes because the "unclarified nature of the future consequences of the contradiction makes it impossible for the (satisfied) system member to maintain that the contradiction is certainly outside of the realm of interest" (Mathiesen, 1974, p. 16). Presenting an alternative to existing explanations and institutional responses to violence in the home means we must adopt alternative methods, explanations, and solutions. The method, as described above, must be concrete and include historical and contemporary contexts. The explanation must consider why wife beating has occurred and continues as a recurrent pattern within the traditional fabric of society, how it operates and is supported by institutional ideologies and responses. The proposed solutions must include short- and long-term alternatives that challenge existing ideologies and institutional responses relating to the problem. This overall alternative enterprise must operate on at least three interrelated levels, including individual, ideological, and institutional.

In constructing alternative explanations we must use terms such as *wife beating* to describe the social problem and *battered women* to denote the victims, instead of more abstract concepts such as *spouse abuse* and *marital violence,* since they give the false impression of an equal problem for both men and women and thereby actually discriminate against women (Dobash, 1981). We must also place the problem in the context of historically structured forms of family relationships and their accompanying ideologies, such as patriarchal domination in capitalist societies, rather than situating it relative to stereotypical sex roles or constellations of attitudes associated with terms such as *sexism.* In using this form of discourse we are refusing to adopt the language of the system and instead adopt that of the alternative.

Proposing the contradictory message and the accompanying solutions also involves rejecting the violence unequivocally rather than setting limits on it by excusing it or rejecting only its most severe and public forms. This involves challenging the patriarchal form of domination associated with the violence and the widespread ideological and institutional supports for it. It involves tackling the causes of the problem itself rather than dealing solely with those who currently suffer from it. Thus, proposals must include fundamental changes directed not only at assisting victims and reacting to offenders but also at the institutional and ideological means by which the problem itself is sustained or eroded.

The alternative to wife beating includes an ongoing confrontation with patriarchal forms of domination and control and a struggle for the development of egalitarian relations between women and men. These actions will encompass both short-term and long-range goals for changes at the individual and institutional levels. Although short-term and fully formed goals directed at assisting individuals, such as refuges organized on feminist principles, legislation, feminist programs for violent men, equal employment opportunities for women, provision for daycare, and many others, should be sought, they should be carefully scrutinized in terms of the short-term effects on the women and men involved and long-term consequences for the problem itself. The achievement of short-term goals should not become an end in itself and imply a termination of action, but should be a part of an unfolding new social order in which violence toward women would cease to be actively taught and institutionally supported and would truly become a deviant and abhorrent act. It is this approach that we have adopted in our own work and that we can see in the work of numerous other social scientists and activists. In Britain and the United States, examples of such work have been undertaken in a wide variety of areas.[2] They are neither unified in their approaches nor are the messages always unequivocally challenging, but they represent a shift in this critical direction.

The Social Scientist
and the Community

Presenting the alternative message in various public arenas in conjunction with community groups is an additional and important aspect of action research. This is a complex process that leads the social scientist into direct contact with grass roots groups, the media, and statutory bodies. It involves the social scientist in social and political processes associated with the deliberations over new legislation directed at altering existing policies and practices of statutory agencies, the dissemination of information and theoretical arguments through the mass media, and the various challenging activities of community groups.

Action researchers are inevitably involved at these various levels, and in this final section we offer examples of the pitfalls associated with this type of activity, indicate the problematics of putting the contradictory and competing message through the media and to members of statutory agencies, and suggest meaningful ways of relating to community groups.

When we first entered this complex arena we did so in a hesitant and rather halting manner. Without the results of our research and with little available evidence on the problem, we were reluctant to offer definitive interpretations to legislators and representatives of the media who sought them. The British media sought out those who were prepared to provide immediate answers, and psychiatrists were willing to do so. The bulk of their interpretations focused on the supposed pathological characteristics of men and women involved in abuse. We entered media presentations partly because we sought to counter and contradict the premature and false explanations offered by members of the psychiatric profession. We stressed that this was an important problem directly related to the status of women and that it required immediate public attention. The media often pressed for sensationalist examples and superficial analysis that reflected their own preconceptions of the problem. It has been, and often continues to be, a struggle to present the contradictory message in a medium that is predictably oriented to presenting the prevailing ideologies regarding women, reducing complex social issues to individual problem and digestible "fact," and seeking to glorify individuals.

Representatives of the Women's Aid Federations have experienced similar problems in having their vast cumulative experience and expertise often ignored by the media. Although the federations assist nearly all of the battered women seeking help and conduct and excellent educational programs for schools, professionals, and the general public, the British media have, until recently, largely ignored these efforts and focused on one refuge and one woman, Erin Pizzey. Pizzey's message is one that is easily accepted. Her speculations regarding the biologically determined "violence-prone" woman (Pizzey & Shapiro, 1981) not only focus attention at the individual level but also blame the victim. No wider socio-cultural explanations need be sought, nor are efforts to change patriarchal capitalist societies necessary. The media elevated Pizzey to the level of a media personality. Battered women are no longer the only or even the primary concern. The media created Pizzey as a phenomenon, and then perpetuated that reality through continued coverage of her personal life. The problems of battered women were no longer especially significant when issues were replaced by personalities.

The difficulties in presenting the alternative are also apparent when attempting the necessary task of confronting professionals with the evidence of their contribution to the continuation of the problem of violence against wives. Social workers, doctors, and police officers deal with battered women on a daily basis, yet their actions often fail to provide assistance and they may even exacerbate a woman's predicament, deflect blame onto her, and increase her sense of isolation. The problem then, is to present professionals with this evidence and offer feminist interpretations and alternative strategies while continuing to compete, rather than becoming irrelevant to the ongoing discourse. We must continue to put forth the alternative message (a "Competing Contradiction"), and not modify it simply to make it more palatable or acceptable to professionals, thus stripping it of its real challenge. We have found this to be an extraordinarily difficult task and realize that our message often runs the risk of becoming a Noncompeting Contradiction, outside of the system's discourse, since professionals resist feminist interpretations that lead to a thorough examination of existing responses and/or seek to reject alternative strategies as impractical and irrelevant.

Throughout this overall reflexive and challenging process of conducting research, constructing explanations of the problem, and presenting the alternative, we have often worked closely with Scottish Women's Aid. Our first contact with Women's Aid workers was at the very beginning of our research. From the onset of this contact we were engaged in a dialogue with members of Women's Aid, one that involved a mutual exchange of knowledge and interpretations. We learned a great deal from members of Women's Aid, and their experience often helped us in expanding our research domain into areas that we had not at first considered important. This does not mean that our analysis always agreed with theirs or that we were captured by their perspective. Through a two-way process we learned from them and, we would like to think, they learned from us and that our research findings contributed to their attempts to assist battered women. For example, our finding that 25% of all violent crimes are wife assaults has provided a firm foundation for the justifiable claim that the problem is widespread and requires urgent attention.

The relationship between social scientists and community groups will always involve dialogue, debate, and political activity (Touraine, 1981). It is unethical to use community groups in a predatory manner, as mere avenues to research subjects, or sources of information, to be used solely for professional ends and discarded once the research results are in. Nor is it acceptable to behave in an arrogant or aloof manner by setting oneself up as the expert, denying the legitimacy of the knowledge and expertise that group members have gained through various forms of direct and continual experience with the problem (Crowe, 1980).

Although action researchers are oriented to community groups, this does not mean that they become mere ideologues and that their research is biased or distorted. Yet, facile claims of this nature are often made and used to impede or denigrate critical, feminist action research and proposed changes in the existing order. It is relevant to note that it is considered legitimate, even laudable, for social scientists to conduct research under the auspices of government agencies oriented to developing social policy or reform, and such support bestows merit on the research and authenticity on its findings. Alternatively, it is often considered illegitimate for the action researcher to conduct research oriented to community action and fundamental social change, and this denigrates the research and the findings. There is no logical or empirical reason why action researchers should be more biased or tainted through association with community groups than those researchers who accept grants from state agencies or those who are simply in pursuit of professional advancement. Indeed, action researchers do not receive large sums of money from the groups with which they are associated. The quality of research must be determined by its own merit and not evaluated according to the power and authority of those who support it or are affected by it.

In conclusion, we have offered a sketch of some of the processes associated with research relating to social action and social change in order to indicate some directions that might be pursued in expanding and developing this kind of work. Developing a more meaningful sociological orientation to explanations of and solutions to social problems can only begin through reflecting upon the process of ongoing research and action. This development cannot come through the present textbook or through a cookbook depiction of social science denuded of all but its technical problems, nor will it have any meaning or utility unless social scientists realize that they are an integral aspect of this overall process.

NOTES

1. For the purposes of this discussion, we will distill Mathiesen's argument and deal in a fairly straightforward manner with what is a very complex argument. Therefore, we would strongly recommend that Mathiesen's *The Politics of Abolition* (1974) be

consulted, and caution that our discussion cannot serve as a substitute for his elaborate and subtle argument.

2. Most of these works include a consideration of historical, institutional, cultural, and/or interactional factors directly related to the problem that are placed in an overall social, economic, and/or political context. They cover topics such as: housing and refuge provision (Ahrens, 1980; Binney, Hankell, & Nixon, 1981; Hanmer, 1977; Klein, 1979; Pahl, 1978; Schechter, 1982; Scottish Women's Aid, 1978; Sutton, 1977; Warrior, 1980; Welsh Women's Aid, 1980), social services (Maynard, 1985; Nichols, 1976; Wilson, 1975), medicine (Stark, Flitcraft, & Frazier, 1979), the criminal justice system (Bannon, 1975; Fields, 1977; Loving, 1980; Pagelow, 1981; Pahl, 1982; Wasoff, 1982; Wasoff, Dobash, & Dobash, 1979), the state (Morgan, 1986), and inequality (Klein, 1979, 1982; Martin, 1976).

REFERENCES

Ahrens, L. (1980). Battered women's refuges: Feminist cooperative vs. social service institutions. *Radical America,* pp. 41-49.

Bannon, J. (1975, August 12). *Law enforcement problems with intra-family violence.* Paper presented at the meeting of the American Bar Association.

Bart, P. B. (1971). Sexism and social science: From the gilded cage to the iron cage, or the perils of Pauline. *Journal of Marriage and the Family, 33*(4), 734-745.

Bernard, J. (1972). *The future of marriage.* New York: Bantam.

Binney, V., Hankell, G., & Nixon, J. (1981). *Leaving violent men: A study of refuges and housing for battered women.* London: Women's Aid Federation.

Bowder, B. (1979, March). The wives who ask for it. *Community Care,* pp. 18-19.

Brownmiller, S. (1975). *Against our will: Men, women and rape.* New York: Simon & Schuster.

Charlton, C. (1972). The first cow on Chiswick High Road. *Spare Rib, 24,* 24-25.

Cicourel, A. (1964). *Method and measurement in sociology.* New York: Fine Press.

Cicourel, A. (1968). *The social organization of juvenile justice.* New York: John Wiley.

Connerton, P. (1976). *Critical sociology.* Harmondsworth, England: Penguin.

Coote, A., & Gill, T., with Richardson, J. (1977). *Battered women and the new law.* London: National Council for Civil Liberties.

Crowe, M. (1980, June 8). Research—behind closed doors. *Equal Times,* pp. 11-13.

Delamont, S., & Ellis, R. (1979). *Statutory and voluntary responses to domestic violence in Wales: A pilot project.* Domestic Violence Project (SRU Working Paper No. 6). Cardiff, Wales: Department of Health and Social Security/Welsh Office.

Dobash, R. E. (1981). When nonsexist language is sexist. In B. Warrior (Ed.), *Working on wife abuse.* Cambridge, MA: Betsy Warrior.

Dobash, R. E., & Dobash, R. P. (1979). *Violence against wives: A case against the patriarchy.* New York: Free Press.

Dobash, R. E., & Dobash, R. P. (1979b, May 3). If you prick me do I not bleed? (A response to Pizzey, Gayford and McKeith). *Community Care,* pp. 26-28.

Dobash, R. E., & Dobash, R. P. (1981). Community response to violence against wives: Charivari, abstract justice and patriarchy. *Social Problems, 28*(5), 563-581.

Dobash, R. E., & Dobash, R. P. (1983). The context specific approach to researching violence against wives. In D. Finkelhor, R. Gelles, G. Hotaling, & M. A. Straus (Eds.), *The dark side of families* (pp. 261-176). Newbury Park, CA: Sage.

Dobash, R. E., & Dobash, R. P. (1984). The nature and antecedent of violent events. *British Journal of Criminology 24*(3), 269-288.

Dobash, R. E., & Dobash, R. P. (1987). The response of the British and American Women's movements to violence against women. In J. Hanmer & M. Maynard (Eds.), *Women, violence and social control* (pp. 169-179). London: Macmillan.

Dobash, R. E., & Dobash, R. P. (in press). *Women, violence and social change in Britain and the United States.* Boston: Routledge & Kegan Paul.

Dobash, R. Emerson, Dobash, R. P., & Davanagh, K. (1984). The contact between battered women and social and medical agencies. In J. Pahl (Ed.), *Private violence and public policy.* Boston: Routledge & Kegan Paul.

Faulkner, R. K. (1973). On respect and retribution: Toward an ethnography of violence. *Sociological Symposium, 9,* 17-35.

Field, M. H., & Field, H. F. (1973). Marital violence and criminal process: Neither justice nor peace. *Social Service Review, 47,* 221-240.

Fields, M. (1977). Wife beating: Facts and figures. *Victimology, 2,* 543-646.

Gaquin, D. A. (1978). Spouse abuse: Data from the national crime survey. *Victimology, 2,* 632-643.

Gayford, J. J. (1968). Sociologist as partisan: Sociology and the welfare state. *American Sociologist, 3,* 103-116.

Gayford, J. J. (1976). Ten types of battered wives. *Welfare Officer, 1,* 5, 9.

Hanmer, J. (1977). Community action, women's aid and the women's liberation movement. In M. Mayor (Ed.), *Women in the community* (pp. 91-108). London: Routledge & Kegan Paul.

Horowitz, I. L. (Ed.). (1964). *The new sociology: Essays in social science and social theory in honour of C. W. Mills.* Oxford: Oxford University Press.

Klein, D. (1979). Can this marriage be saved? Battery and sheltering. *Crime and Social Justice, 12,* 19-33.

Klein, D. (1982). The dark side of marriage: Battered wives and the domination of women. In A. Rafter & A. Stanko (Eds.), *Judge, lawyer, victim, thief* (pp. 83-109). Boston: Northwestern University.

Lion, J. R. (1977). Clinical aspects of wifebattering. In M. Roy (Ed.), *Battered women: A psychosociological study of domestic violence* (pp. 126-136). New York: Van Nostrand Reinhold.

Loving, N. (1980). *Responding to spouse abuse and wife beating: A guide for police.* Washington, DC: Police Executive Research Forum.

Lukacs, G. (1971). What is orthodox marxism? In *History and class consciousness* (R. Livingstone, Trans.). London: Merlin.

Martin, D. (1976). *Battered wives.* San Francisco: Glide.

Marx, K. (1970). *Contribution to the critique of political economy.* (M. Dobb, Ed.). Moscow: Progress.

Mathiesen, T. (1974). *The politics of abolition.* London: Martin Robertson.

Maynard, M. (1985). The response of social workers to domestic violence. In J. Pahl (Ed.), *Private violence and public policy.* Boston: Routledge & Kegan Paul.

Morgan, P. (1986). Constructing images of deviance: A look at state intervention into the problem of wife beating. In N. Johnson (Ed.), *Marital violence* (pp. 60-76). Boston: Routledge & Kegan Paul.

National Women's Aid Federation (1975). *Battered women need refuges: A report from the National Women's Aid Federation.* England: Author.

National Women's Aid Federation (1978). He's got to show her who's boss—The National Women's Aid Federation challenges a man's right to batter. *Spare Rib, 69*(15), 18.

Nichols, B. B. (1976). The abused wife problem. *Social Casework, 57,* 27-32.

Nielsen, J. M., Eberle, P., Leidig, M. W., & Walker, L. E. (1979, August). *Why women stay in battering relationships.* Paper presented at the meeting of the American Sociological Association, Boston.

Oakley, Ann (1974). *The sociology of housework.* New York: Pantheon.

Pagelow, M. (1981). *Woman battering.* Newbury Park, CA: Sage.

Pagelow, M. (1986). The battered husband syndrome. Social problem or much ado about nothing. In N. Johnson (Ed.), *Marital violence* (pp. 172-194). Boston: Routledge & Kegan Paul.

Pahl, J. (1978, November). *A refuge for battered women: A study of the role of a women's centre.* London: Her Majesty's Stationery Office.

Pahl, J. (1982, November). Police response to battered women. *Journal of Social Welfare Law,* pp. 337-343.

Pahl, J. (1985). *Private violence and public policy.* Boston: Routledge & Kegan Paul.

Parliamentary Select Committee on Violence in Marriage (1975). *Report from the Select Committee on violence in marriage together with the proceedings of the committee: Vol. 2. Report, minutes of evidence and appendices, session 1974-75* (HC 553-4). London: Her Majesty's Stationery Office.

Pizzey, E. (1974). *Scream quietly or the neighbours will hear you.* Harmondsworth, England: Penguin.

Pizzey, E., & Shapiro, J. (1981). Choosing a violent relationship. *New Society, 56,* 133-135.

Pleck, E., Pleck, J., & Bart, P. (1977). The battered data syndrome: A reply to Steinmetz. *Victimology, 2,* 680-683.

Rose, H. (1978). In practice supported, in theory denied: An account of an invisible urban movement. *International Journal of Urban and Regional Research, 2,* 521-537.

Rose, H. (1985). Women's refuges: Erecting new forms of welfare? In C. Ungerson (Ed.), *Women and social policy.* London: Macmillan.

Rose, H., & Rose, S. (1976). The radicalisation of science. In H. Rose & S. Rose (Eds.), *The radicalisation of science: Ideology of/in the natural sciences* (pp. 1-31). London: Macmillan.

Rowbotham, S. (1973). *Woman's consciousness, man's world.* Harmondsworth: Penguin.

Schechter, S. (1982). *Women and male violence.* Boston: South End Press.

Schultz, L. G. (1960). The wife assaulter. *Journal of Social Therapy 6*(2), 103-112.

Scottish Women's Aid (1978). *Battered women in Scotland: Your rights and where to turn for help.* Edinburgh: Ainslie House.

Shainess, N. (1986). *Sweet suffering.* New York: Pocket Books.

Smith, D. E. (1974). Women's perspective as a radical critique of sociology. *Sociological Inquiry, 44*(1), 468-487.

Snell, J. E., Rosenwald, R., & Roby, A. (1964, August). The wifebeater's wife: A study of family interaction. *Archives of General Psychiatry, II,* 107-112.

Stark, E., Flitcraft, A., & Frazier, W. (1979). Medicine and patriarchal violence: The social contruction of a (private) event. *International Journal of Health Services, 9*, 461-493.

Steinmetz, S. K. (1977). The battered husband syndrome. *Victimology, 2*, 499-509.

Storr, A. (1974). *Human aggression.* Harmondsworth, England: Penguin.

Straus, M. A. (1977). Wife beating: How common and why? *Victimology*, 443-458.

Straus, M. A. (1979). Measuring conflict and violence: The conflict tactics (CT) scales. *Journal of Marriage and the Family, 40*(1), 75-88.

Straus, M. A. (1980). Victims and aggressors in marital violence. *American Behavioral Scientist, 23*, 681-704.

Straus, M. A., & Gelles, R. (1986). Societal change and change in family violence from 1975 to 1985 as revealed by two national surveys. *Journal of Marriage and the Family, 48*, 465-479.

Straus, M., Gelles, R., & Steinmetz, S. (1980). *Behind closed doors.* New York: Doubleday.

Sutton, J. (1977). The growth of the British movement for battered women. *Victimology, 2*, 576-584.

Taylor, I., Walton, P., & Young, J. (1973). *The new criminology: For a social theory of deviance.* London: Routledge & Kegan Paul.

Toch, H. (1969). *Violent men: An inquiry into the psychology of violence.* Chicago: Aldine.

Touraine, A. (1981). *The voice and the eye, an analysis of social movements* (Maison des science de l'Homme & CUP, Trans.). Cambridge: Cambridge University Press.

U.S. Commission on Civil Rights (1979). *Battered women: Issues of public policy.* Washington, DC: U.S. Government Printing Office.

Walker, L. (1977). Battered women and learned helplessness. *Victimology, 2*, 528-531.

Warrior, B. (1980). *Working on wife abuse.* Cambridge, MA: Author.

Wasoff, F. (1982). Legal protection from wifebeating: The processing of domestic assaults by Scottish prosecutors and criminal courts. *International Journal of the Sociology of Law, 10*, 187-204.

Wasoff, F., Dobash, R. E., & Dobash, R. P. (1979). The current evidence and legal remedies regarding battered women. *Journal of the Law Society of Scotland, 14*(5), 178-183.

Weber, M. (1949). *The methodology of the social sciences* (E. Shils & H. A. Finch, Trans. and Eds.). New York: Free Press.

Welsh Women's Aid (1980). *The housing needs of battered women in Wales.* Cardiff, Wales: Author.

Willer, D., & Willer, J. (1973). *Systematic empiricism: A critique of a pseudoscience.* Englewood Cliffs, NJ: Prentice-Hall.

Wilson, E. (1975). Battered wives: A social worker's viewpoint. *Royal Society of Health Journal, 95*, 294-297.

Wilson, E. (1977). *Woman and the welfare state.* London: Tavistock.

Yllö, K. (1983). Using a feminist approach in quantitative research: A case study. In D. Finkelhor, R. J. Gelles, G. T. Hotaling, & M. A. Straus (Eds.), *The dark side of families* (pp. 227-288). Newbury Park, CA: Sage.

3

Fear of Crime and the Myth of the Safe Home

A Feminist Critique of Criminology

ELIZABETH A. STANKO

Last year, I was living in a neighborhood that was terrorized by a serial rapist. Two of the three women raped by this assailant were under-graduates from my own university. During the following months, I experienced a more acute fear about rape and other forms of male violence, as did other neighborhood and university women. I changed the front and back locks on my house for additional security and, after dark, restricted my movements outside the house. Because the rapist's strategy of attack involved entering women's homes, I felt unsafe in my home. As the initial crisis of the rapist waned (the attacks just stopped after two months, the man was never apprehended), the illusion of safety inside my own home returned.

I knew I had experienced what criminologists refer to as "fear of crime." This fear, according to criminologists, is associated with a diffuse anxiety or concern about being a victim of crime, particularly a crime of violence. This experience, however, was different from the other experiences of feeling unsafe outside my own home (a common experience of most women) because I tried to grasp what it must be like to live within an unsafe home. As a feminist who has been involved in the battered women's movement (I helped found a shelter in my home town), I know that this feeling of unsafety is a continuous experience of countless women and children who are battered and sexually abused in their own homes. Yet, as a criminologist, I have no academic language or analysis to account for "fear of crime" in association with the home being an unsafe, fear-producing environment.

The myth of the safe home is deeply entrenched in the minds of most Americans. This myth is supported by academics and policy makers who fail to recognize the potential danger of the home as a locus of violence against women. Why, for instance, do images of serious crime, particularly interpersonal violence, continuously focus on street crime—crime supposedly committed by strangers—rather than on the inter-personal violence that exists at such high levels in American households? What does it mean to women experiencing violence from familial and familiar assailants to confront thinking that presumes the home and relationships with known others as "safe," rather than as potentially violent? How does this thinking affect the lives of women living within violent households? In conceptualizing the problem of interpersonal violence, do men take their personal safety on the street or in the home for granted? As many working in the area of woman battering already know, the myth of the safe home helps to maintain and reproduce society's blinders, obscuring many of women's widespread experiences of male violence within the home. The purpose of this chapter is to examine how the growing attention to the phenomenon of "fear of crime" contributes to the myth of the safe home.

Conceptualizing Fear
From a Male Point of View

> Male, as opposed to female, activities are always recognized as predomi-nately important, and cultural systems give authority and value to the rules and actions of men. (Rosaldo, 1974, p. 19)

A feminist critique of criminologists' concept "fear of crime" begins with recognizing the cultural meanings linked to the abstract categories of the public and the private. These categories are important for they incorporate notions about sexual stratification and male dominance. The public realm is predominately men's domain. Affairs of the state, the workplace, and the traditional "protecting" institutions, like the military and the criminal justice system, still largely belong to and are controlled by men. Women's traditional domain, the private sphere of the home, occupies a subordinate position within a society bounded by status and prestige (Rosaldo, 1974).

In examining the literature in the area of "fear of crime," it seems that criminologists, too, have created a public-private dichotomy, one which associates public space with danger and private space with safety. This dichotomy can be found in scrutinizing criminologists' study of men's and women's concern about crime on the streets, a topic about which we now have a wealth of information. Note, too, that the language of the discipline focuses on "citizen" concern—a gender neutral reference—in their descriptions of who is afraid of crime and how fear alters individuals' daily lives. The gender neutral term automatically mutes any difference between men and women. Surveys conducted by national TV networks, polling centers, and victimization researchers indicate that women and men are aware of crime and take steps to avoid situations where they might be victimized. They also report anxiety, "fear," of being a victim of crime. Not only are individuals concerned about the effect of crime on their lives, but they alter their behavior—by moving, avoiding certain "dangerous" areas, staying at home at night—because of the effects or the perceived effects of street crime (Balkin, 1979; Baumer 1978; Clemente & Kleiman, 1977; Dubow, McCabe, & Kaplan, 1979; Garofalo, 1979; Hindelang, Gottfredson, & Garofalo, 1978; Lewis & Maxfield, 1980; Maxfield, 1984; President's Commission, 1967; Skogan & Maxfield, 1981; Tyler, 1980).

Criminologists treat the existence of "fear of crime" as a "social fact" (Liska, Lawrence, & Sanchirico, 1982) rather than an individual ailment. But what women and men are afraid of is much less clear. While individuals cite interpersonal violence as their number one concern, their fear, according to researchers, arises from their feelings of being unsafe on the street and their perceived risk and/or experiences with predatory (person to person) crime (Maxfield, 1984). A curious paradox exists among gender, fear, and risk of victimization. Victimization survey findings indicate that men are at greater risk to victimization from interpersonal violence. Yet, women and the elderly, the least likely to be victimized, according to these same surveys, report the highest levels of fear of being criminally victimized, almost three times the levels of men (Balkin, 1979; Clemente & Kleiman, 1977; Hindelang, Gottfredson, & Garofalo, 1978; Skogan & Maxfield, 1981).

Researchers attach expressions of fear of crime to the safety or the unsafety of the public streets. To do so, criminologists construct the concept "fear" by querying citizens about how safe they feel on the street, after dark, in their own neighborhoods. "Real crime," that which is assumed to engender fear, is typically linked with violence committed by strangers in public places. The President's Commission on Law Enforcement and the Administration of Justice (1967), in its series of reports which set the agenda for criminal justice inquiry since 1967, noted that fear of crime was "not a simple fear of injury or death or even of all crimes of violence, but, at bottom, a fear of strangers" (p. 52). As such, the street—the public space—is the location where criminal violence can and does occur (Silberman, 1978). Police and politicians, who together like to assure American citizens about the need to "protect" the streets from crime, express concern about the safety of public space. Indeed, fear about crime and being a victim of crime outside the home has become troublesome for American police and politicians: It upsets the public's confidence in the state's promise to protect its citizens (Hanmer & Stanko, 1985).

Within current conceptions about fear of crime, researchers treat the home as a safety zone, a respite from the unknown dangers of the street. This is where women are told to remain if there is a dangerous stranger about. Researchers do not attribute serious, interpersonal crime against women—battering from partners and intimate companions, sexual assault/rape from those familiar and familial, to the type of victimization, "which engenders fear to walk the streets" (Liska, Lawrence, & Sanchirico, 1982, p. 764). As criminologists and criminal justice policy makers continue to use images about random violent crime in discussions of interpersonal violence, they bypass, for the large part, women's experiences of interpersonal violence, which more often involve intimates who victimize them in their own homes.

To a large extent, the theoretical framework surrounding the study of interpersonal violence and "citizen" fear about it can be said to be "masculinist" because it focuses on the public sphere—street crime—and virtually ignores so-called "private violence." As we will examine next, the counting of crime and the intervention into what comes to be characterized as real crime also emphasizes the "public" sphere, once again overlooking women's experiences of fear in their own homes.

Criminal Victimization: The Construction of Stranger Violence

Police policy and policing practice shape the concept of what constitutes serious, fear-producing crime. Prior to the development of crime surveys, or victimization surveys as they are also called, all information about serious crime and its occurrence came from police reports. As Ericson (1981), McCleary, Nienstedt, & Erven (1982), and others note, police recording and response practices influence the counting of serious crime on stranger violence. As feminist researchers have shown, instances of wife battering and other forms of male violence within the home have traditionally been excluded from official police action (Martin, 1976; Stanko, 1985). Rather than a blatant abuse of discretionary power, the reluctance of police to arrest woman-batterers is part of the normal exercise of duty (Berk & Loseke, 1981; Black, 1970; Oppenlander, 1982; Stanko, 1985). Moreover, those police who treat complaints of battering as serious crime may face an unresponsive prosecution and judicial system as well (Stanko, 1982). Failure of police to record incidents of woman battering relegates many of these offenses to an official limbo: but where there is no record, is there no fear?

Criminologists began to address the limitations of police generated information about crime incidence in the 1980s. Researchers conducted surveys to inquire about individuals' experiences with crime, to ask whether they sought the assistance of the police when they encountered such an experience, and to explore their feelings about the safety of the streets. Victimization studies, bound within traditional understandings about serious crime (that it is violence committed largely by strangers), use official categories of crime as their base, and focus on crimes such as rape, robbery, assault (crime categories of the Uniform Crime Reports, Index I) as the most bothersome and fearful for citizens. This emphasis on interpersonal violent crime spotlights street crime committed by strangers and neglects other forms of crime that also might produce fear, for instance, the illegal dumping of toxic waste (Box, 1984; Johnson & Wasielewski, 1982; Reiman, 1984).

Crime survey researchers consistently find that approximately one half of all serious crime—robbery, assault, rape—is not reported to the police. In explaining why criminal events are not reported to police, researchers cite various factors that influence an individual's decision to involve the police in what could, by statute, be defined as criminal violence and serious crime. Some of these factors are how "private" individuals feel that a "dispute" is, their feeling that the police would not think the matter serious, their feelings that even if reported nothing could be done to resolve the matter, or their feelings that despite its statutory seriousness, the matter was not important enough to report to police (Bureau of Justice Statistics, 1983).

For a variety of reasons, interpersonal violence committed by intimates, friends, and acquaintances tends to be underreported in victimization surveys. These are the very crimes that are most likely to affect women (Stanko, 1987). Diana Russell, in her comprehensive book *Sexual Exploitation,* illustrates the effect of underreporting on understanding rape. Her 1978 survey of 930 women in the San Francisco area uncovered rape incidence 24 times that reported by the FBI Uniform Crime reports (1985, p. 46). Russell's findings, also collected from questionnaires, expose a masculinist framework from which most information about women's victimization is gathered, reported, and analyzed. As a result, much crime victimizing women that takes place within the home does not find its way into subsequent analyses of women's risk of interpersonal violence, perceptions of danger, and feelings of fear—analyses that inform policy makers' crime reduction programs, which are geared toward street crime.

There is another reason for underreporting male violence to women. Through folklore or through experience, women know about police reluctance to become involved in so-called "private" disputes. Women who fear reprisal from violent men or who feel that even if the police were contacted they would not intervene may not contact the police. Reviews of the literature in the area of battering highlight women's experiences with reporting interpersonal violence to police as a negative experience (Martin, 1976; Pagelow, 1985). Police responses to calls for assistance in "dds"—domestic disputes—linked with women's anticipation of those responses, remove many instances of wife battering from the ranks of recorded serious criminal violence. Moreover, there is some evidence that battered women's fear about their vulnerability to victimization from strangers may also increase, perhaps because they feel less protected by the police (Finkelhor & Yllö, 1985; Russell, 1982; Stanko, 1985; Tyler, 1980).

Women's silence about intimate violence is not limited to the police. Few battered women report violence by husbands or boyfriends to crime survey researchers, perhaps for fear of similar reprisal or because they feel that researchers, too, would not treat their experiences as criminal violence. The recent publication of the British crime survey notes the likelihood that there will be "some undercounting of non-stranger violence" (Hough & Mayhew, 1985, p. 16). "Many such victims may be unprepared to report incidents of this nature to an interviewer; they may not feel that assaults of this sort fall within the survey's scope, or they may feel embarrassment or shame. *Indeed, their assailants may be in the same room at the time of interview*" [emphasis added] (Hough & Mayhew, 1985, p. 21).

Despite the shortcomings on the reporting of intimate familial and familiar violence, though, criminologists have published a solid body of literature based on crime surveys about interpersonal violence, specifying its incidence, its victims, its surrounding circumstances, as well as the gender, age, race, area of residence, marital status and so forth of those reporting an experience of criminal victimization (Hindelang, Gottfredson, & Garofalo, 1978). As a reflection of the data collected in crime surveys, it appears that young, single, Black, Hispanic, or Asian men who live in urban areas have the highest likelihood of being victims of interpersonal violence (particularly assault) and have the greatest probability of sustaining injury as a consequence of that victimization. Hindelang, Gottfredson, and Garofalo (1978) and Skogan and Maxfield (1981) suggest that this population is typically victimized by individuals with similar demographic characteristics. The focus of explanations and theories about personal victimization turns to explaining interpersonal violence among men, simply because men have higher reported levels of having experienced forms of interpersonal criminal violence with the exception, of course, of rape. If the dynamics of male-male interpersonal violence indeed differs from male-female violence (or for that matter female-male and female-female) then those differences are not accounted for in theories of personal criminal victimization.

The risk of criminal victimization, according to Cohen and Felson (1979), depends on one's daily routine. Criminologists responsible for the "routine activities" perspective, see crime as reflecting the nature of individuals' normal, everyday patterns of interaction. Directed to explanations of "direct-contact (person-person) predatory violations" this perspective posits that criminal activity "can only be sustained by feeding on other activities" (1979, p. 590). Hindelang et al.'s lifestyle perspective (1978) and that of Gottfredson (1984) note that the frequency of being out of the home, combined with being a young male who drinks alcohol, increases the risk of personal victimization.

According to these prevailing theories, public space is associated with interpersonal violence and criminal violence is linked with leaving the safety of one's home. Cohen and Felson, while recognizing the existence of family violence, conclude that "household and family activities entail lower risk of criminal victimization than non-household-non-family activities, despite the problems in measuring" family violence (1979, p. 594). However, this observation may be true only for men and their experiences of interpersonal violence. Hindelang et al. (1978) found that men are most likely to be assaulted or robbed away from their homes and by strangers. And Messner and Tardiff (1984) report that men are most likely to be murdered away from home.

When it comes to explaining violence against women, the current explanations require rethinking. From the start, women do not share an important demographic characteristic with those who victimize them— their gender. While men may be more at risk outside the home, women are very much at risk in their own homes. Women are more likely to be killed by family members, near or in their own homes (Messner & Tardiff, 1984). Physical and sexual assaults, too, commonly take place within the home (Berk & Loseke, 1981; Butler, 1979; Herman, 1981; Pagelow, 1985; Russell, 1984; Stanko, 1985; Straus, Gelles, & Steinmetz, 1980). With the exception of murder, these are precisely the types of crimes most likely to be underreported to both the police and crime survey researchers (Hanmer & Saunders, 1984; Russell, 1982).

Have fear and risk of violence become a problem of safe streets? According to criminologists and policy makers, "fear of crime," a growing concern of governmental policy makers, is prompting recent programs aimed at removing graffiti and breaking up groups that loiter on the street corners (Sherman, 1983). In addition to efforts to clean up the streets, the U. S. Attorney General's Task Force on Family Violence, in an effort to turn some attention to family violence, put forth a number of recommendations for altering criminal justice policy and practice. In it, there is an attempt to address the failure of police to treat family violence as serious crime. But they do so by maintaining the notion that the home can be made a "safe place."

The Task Force is straightforward about one thing: Many violent acts toward "loved" ones are criminal in nature and should be treated as such by police, prosecutors, and others involved in the criminal justice process. By recognizing acts of family violence to be criminal acts, the Task Force believes abusers will be subject to the wrath of the criminal justice system—arrest, conviction, and the threat of imprisonment.

While the Task Force encourages the criminal justice system to intervene in instances of family violence, it also binds any and all solutions to the problem of interpersonal, familial crime to the maintenance of the family, a difficult contradiction with which to contend. As such, the Task Force report falls short on a number of accounts. The Task Force neutralizes the gender of those victimized most often, as well as the gender of their assailants. Further, it neglects to address how other segments of the criminal justice system uphold the concept of serious crime as crime that is generally committed by strangers. The Task Force's failure to recognize the contribution of gender stratification to violence within the home and the effects of that stratification on all aspects of women's lives restricts the discussion of family violence to one focusing on one, albeit undesirable, aspect of family dynamics. In their comprehensive study of battered women in Scotland, Dobash and Dobash note that there is overwhelming evidence that "women in their position as wives . . . become the 'appropriate' victims of violence in the home" (1979, p. 426). The Task Force, however, uncritically clings to the notion that the traditional family unit is the "fundamental unit upon which society is built," rather than a unit that in many ways contributes to violence within the family.

More importantly, despite its recommendations concerning the importance of treating criminal violence among intimates as "crime," the Task Force does not take on the myth of the safe home. A change in how criminal violence is understood and reinforced by everyday practice is critical to providing an impetus to criminal justice personnel to actually treat intimate, familial violence as criminal behavior. As it stands, the conceptualization of violent crime remains firmly linked to acts randomly perpetuated by strangers against seemingly innocent, undeserving victims. While women express fear about random crime committed by strangers, they have also experienced interpersonal violence from intimates. How does this experience affect their feelings about personal safety?

Fear of Crime: What Threatens Women's Personal Safety?

Explanations of the gap between women's and men's reported fear of crime point to gender experiences and role expectations (Balkin, 1979; Clemente & Kleiman, 1977; Hindelang, Gottfredson, & Garofalo, 1978; Lewis & Maxfield, 1980; Maxfield, 1984; Riger & Gordon, 1981; Riger, Gordon, & LeBailly, 1978; Skogan & Maxfield, 1981). Researchers tacitly accept that men are reluctant to admit fear and that women, on the other hand, anticipate their social and physical vulnerability to criminal victimization and therefore take more precautions to avoid attack. In general, though, explanations about the presence of or lack of fear seem to include speculation about whether these fears are "real," "founded" or not. Are women overreacting to the conditions of their physical safety? Is there an acceptance on the part of researchers that there is no necessary relationship between women's expressed fear of crime and their actual risk of interpersonal violence?

The existence of high levels of women's fear of crime obviously necessitates some explanation. Accounting for women's fear of crime, Skogan and Maxfield (1981) suggest that women's fear (and the elderly's, another group reporting high levels of fear and who are also primarily women) is a perception of their social and physical vulnerability. To them, physical vulnerability concerns "openness to attack"; powerlessness to resist; exposure to significant physical and emotional consequences if attacked; and social vulnerability that involves "daily exposure to the threat of victimization and limited means for coping with the medical and economic consequences of victimization" (Skogan & Maxfield, 1981, pp. 77-78).

This understanding of vulnerability, some researchers suggest, manifests itself in women's fear of rape (Gordon, Riger, LeBailly, & Heath, 1980; Riger, Gordon, & LeBailly, 1978). Riger and Gordon (1981, p. 86) propose that women's fear is proportionate to their subjective estimates of risk of rape. They conclude that estimates of risk, plus women's perceptions of their physical competence and their "attachment of their communities" contribute to women's feelings of unsafety on the streets. Yet, there is an undercurrent running through even this recognition of women's fear: it is still a perception, not a reflection of actual experience (perhaps because it hasn't been documented through crime surveys?).

I believe there is another explanation. Women's fear of victimization is, in fact, a logical assessment of women's and the elderly's ability to defend themselves in the face of male assailants (Stanko, 1987). In a sense, women's vulnerability—and women's recognition of that vulnerability through expressions of fear—is itself a mechanism of social control over women. Indeed, part of men's feelings of personal safety and women's of unsafety, is rooted in the fact that men's safety, in many ways, depends on women's vulnerability. Men, for the most part, are able to predict that women will not endanger their physical—and sexual—well-being on the street or in the home. Women, on the whole, might also feel that women will not typically endanger them on the street. Both men and women are on guard to men as potential assailants. However, men, as a gender, are taught to defend themselves and have learned how to fight, anticipate danger and so forth. Women are taught to rely on men's benevolence for their protection from other men. This is a precarious position for women who are abused by their "protectors."

While women's fear remains an anomaly of perception for criminologists, feminists are beginning to link women's fear of crime—which might better read women's fear of men—to women's experiences of men's threatening and / or violent behavior, experiences that may not be considered serious crime by the police and others (Stanko, 1985). Obscene phone calls intrude into the safety of the home and sexual harassment creates an intimidating atmosphere on the street or at work (MacKinnon, 1978). Indecent exposure threatens and frightens women (Hanmer & Saunders, 1984; McNeill, 1987). While these various forms of intrusions may not always cause physical injury to women, they create an atmosphere of unsafety, both inside and outside the home.

Unsafety and fear are not only connected to experiences of interpersonal violence, but to women's perceptions of unsafety in contemporary society. Serial rapists and murderers, too, contribute to an atmosphere—at home or on the street—rife with acute fear. The reaction of women in Dallas in 1985 to a series of murders involving young women, for example, included women arming themselves, altering the routines of the most mundane of tasks, and attending rape awareness and self-defense classes en masse. In Worcester, Massachusetts in 1985, in response to the serial rapist mentioned earlier, I, along with many of my friends and students, altered a number of my routine patterns and still felt unsafe in my own home, even with the doors locked. We heightened our precaution on the street and at the same time felt extremely vulnerable in our own homes. And what is the advice police give to women during situations when a serial rapist/ murderer is about? Stay home!

While women's fear, as captured by crime surveys, may be saying a great deal about the context of women's lives, there should be more serious concern about the particular effect of women's fear of crime on women battered and sexually abused in their own homes. Russell's (1982, p. 221) survey indicates that married women, currently in violent relationships, are more afraid of sexual assault outside the home, and thus fear the unknown, more than the known male who is violent to them. Fear of the unknown—be it a fear of life without marriage or fear of institutional victimization—may also delay a woman's escape from violence within the home. Finkelhor and Yllö (1985), in their in-depth examination of marital rape, found that women's fear of their rapist-husbands lasted much longer than their marriages. "Often it was very deeply ingrained, and generalized to other men. Some of the marital rape victims had lived in terror for years, never knowing when a physical or sexual assault might come," the authors state. "This insecurity became almost instinctual and lingered even when the husband was no longer physically present, for it was hard to get away from the psychological presence of a brutal husband" (1985, pp. 130-131). Can women feel safe around male strangers when those familiar to them have violated their physical and sexual safety? Or can they feel safe when they commonly assume that their physical and/or sexual violations would not be treated as serious crime by the police? Or can they feel safe when a roving stranger who is violent to women strikes seemingly randomly in a particular area over a period of time?

Part of women's silence around physical and sexual abuse in the home, I believe, can be attributed to the barriers preventing women from speaking about their homes as anything but sanctuaries. The prevailing myths about the home as haven are incorporated into the everyday thinking of (primarily male) criminologists and criminal justice personnel. Therefore, the feminist argument that the home may be a dangerous place for women confronts deeply ingrained and hostile beliefs that support the ideology of the home as man's haven.

Women's reported fear of crime and the growing evidence of their experiences of interpersonal violence from known assailants questions the prevailing theoretical explanations for the risk of victimization of interpersonal violence and the possible fear its risk evokes. Moreover, I believe that the current focus by U. S. policy makers and criminologists toward reducing citizen fear (particularly women's fear) about criminal violence (Sherman, 1983) is misguided because it concentrates on crime that is committed outside the home. This attention to violence committed by strangers obscures the possible fear-producing effects of violence within the home, and militates against the inclusion of intimate violence, largely perpetrated against women and girls, from being considered serious crime. By retaining the ideology of the safe home, we retain an important contributor to women's subordinate status within a gender-stratified society.

REFERENCES

Attorney General's Task Force on Family Violence (1984). *Final report*. Washington, DC: U. S. Government Printing Office.

Balkin, S. (1979). Victimization rate, safety, and fear of crime, *Social Problems, 26*, 343-358.

Baumer, T. L. (1978). Research on fear of crime in the United States, *Victimology, 3*, 254-264.

Berk, D., & Loseke, R. (1981). Handling family violence: Situational determinants of police arrest in domestic disturbances. *Law and Society Review, 15*(2), 317-346.

Berk, D., Loseke, R., & Rauman, R. (1983). Mutual combat and other family violence myths. In D. Finkelhor, R. J. Gelles, G. T. Hotaling, & M. A. Straus (Eds.), *The dark side of families.* Newbury Park, CA: Sage.

Black, J. (1970). The production of crime rates. *American Sociological Review, 35*(4), 733-748.

Box, S. (1984). *Power, crime and mystification.* London: Tavistock.

Bureau of Justice Statistics (1983). *Report to the nation on crime and justice.* Washington, DC: U. S. Government Printing Office.

Butler, S. (1979). *The conspiracy of silence.* New York: Bantam Books.

Clemente, F., & Kleiman, M. (1977, December). Fear of crime in the United States: A multivariate analysis. *Social Forces, 56,* 519-531.

Cohen, E., & Felson (1979). Social change and crime rate trends: A routine activities approach. *American Sociological Review, 44,* 588-608.

Dobash, R. E., & Dobash, R. P. (1979). *Violence against wives: A case against patriarchy.* New York: Free Press.

Dubow, F., McCabe, E., & Kaplan, G. (1979). *Reactions to crime: A critical review of the literature.* Washington, DC: U.S. Government Printing Office.

Ericson, V. (1981). *Making crime: A study of detective work.* Toronto: Butterworths.

Finkelhor, D., & Yllö, K. (1985). *License to rape: Sexual abuse of wives.* New York: Holt, Rinehart & Winston.

Garofalo, R. (1979). Victimization and the fear of crime. *Journal of Research in Crime and Delinquency, 16,* 80-97.

Gordon, M., Riger, S., LeBailly, R., & Heath, L. (1980). Crime, women and the quality of urban life. *Signs, 5,* 144-160.

Gottfredson, G. (1984). *Victims of crime: The dimension of risk.* London: HMSO.

Hanmer, J., & Stanko, A. (1985, November). Stripping away the rhetoric of protection: Women, law and the state. *International Journal of the Sociology of Law.*

Hanmer, J., & Saunders, D. (1984). *Well founded fear.* London: Hutchinson.

Herman, J. (1981). *Father-daughter incest.* Cambridge: Harvard University Press.

Hindelang, M., Gottfredson, D., & Garofalo, R. (1978). *The victims of personal crime.* Cambridge, MA: Ballinger.

Hough, H., & Mayhew, M. (1983). *The British crime survey.* London: HMSO.

Hough, H., & Mayhew, M. (1985). *Taking account of crime: Key findings from the 1984 British crime survey.* London: HMSO.

Johnson, J., & Wasielewski, L. (1982). A commentary on victimization research and the importance of meaning structures. *Criminology, 20*(2), 205-222.

Lewis, D. A., & Maxfield, M. (1980). Fear in the neighborhoods: An investigation of the impact of crime. *Journal of Research in Crime and Delinquency, 17,* 160-189.

Liska, E., Lawrence, J., & Sanchirico (1982). Fear of crime as a social fact. *Social Forces, 60*(3), 760-770.

MacKinnon, A. (1978). *Sexual harassment of working women.* New Haven: Yale University Press.

Martin, D. (1976). *Battered wives.* San Francisco: Glide.

Maxfield, G. (1984). *Fear of crime in England and Wales.* London: HMSO.

McCleary, R., Nienstedt, B. C., & Erven, J. M. (1982). Uniform crime reports as organizational outcomes: Three time series experiments. *Social Problems, 29,* 361-372.

McNeill, S. (1987). Flashing: Its effects on women. In J. Hanmer and M. Maynard (Eds.), *Women, violence and social control.* London: Macmillan.

Messner, F., & Tardiff, K. (1984). *The social ecology of urban homicide: An application of the routine activities approach.* Paper delivered at the American Criminology annual meetings, Cincinnati, Ohio.

Oppenlander, N. (1982). Coping or copping out: Police service delivery in domestic disputes. *Criminology, 20,* 449-466.

Pagelow, M. (1985). *Family violence.* New York: Praeger.

President's Commission on Law Enforcement and Administration of Justice (1967). *Task force report: Crime and its impact—an assessment.* Washington, DC: U.S. Government Printing Office.

Reiman, H. (1984). *The rich get richer and the poor get prison.* New York: John Wiley.

Riger, S., & Gordon, M. (1981). The fear of rape: A study in social control. *Journal of Social Issues, 37,* 71-92.

Riger, S., Gordon, M., & LeBailly, R. (1978). Women's fear of crime: From blaming to restricting the victim. *Victimology, 3,* 274-284.

Rosaldo, M. Z. (1974). Women, culture and society: a theoretical overview. In M. Z. Rosaldo & L. Lamphere (Eds.), *Women, culture and society.* Palo Alto, CA: Stanford University Press.

Russell, D.E.H. (1982). *Rape in marriage.* New York: Macmillan.

Russell, D.E.H. (1984). *Sexual exploitation.* Newbury Park, CA: Sage.

Sherman, L. (1983). *Experiments in fear reduction: Houston and Newark program and evaluation plans.* Washington, DC: Police Foundation.

Silberman, C. (1978). *Criminal justice, criminal violence.* New York: Random House.

Skogan, W., & Maxfield, M. (1981). *Coping with crime.* Newbury Park, CA: Sage.

Stanko, E. A. (1982). Would you believe this woman: Prosecutorial screening for "credible" witnesses and a problem of justice. In N. H. Rafter & E. A. Stanko (Eds.), *Judge, lawyer, victim, thief: Women, gender and criminal justice.* Boston: Northeastern University Press.

Stanko, E. A. (1985). *Intimate intrusions.* London: Routledge & Kegan Paul.

Stanko, E. A. (1987). Typical violence, normal precaution: Men, women and interpersonal violence in the U.S., England, Wales and Scotland. In J. Hanmer & M. Maynard (Eds.), *Women, violence and social control.* London: Macmillan.

Straus, M. A., Gelles, R. J., & Steinmetz, S. (1980). *Behind closed doors.* New York: Doubleday.

Tyler, T. J. (1980). The impact of directly and indirectly experienced events: The origin of crime related judgments and behaviors. *Journal of Personality and Social Psychology, 39*(1), 13-28.

PART II

Feminist Research

4

Wife Abuse, Husband Abuse, or Mutual Combat?

A Feminist Perspective on the Empirical Findings

DANIEL G. SAUNDERS

A key element of feminist theories of woman abuse is that men use physical violence to maintain male dominance in the family. Women as individuals and as a class are regarded as the primary victims. A challenge to this view came in the 1970s with the concepts of the *battered husband syndrome* and *mutual combat* in marriage. While some authors continue to suggest that "men are battered too," most social activists argue that women are violent only to protect themselves and their children. From this feminist perspective, to label self-defense *husband abuse* serves to direct attention away from the victimization of women and the function of male dominance.

A review of the assumptions and empirical findings regarding male versus female violence in the home is not simply of academic interest

AUTHOR'S NOTE: The study reported here and the writing of this manuscript were supported in part by grant 77-0620SC29636 from the Wisconsin Council on Criminal Justice and grants MH-1516106 and MH-1713901 from the National Institute of Mental Health. Portions of this chapter appeared in an article "When battered women use violence: Husband abuse or self-defense?" in *Victims and Violence,* Vol. 1, No. 1, 1986. © Used by permission, Springer Publishing Company, New York.

The author would like to thank Patricia Size for her help in gathering the data, the members of the Family Violence Seminar at the University of New Hampshire for their comments on an earlier draft of this manuscript, and Michelle Wilderman for her help in typing the manuscript.

since many reports on battered husbands have been used to attack social remedies for battered women. As a recent example, Fathers United for Equal Justice in New Hampshire called for the creation of a "Commission on the Status of Men," stating that "Little mention is ever made . . . that most abused spouses are husbands, and that women actually have higher rates of aggressive actions of violence in the home. They start most of the hassles in the family and then enlist the aid of the legislature and the courts when they are unable to prevail" (Fathers Group, 1984). When the controversy over the "battered husband syndrome" arose in the 1970s, the feminist activists' mistrust of the social sciences seemed confirmed by academic and subsequent media accounts of the "battered husband syndrome." Such accounts created fears that services for battered women would be deemed biased, leaving them vulnerable to funding cuts.

Unfortunately, current social science research cannot yet answer the question of whether physical violence between spouses is best conceptualized as wife abuse, husband abuse, or as mutual combat. For one thing, few studies have carefully examined the motives behind the use of physical force, the physical consequences of abuse as used by men or by women, or the contexts in which men or women choose to use violence against their partners. Furthermore, the field is marked by conceptual confusion. Does "fighting back," for example, mean self-defense, retaliation, or both? Last, social scientists and social activists have been polarized into opposing camps, which makes it difficult to resolve this controversy with scientific and moral integrity.

It is my belief that quantitative social science research can clarify whether battering is best understood as wife abuse, husband abuse, or mutual combat. At the same time, I believe that a feminist perspective can inform and guide empirical study in productive ways. In this chapter, I will first describe my feminist framework to set the stage for my conceptual and empirical analyses. I will then critically review the literature on the "battered husband syndrome," examine conceptual problems with the notions of self-defense and retaliation, and summarize the findings of an exploratory study on battered women's motives for using violence against their partners.

A Feminist Framework

I begin with the assumption that research used for social change does not compromise one's scientific ideals because all research is tied to values. For example, there is ample documentation that sexist beliefs have influenced research conclusions in studies of male-female aggression (see for example, Salzman, 1979). In the words of Ruth Bleier: "Science is a cultural institution. While the structure of science has its edges pure and probing into the knowable unknown, its massive core, like all institutions, embodies, protects, and perpetuates the thoughts and values of those who are dominant in the society that produces it. To ignore this is to ignore the obvious. Scientists are human beings born into and molded by an insistent and obtrusively value-laden culture" (1979, p. 49).

There are times when the values of social change and the values of science seem contradictory. As a counselor, activist, and researcher in the area of woman abuse, I have felt tension as I try to be true to the values of social science and of social justice and equal rights. A guiding principle of my research is that certain values of feminist activism and social science support each other. One source of tension seems to arise from the simple fact that social action usually means immediate action, whereas the knowledge gained from science takes a long time to acquire. As a counselor, I am faced with a similar dilemma: a client in pain needs help even if I do not know the most effective intervention for the problem presented. Yet action that is not well informed can be less than optimal, ineffective, or worse, counterproductive. Movements for social justice, then, need to use the scientific search for truth as a guide. For example, social science can help document the extent of inequality, uncover its causes and assess the effectiveness of social remedies. It cannot conclude that change is needed in the first place.

In my research work, as in my counseling work, there are various theoretical frameworks that I lay over the data that I see. Sometimes no single framework fits best and there remains an awkward integration of two or three frameworks. For example, the proposition that men who batter are uncommonly jealous can be investigated and/or interpreted from a psychological perspective ("perhaps he has an obsessive-compulsive personality disorder"), a family dynamics perspective ("perhaps she flirts with other men"), or a sociocultural perspective ("perhaps he's exaggerating the male dominance common to all men in our society"). I may also try more than one social theory—feminist, socialist, and so on. This interplay between data and theory can occur within the researcher or among researchers. I believe that a key value for the researcher is an openness to new information and the struggle to see the filter of one's own socialization. Likewise, as an activist or counselor, I need to balance the single-mindedness of purpose with the open-mindedness of gathering the least biased information and an openness to a multiplicity of causes of human suffering.

Another source of tension between activists and researchers is the perception by many activists that science always supports the status quo. The Dobashes (1981), however, describe the construction of "a new liberal agenda" in the mid-1960s that had "a profound and diverse impact on social science. . . . The civil rights movement, the Vietnam war, the upheavals in cities and on campuses, and the Women's Liberation Movement all provided evidence of the conflict conception of the world, and many sociologists sought to contribute to these struggles by trying to work in a manner that would capture the dynamic processes of conflict and social change that were missing from the reigning orthodoxy" (p. 446). Given the roots of feminist research in broader social research, it may not be surprising that male and female authors publishing in social science journals do not appear to differ in the use of feminist methods and their level of feminist content (Lykes & Steward, 1983; Walker & Thompson, 1984). My own work stems in part from the social movements listed by the Dobashes. I have not seen feminist research as generally identified with female researchers. A special issue of the *International Journal of Women's Studies* (Stark-Adamec & Adamec, 1985) illustrates well the collaboration of male and female researchers and their contributions to a growing number of quantitative feminist studies on women's victimization.

While there is general agreement about what constitutes the content of feminist research, there seems to be little agreement about what constitutes feminist research methodology. The methods range from exclusively quantitative to exclusively qualitative in nature. In a review of articles in the *Journal of Marriage and the Family,* there was no relationship between ratings of feminist content and ratings of feminist methods (Walker & Thompson, 1984). Among the disadvantages of a quantitative approach are a lack of richness in the meanings and explanations of individual responses. Among the advantages of quantitative methods are the use of clear definitions of variables, the ability to replicate studies, and the ability to make generalizations that allow for prediction and intervention.

When a feminist framework is applied using more traditional methods, it aims to reduce sexist bias by raising critical questions about the research process. The researcher can reduce bias by asking a number of questions: (1) Will an answer to the research question lead to greater equality between the sexes? (2) Are the variables operationalized in the most meaningful way? For example, is the act of violence or its effects the best measure of violence? (3) Is there bias in the data collection? For example, what influence does the sex of the interviewer have? (4) Does the analysis need certain explanatory variables (e.g., gender) to make it meaningful? (5) Does data interpretation include one or more feminist frameworks? (6) Is the report free of sexist language? (7) Does the author spell out the limitations in such a way that the reader is warned about false conclusions that may harm women? My approach in this chapter is to use the substance of feminist research but rely primarily on the quantitative methods of traditional science. The substantive issues include a power analysis of gender relationships, recognition of women's oppression, and attention to complex explanatory models.

Definition of Terms

The term "battered women" is used here in the broad sense to mean female recipients of all forms of physical force by their intimate partners who intend to hurt them. The full range of severity is included, from slaps to beatings to the use of weapons. This definition is more in line with legal definitions of "battery" than the popular definition (LaFave & Scott, 1972). "Minor violence," for example, slapping and shoving, is included in the definition because of its high probability of escalating to severe violence (Dobash & Dobash, 1979; Pagelow, 1981; Walker, 1984) and because one episode of violence of any intensity may shift the power balance in the relationship by making the woman more passive (see Walker, 1984). Unless otherwise noted, the terms *marital violence* and *wife abuse* will be used for the sake of convenience to refer to both married and unmarried couples.

Wife Abuse, Husband Abuse, or Mutual Combat? A Review of Literature

In order to answer the question of whether battering in families is primarily wife abuse, husband abuse, or mutual combat, several questions must be answered: (1) What is the empirical evidence regarding whether men use physical violence in marriages more than, less than, or equal to their wives? (2) Are men and women equally victimized or harmed when their partners use physical force against them? (3) Do men and women use violence for similar reasons, that is, what are their respective motives? (4) What are the conceptual issues concerning the definition of *self-defense* between husbands and wives?

Rates of Violence
Employed by Husbands and Wives

The initial studies of marital violence by Murray Straus and his associates were meant to be incidence surveys, and questions were not asked about the motives and consequences of the violence (Gelles, 1974; Steinmetz, 1977; Straus, 1980; Straus, Gelles, & Steinmetz, 1980). These researchers were surprised to find approximately equal rates of violence, both severe and nonsevere, committed by both husbands and wives. The findings were consistent between their nonrandom surveys and their survey of over 2,000 households representative of the U.S. population. The researchers did, however, point out a number of reasons why woman abuse should remain the focus of intervention: husbands had the higher rates of the most dangerous behavior; husbands repeated their violence more often; husbands were likely to do more damage because of size differences; women are economically trapped in marriage more often than are husbands; and many women may use violence to defend themselves. Other researchers have also found that men are responsible for the most severe forms of violence (Gaquin, 1977-78; Makepeace, 1983).

Despite the qualifications given by Straus and others to their studies, a considerable amount of controversy erupted in the late 1970s over questions of the nature and scope of violence perpetrated by wives against their husbands. Reports of a "battered husband syndrome" (Langley & Levy, 1977; Steinmetz, 1977-78) of a magnitude equal to that of the problem of battered wives met with charges of a "battered data syndrome" (Pleck, Pleck, Grossman, & Bart, 1977-78), since the claims about "battered husbands" appeared to be based on incomplete tables and projections to the entire U.S. population made from one or two nonsevere cases (see Pagelow, 1984 for review). Reports of "mutual combat" by couples were met with the charge that mutual combat was a "myth," since victims who sustained injuries and sought help were overwhelmingly female (Berk, Berk, Loseke, & Rauma, 1981).

The study reported later in this chapter focuses on those cases that some authors might call "mutual combat" (see Steinmetz, 1980): cases in which both partners have been violent, although not necessarily at the same time. In the nationally representative survey of family violence (Straus et al., 1980), this type of relationship was the most common, accounting for 49% of the relationships that contained violence during the survey year (Straus, 1980). Relationships in which only the husband or wife was violent were less common among the relationships containing violence (28% and 23% respectively). Of all the wives who were subjected to violence during the survey year, 64% were also violent during that time.

Supporting the findings of the first national study of family violence (Straus et al., 1980), it was discovered in several studies that from 23% to 71% of battered women used violence at least once against their abusers. These studies included a random survey of one New York county (Nisonoff & Bitman, 1979, n = 296); battered women who sought help for attempted suicide (Oswald, 1980, n = 263); a nonrandom survey of help-seeking and nonhelp-seeking battered women (Walker, 1984, n = 403); and battered women seeking help from shelters (Fojtik, 1977-78, n = 100; Pagelow, 1981, n = 267).

Very recently, Straus and Gelles (1986) released the findings of their second national survey on family violence. They report that violence by wives remains at levels comparable to those by husbands. However, they do not provide data on the crucial questions of self-defense and injury. This chapter focuses on data from the first national survey. Nevertheless, the issues raised are generally applicable to the most recent survey as well.

Extent of Husband and Wife Victimization

Reporting the rates of violence by each partner tells us nothing about the extent of victimization each suffers. Straus (1980) further analyzed the national study data and found that when both partners were violent (n = 159), 44% of the husbands used a higher level of violence than their partners, compared with 23% of the wives who used a higher level of violence. Furthermore, wives' increases in minor violence were associated with a sharp increase in the number of severe assaults by their partners. The same pattern did not hold for wives' use of severe violence; their use of severe violence was not frequent until it was associated with receiving 10 or more acts of "minor" violence in the previous year.

Studies of police reports using sample sizes ranging from 120 to 3,000 also indicate the greater victimization of wives, who are reported as sole victims about 90% of the time (Berk et al., 1981; Dobash & Dobash, 1979; Kenny, 1981; McLeod, 1984; Saunders, 1980; Vanfossen, 1979). Reports to the police are likely to involve the most severe forms of violence (Saunders & Size, 1980; Schulman, 1979). There remains the possibility, however, that battered husbands are more ashamed to report abuse and therefore official statistics are lower for husbands (see Steinmetz, 1977-78).

Although men appear in the minority when the violence is reported as a crime, studies that use this narrow definition show that men are proportionately more likely to be injured. McLeod's (1984) analysis of the National Crime Survey and of police reports showed that women are more likely to use weapons and, as a result, men are somewhat more likely to sustain injuries (52%-55% compared with 73%-77%). She found that, contrary to one of the propositions of those who present the battered husband hypothesis, male victims were not overly represented among the aged or economically dependent.

An increased risk of victimization for women is likely to occur because of size differences and women's relative lack of experience with fighting. Men who batter average 45 pounds heavier and 4 to 5 inches taller than their partners (Pagelow, 1981; Walker, 1984). The male batterers' weights tend to be at the national norm while there is some evidence that battered women's weights are below the national norm for women (Pagelow, 1981). Wives' higher risk of sustaining (and sustaining severe) injuries from domestic assaults are supported by surveys of three types of samples: a representative crime victimization survey (Gaquin, 1977-78); police reports (Berk et al., 1981; Saunders, 1980), and a nonrandom community sample (Irwin, 1981). Greenblat (1981) and Adler (1981) present interview data that illustrate the differences between male and female violence. In some cases, both partners knew that the women's hardest punches did not hurt their partners, and, in fact, the men laughed at the women's efforts. In a table of quantitative data, however, this would count as "husband abuse."

Why Battered Women
Use Physical Force
Against Their Husbands

If women use violence, it is more likely to be against a violent partner than a nonviolent one. In comparing how often 203 women employed violence against abusive mates or against other nonabusive mates, Walker (1984) found that, with abusive mates, 23% of these women "occasionally" and 1% "frequently" used physical force. But with a nonabusive mate, only 4% of these same women used physical force "occasionally" and none used it "frequently." This difference suggests that battered women's physical aggression is a function of the type of relationship and is not a general characteristic of the women. Factors other than the particular marital situation, however, also predict whether a wife uses violence. In an analysis of the national data, wives who both used and received violence were much more likely to have been punished as a teenager (30%) than wives who did not use violence and had either violent (21%) or nonviolent partners (17%) (Straus, 1980). Wives who used violence against their partners were also more likely to approve of marital violence and of physical punishment for children. The causal order here is not clear. However, the evidence from Walker's study just cited indicates that many women displace aggression from their husbands onto their children.

Very little is known about the extent to which the violence of battered women is motivated by self-defense. The factors associated with homicide by battered women have begun to be investigated and they appear to support the self-defense explanation for battered women's violence. An analysis of spousal homicide in one city showed that wives were seven times more likely than husbands to have used violence in self-defense (Wolfgang, 1957). McCormick (1976) reported that 40% of the women jailed for spousal killing (n = 132) in her study had been subjected to chronic physical abuse in their marriages and that this abuse was the dominant factor in the murder. Totman (1978) found that women who killed their partners were likely to feel they had exhausted all their alternatives in seeking help. Browne (1986) compared battered women who had killed or nearly killed their partners and those who had not. Factors associated with homicide centered around the man's behavior, including the frequency of abuse, the severity of the woman's injuries, forced sex, the man's threats to kill, and his frequency of intoxication.

Indirect evidence for battered women's use of self-defense comes from the national family violence study (Straus et al., 1980). Husband's threats to use weapons were highly associated with their actual use, whereas for wives, threats to use weapons were not nearly as highly associated with the actual use of weapons (81% versus 13% shared variance; Straus, personal communication) and were even less highly associated with other forms of violence (Straus, 1979). The men's use of threats suggests premeditation and an attempt to control; the women's use of weapons with little associated violence and no threats suggests a self-defense motive.

Two surveys of battered women, both help-seeking samples, asked about self-defensive violence. In one survey, 29% of the women (Pagelow, 1981, n = 267), and in another, 41% (Fojtik, 1977-1978, n = 123), reported the use of self-defensive violence. Frieze and her associates (Frieze, Noble, Zomnar, & Washburn, 1980), unlike the Browne study of battered women who killed, found that battered women who fought back were the ones who were mildly abused rather than severely abused and that few women were as violent as their husbands. No study could be found that asked about the frequencies with which battered women used self-defensive violence or that detailed the sequence of events when both partners were violent in a single episode.

Self-Defense: Conceptual Issues

Some reports of battered women's violence contain questionable assumptions. For example, it is often assumed that retaliation (Straus, 1980), or "fighting back" (Pagelow, 1981), and self-defense are mutually exclusive concepts and that "severe violence" in response to "minor violence" cannot be called self-defense (Straus, 1980). Criminal law textbooks and recent court decisions help to clarify these issues. A widely used text defines self-defense as follows: "One who is not the aggressor in an encounter is justified in using a reasonable amount of force against his adversary when he reasonably believes (1) that he is in immediate danger of unlawful bodily harm from his adversary and (2) that the use of such force is necessary to avoid this danger" (LaFave & Scott, 1972, p. 391). Women's size and social conditioning are now recognized as important factors for juries to consider in determining self-defense. In rejecting the traditional jury instructions in the appeal of the Wanrow murder case, the court stated:

> In our society, women suffer from a conspicuous lack of access to training in, and means of developing, those skills necessary to effectively repel a male assailant without resorting to the use of a deadly weapon . . . . The respondent was entitled to have the jury consider her actions in the light of her own perceptions of the situation, including those perceptions which

were the product of our nation's "long and unfortunate history of sex discrimination"... (The challenged instructions) leaves the jury with the impression that the objective standard to be applied is that applicable to an altercation between two men. The impression—that a 5'5" woman with a cast on her leg and using a crutch must, under the law, somehow repel an assault by a 6'2" intoxicated man without employing weapons in her defense... violates the respondents' right to equal protection under the law. (*State of Washington v. Wanrow*, p. 559)

Therefore, battered women are justified in using enough force to stop an attack, which in most cases means using more "severe" violence than their attackers use.

Likewise, self-defense pleas in homicide cases are not nullified when extreme terror mixes with extreme rage (Schneider & Jordan, 1978). It seems reasonable to expect victims of battery or sexual abuse who defend themselves from lethal or nonlethal attacks to combine anger with their fear. Walker's (1984) research on battered women's emotional responses after being assaulted supports this expectation. Thus, retaliation (angrily trying to hurt the other) while one is being attacked may be indistinguishable from self-defense (see Pagelow, 1984).

There may exist a double standard in definitions of retaliation and self-defense. When battered women defend themselves, there may be a tendency to label it retaliation (Edwards, 1985). Men tend to label violent responses to verbal abuse as "self-defense" whether the verbal abuse is from a woman or a man, hence the phrase "them's fightin' words" heard in cowboy movies. The men are defending their self-image rather than defending themselves from physical harm. Saving face is a particularly strong motive when the woman is, or is suspected to be, sexually unfaithful. Men are traditionally given light sentences if they kill an unfaithful wife "in the heat of passion." Women are not afforded the same leniancy.

Other differences from traditional legal interpretations exist for battered spouses. Great force may frequently be used by battered women who recognize their partner's behavior patterns and fear that another beating is imminent. In the words of one legal scholar: "After presenting evidence of prior beatings at the hands of her husband, the battered wife should be able to maintain a strong claim of self-defense based on the apprehension of an imminent danger caused by her husband's otherwise trivial or seemingly innocuous conduct" (Kieviet, 1978, p. 223). Self-defense pleas usually require the defendant to show that it was impossible to withdraw safely from the threatened harm. When the victim and attacker live together, however, most jurisdictions recognize that one should not have to flee one's own home to seek safety (Fiora-Gormally, 1978).

Although men would be expected to be more traditional and give harsher penalties to women who kill, in one study of college students' attitudes about battered women's use of violence this was not the case. Men and women did not differ in their levels of justification for the violence or in the length of the prison sentence they would recommend (Simons, 1983). Social class did play a role, however; those of higher social class viewed the violence as less justified and recommended a longer sentence.

The above literature review reveals that wives tend to be more greatly victimized than husbands and that wives' violence may be in self-defense. Yet the current research on battered women's motives has not carefully examined how much violence is in self-defense and whether self-defense and retaliation are mutually exclusive motives, as their dictionary definitions suggest. I will present the findings of an exploratory study that sought a more comprehensive understanding of why women use physical violence against their partners.

Battered Women's
Motives for Violence:
A Preliminary Analysis

The way I conceptualized my research questions was strongly influenced by a feminist perspective. Although I was exploring possible gender differences regarding the use of violence, I was specifically interested in understanding women's frame of reference. Rather than assuming that I knew why they were violent, I asked them to describe the interpersonal contexts and their motives that led them to use physical force. The major question explored was: What is the proportion of times that battered women report their use of violence as "defensive," "retaliatory," or "first strike?" Based on the studies of spousal homicide cited earlier, it was hypothesized that most of the violence of battered women would be in self-defense. A second question was whether the women would distinguish self-defensive violence from violence labelled "fighting back," which some authors define as retaliation or "getting even" (Straus, 1980). From the studies showing a link between anger and fear in the women following attacks, it was hypothesized that there would be a correlation between reports of self-defense and "fighting back."

Method

Sample. Of the 52 battered women who participated in this study, 23% were married, 56% separated or divorced, and 19% single. The average number of years of education was 12.2 (SD = 2.0); 8% of the women held college degrees. The average length of their violent relationships was 7.7 years (SD = 7.61). Forty-five of the women had sought help from a shelter while the rest used a counseling agency. The women seeking help from the shelter were younger and had fewer children than the women in counseling, but the women did not differ significantly in education, income, or marital status.

Procedures. The subjects were taking part in a larger study on the police response to battered women (Saunders & Size, 1980). Agency personnel solicited participation in the study from 56 battered women who were successively admitted to the shelters or counseling agency. Four women refused to participate because some of the items caused emotional upset or because the questionnaire was lengthy. The questionnaires were self-administered after the women became acclimated to shelter life and completed informed consent procedures. Anonymous self-administration was used to help reduce social desirability response bias.

Measures

The subjects completed modified Conflict Tactics Scales (CTS) (Straus, 1979), reporting on the frequency of different levels of violence used by their partners and themselves over the course of the relationship. The CT Scales have good evidence of internal reliability and concurrent and construct validity (see Straus, 1979). In efforts to make the scale less threatening, women were asked to report on verbal abuse and then on acts of physical abuse of increasing intensity. The instructions were framed in the context of a "dispute" and thus may not have uncovered violence originating from conflict outside of the relationship. The frequency categories used for this study were: never, once, occasionally, once a month or less, regularly (about once a month), and more than once a week.

Two identical sets of questions about motivation were placed in the CT Scales completed by each woman. One set followed three relatively nonsevere forms of violence ("threw something"; "pushed, grabbed, or shoved"; "slapped") and the other followed the items reflecting more serious forms of violence ("kicked, bit, or hit with a fist" through "used a knife or gun"). The questions were: (1) "What percentage of these times (above) do you estimate that you acted in self-defense, that is, protecting yourself from immediate physical harm?" (2) "What percentage of these times were you trying to fight back? (3) What percentage of these times did you assault your partner before he actually attacked you or threatened you with a weapon?" After each question there was a line with 0% and 100% at either end and percentage points spaced equally and numbered by 10s. Respondents were instructed to "Mark anywhere on the line." Note that respondents were not asked to divide 100% among the motivation items, but to assign a percent to each type of motivation. In other words, the forms of motivation were not stated in mutually exclusive terms. Note also that the definition of self-defense used here could be interpreted as based either on the victim's perceptions of being endangered or on an objective standard of danger. The initiation of an assault, question "c," could, when the respondent feared for her life, be self-defensive but was not clearly defined as such in this study.

An 18-item version of the Marlowe-Crowne Social Desirability Scale (Crowne & Marlowe, 1964) was used to detect possible bias from subjects' attempts to respond in a socially desirable manner. Social desirability response bias is a common source of invalidity in self-report measures. The version used here correlated .95 with the original 33 item version. The scale's concurrent validity has been shown by its correlation in expected directions with the validity scales of the Minnesota Multiphasic Personality Inventory (Crowne & Marlowe, 1964).

Results

Table 4.1 shows the percentage of women who ever engaged in various types of violence. It shows that 75% engaged in some form of nonsevere violence, about one half having thrown something or slapped, and slightly more than one half reporting that they "pushed, grabbed, or shoved." Two of the categories labelled severe violence were engaged in by 50% to 60% of the women. These were "kicked, bit, or hit with fist" and "hit or tried to hit with something." About 8% of the

TABLE 4.1
Percentage and Mean Frequency Scores
of Women Who Used Violence

	% Who Ever Engaged in Behavior	Frequency Score[a]	
		M	SD
Nonsevere violence			
threw something at him	49.0	1.2	1.9
pushed, grabbed, or shoved	55.1	1.7	2.4
slapped	44.9	1.4	2.3
total	75.0		
Severe violence			
kicked, bit, or hit with fist	51.9	1.7	2.4
hit or tried to hit with something	59.6	1.7	2.2
beat him up	7.7	.3	.2
threatened with knife or gun	11.8	.3	.2
used a knife or gun	7.8	.3	1.2
total	73.1		
Total—all violence	82.7		

a. Frequency scores were calculated as follows: never = 0; once = 1; occasionally = (number of times behavior occurred)/(number of years of relationship, rounded off to a number between 2 and 5); once a month = 6; about once a week = 7; more than once a week = 8.

women admitted "beating up" their partners or using a knife or a gun. About 12% of the women threatened their partners with a knife or gun. The most severe forms of violence were not only used by the fewest number of women but, if used, were used least often. Only one of the eight CTS items was significantly correlated with social desirability scale ("slapped you," $r = -.28$, $p = .024$). This correlation is not significant when the experimentwise error rate is used (.05 alpha divided by the number of correlations). It was necessary to split the alpha level because when more than one correlation is made, each additional one increases the likelihood that chance alone will explain the findings.

Table 4.2 shows the percentage of women who reported self-defensive violence, fighting back, or initiating an attack, broken down by four levels of frequency and two levels of severity. Only one of the six measures of reported motives was significantly correlated with the social desirability scale (fighting back with severe violence, $r = .36$) and the correlation was in the opposite direction expected. The women reported that self-defense was the most common motive for both nonsevere and

TABLE 4.2
Percentage of Women Using Different Motives
for Violence by Frequency of Violence

Motive	Frequency[a]			
	0	5-40	50-95	100
Nonsevere violence				
self-defense				
total	21	23	33	23
of those violent	–	31	44	31
n	11	12	17	12
fighting back				
total	35	15	33	17
of those violent	–	21	44	23
n	18	8	17	9
initiate attack				
total	73	19	6	2
of those violent	–	26	8	3
n	38	10	3	1
Severe violence				
self-defense				
total	29	11	31	29
of those violent	–	16	42	39
n	15	6	16	15
fighting back				
total	40	12	25	23
of those violent	–	16	34	32
n	21	6	13	12
initiating attack				
total	88	10	2	0
of those violent	–	13	3	0
n	46	5	1	0

a. Frequencies are not shown between 40% and 50% because no violence was reported for those frequencies.

severe violence. About 40% of the women who used severe violence reported that all of this violence was in self-defense; another third of the women said that all of their severe violence was "fighting back." In contrast, only one woman (3%) reported that she initiated most of the violent encounters with severe violence. A similar pattern existed for the nonsevere violence: about 30% of the women who were violent said that all of their nonsevere violence was in self-defense; another 23% described all of their violence as "fighting back." Four women (11%)

TABLE 4.3
Correlations Between Different Perceptions of Violence
Within Each Level of Violence

| | Nonsevere | | Severe | |
	Fighting Back	Initiating Attack	Fighting Back	Initiating Attack
Self-defense	.55**	−.23	.36**	−.15
Fighting back		.04		.01

$*p < .05; **p < .01; ***p < .001.$

TABLE 4.4
Correlations of Different and Similar Perceptions of
Violence Across the Two Levels of Violence

| | | Severe | |
Nonsevere	SD	FB	IA
Self-defense	.82***	.25	.04
Fighting back	.35*	.48***	.12
Initiating attack	−.27	−.04	.44***

$*p < .05; **p < .01; ***p < .001.$

said that much of their nonsevere violence (50%-100%) was initiated by them.

Table 4.3 presents the correlation matrices between different motivational items within each violence severity level. The patterns are identical. For each level of severity, self-defense and fighting back are positively and significantly correlated with each other; however, self-defense and initiating an attack are negatively correlated in this study, and there is no relationship shown between fighting back and initiating an attack. The positive relationship between self-defense and fighting back also holds across the levels of severity, as shown in Table 4.4. The results in Table 4.4 also show a high degree of consistency in reported behavior among the same motivations across the levels of violence and thus support the validity of the measures. When all of the above correlations were calculated after controlling for social desirability response bias, the results were the same.

Discussion

As in the surveys of battered women cited in the introduction, many of the women in this study reported using violence against their partners. Each type of violence they reported had rates above those for the total sample of wives in a national survey (Straus et al., 1980). Relatively few women, however, reported using violence that was likely to cause serious injuries, for example, "beating up" or the use of a weapon.

A unique aspect of the present study was its focus on battered women's motives for violence. The most frequent motive for violence reported by these women was self-defense. Only a few women reported that they ever initiated an attack of severe violence. The concepts of self-defense and "fighting back" tended to be merged into a single concept for these women.

Among those women who initiate violence, some authors speculate that the women sense impending violence from their partners and initiate the attack in order to stop the overwhelming build-up of tension (Gelles, 1974; Lewis, 1981; Walker, 1984). Under particular circumstances, when the women are convinced that they or their children are in imminent danger of death or great bodily harm, they are legally justified in using force even when danger does not exist in an objective sense and the man is not threatening or attacking. The methods of this study were not able to uncover such "preemptive strikes" as a possible motive; however, the results of this study show that neither self-defense nor fighting back were correlated with initiating an attack.

A self-defense motive is also not ruled out when abused women have strong anger mixed with their fear. Many women in this study did not distinguish between self-defense and fighting back, which is compatible with legal definitions of self-defense. For instance, one of the options women are taught to use in response to sexual assault is to inflict pain on their assailants. It is also possible that the women's primary motive was to injure and that a claim of self-defense was used to justify these actions. The results still indicate, however, that most episodes of violence for these women were initiated by the husbands.

The results of this study underscore Greenblat's (1981) and the Dobashes' (1981) contention that marital violence events need to be studied in context and that researchers must employ caution in how they apply labels to simple counts of events. The use of certain terms applied to both partners—for example, "victim," "combatant," "aggressor," and "battered"—may have unfortunate consequences. Such terms shape our perceptions of events, help to define social problems, and may eventually determine what services are provided. To say that men and women reach equality when it comes to marital violence literally adds insult to injury for the group of women who often fear for their lives and never initiate an attack, but who strike back in self-defense. The consequences of violence also need to be studied. A shove by a woman may enrage her partner; a shove by a man can knock a woman down and cause a concussion. A woman's punch may only cause laughter, whereas a man's can cause a full range of injuries. In a study of spousal homicide, for example, beatings were the cause of death for a third of the wives; wives who killed, on the other hand, almost always used weapons (Chimbos, 1978).

Even though many battered women may aggressively defend themselves from attack and may be legally justified in doing so, it would be a mistake to assume that aggression works for victims. Available evidence indicates that such action will probably make things worse. In Fojtik's (1977-78) survey of help-seeking battered women, 77% of those who tried to defend themselves reported that it escalated the violence. Bowker (1983) also found that an aggressive response escalated the man's violence. He found that the most successful strategies women used in stopping their husbands' attacks were threats of divorce or threats to invoke criminal justice sanctions. Bowker concluded that this method worked because it improved the balance of power between the partners.

The limitations of the present study and its exploratory nature require that its findings be taken cautiously. A major problem in the methodology was that respondents were not asked about their behavior and possible motives for one specific incident at a time. Since correlations were made among frequencies applied over the course of the entire relationship, one cannot know about the correlations using incidents as the unit of analysis. Another limitation of the study is the nature of the sample. Most of the women were seeking help from a shelter and thus were more likely than other battered women to be from a low income group and to have experienced severe abuse (Washburn & Frieze, 1981). Women seeking shelter, calling the police, or going to the emergency room are not likely to be found in relationships in which couples keep their violence at low levels (Schulman, 1979; Steinmetz, 1980). A representative survey asking about the sequence of events, motives, and outcomes would provide much more conclusive findings than those of the present study. Reports from both partners would add to the validity of such a study, as well as questions about motives.

Considering all that needs to be studied in order to answer carefully the question of whether husbands and wives use physical violence for similar reasons, a difficult ethical dilemma becomes apparent. Early exploratory studies provide important data for understanding the scope of family violence and can be instrumental in convincing the public of the need for victim services. Yet exploratory studies are often descriptive in nature and do not include the study of explanatory variables. For example, some studies revealed that blacks employed violence in the family more than whites did, which may have confirmed popular social stereotypes of black families as abusive. More complete analysis of the data, however, revealed that although blacks reported higher rates of marital violence than whites, this was generally explained by income differences (Cazenave & Straus, 1974). Similarly, as my review of the literature suggests, studies of the rates of violence led to heated debate about wife abuse versus husband abuse, but these studies could not answer the critical question of why men or women employed violence in the first place. On the one hand, it seems that research reports should be withheld until more comprehensive studies can be completed, in order to prevent harm. On the other hand, when many women are injured daily, it seems unethical to delay publishing findings that potentially could lead to services in the near future.

Because of my feminist values, I try to be more aware of the ethical implications of my research. A feminist perspective also contributes a great deal to how I design my research instruments, how I conduct my research, and how I interpret my data. A feminist analysis in family violence research is especially appropriate given the role of the patriarchy in causing and maintaining the problem (Dobash & Dobash, 1979; Yllö, 1983) and the criticism that family violence and other aggression research is sexist (Bleier, 1979; Wardell, Gillespie, & Leffler, 1983). A feminist perspective compels one to ask about differences of power when viewing male-female relationships. Applied to the research on marital violence, a feminist perspective leads to some of the questions posed in this chapter: Do the physical and social differences of power between the sexes lead to different consequences when men and women are violent? Are the motives for violence different for men and women? The study presented in this chapter is an example of how quantitative methods of inquiry can be integrated with a feminist theoretical analysis. By applying a feminist perspective, the researcher who uses quantitative methods, rather than losing objectivity, has one more theoretical model to use when formulating questions, designing studies, and interpreting results (see for example, Walker, 1984, pp. 110-112).

Summary

When a feminist perspective is employed to examine whether husbands and wives use violence with equal frequency and are equally victimized by the abuse, we learn that some new research strategies are needed. Instead of simply counting the number of times husbands and wives use violence, we must ask men and women about their motives for violence and about the physical consequences of the violence. The study reported in this chapter suggests that although women use violence as frequently as men, they usually employ it in self-defense.

As a feminist researcher, I try to bring a different perspective to my understanding of the current research literature. Instead of accepting the data at face value, I carefully examine how it was gathered and interpreted. I am especially interested in whether the researcher recognizes the inequality between men and women, which is a critical dimension of the family context. In my own study, I combined my feminist values with quantitative research techniques. The content of feminist research, notably the assumption of women's oppression, the need for a gender analysis, and the use of complex explanatory variables were used while relying on the tools of more traditional, quantitative methods. Thus, social science, rather than being a tool of the status quo, is used as a tool for social change.

REFERENCES

Adler, E. M. (1981). The underside of married life: Power, influence, and violence. In L. H. Bowker (Ed.), *Women and crime in America* (pp. 300-320). New York: Macmillan.

Berk, R. A., Berk, S., Loseke, D. R., & Rauma, D. (1981). Mutual combat and other family violence myths. In D. Finkelhor, R. J. Gelles, G. T. Hotaling, & M. A. Straus (Eds.), *The dark side of families: Current family violence research* (pp. 197-212). Newbury Park, CA: Sage.

Bleier, R. (1979). Social and political bias in science: An examination of animal studies and their generalizations to human behavior and evolution. In R. Hubbard & M. Lowe (Eds.), *Genes and gender* (Vol. II, pp. 49-70). New York: Gordian Press.

Bowker, L. H. (1983). *Beating wife-beating.* Lexington, MA: Lexington Press.

Browne, A. (1986). Assault and homicide at home: When battered women kill. In M. J. Saks & L. Saxe (Eds.), *Advances in applied social psychology* (Vol. III). Hillsdale, NJ: Lawrence Erlbaum.

Cazenave, N. A., & Straus, M. A. (1979). Race, class, network embeddedness and family violence: A search for potent support systems. *Journal of Comparative Family Studies, 10,* 280-299.

Chimbos, P. D. (1978). *Marital violence: A study of interspouse homicide*. San Francisco: R & E Research Associates.

Crowne, D. P., & Marlowe, D. (1964). *The approval motive: Studies in evaluative dependence*. New York: John Wiley.

Dobash, R. E., & Dobash, R. P. (1981). Social science and social action: The case of wife beating. *Journal of Family Issues, 2*(4), 439-470.

Dobash, R. E., & Dobash, R. P. (1979). *Violence against wives: A case against the patriarchy*. New York: Free Press.

Edwards, S.S.M. (1985). A socio-legal evaluation of gender ideologies in domestic assault and spousal homicides. *Victimology: An International Journal, 10*(1-4),186-205.

Fathers group wants commission for status of men. (1984, May 10). *Seacoast Woman,* Portsmouth, NH, p. 15.

Fiora-Gormally, N. (1978). Battered women who kill: Double standard out of court, single standard in? *Law and Human Behavior, 2*(2), 133-165.

Fojtik, K. M. (1977-78). The NOW domestic violence project. *Victimology: An International Journal, 2*(3-4), 653-657.

Frieze, I. H., Noble, J., Zomnar, G., & Washburn, C. (1980). *Types of battered women*. Paper presented at the annual meeting of the Association for Women in Psychology, Santa Monica, CA.

Gaquin, D. A. (1977-78). Spouse abuse: Data from the national crime survey. *Victimology: An International Journal, 2,* 632-643.

Gelles, R. J. (1974). *The violent home*. Newbury Park, CA: Sage.

Greenblat, C. (1981). *Physical force by any other name . . . ; quantitative data, qualitative data, and the politics of family violence research*. Paper presented at the National Conference for Family Violence Researchers, University of New Hampshire.

Irwin, J. K. (1981). Interpersonal needs orientations and violence in the conjugal dyad. (Doctoral dissertation, Hofstra University, 1980). *Dissertation Abstracts International, 41*(12), 4742-B.

Kenny, M. A. (1981). Family relationships in domestic violence disturbances. *Dissertation Abstracts International, 41*(8):3734-A.

Kieviet, T. G. (1978). The battered wife syndrome: A potential defense to a homicide charge. *Pepperdine Law Review, 6*(1), 213-229.

LaFave, W. R., & Scott, A. W. (1972). *Handbook of criminal law*. St. Paul: West.

Langley, R., & Levy, R. C. (1977). *Wifebeating: The silent crisis*. New York: Dutton.

Lewis, E. M. (1981). The effects of intensity and probability on the preference for immediate versus delayed aversive stimuli in women with various level of interspousal conflict. (Doctoral dissertation, University of Illinois at Chicago Circle, 1980). *Dissertation Abstracts International, 41*(10), 3897-B.

Lykes, M. B., & Steward, A. J. (1983). *Evaluating the feminist challenge in psychology: 1963-1983*. Paper presented at the annual meeting of the American Psychological Association, Anaheim, CA.

Makepeace, J. M. (1983). Life events stress and courtship violence. *Family Relations, 32,* 101-109.

McCormick, C. (1976). *Battered women—the last resort*. Unpublished manuscript, Cook County Department of Corrections, Chicago.

McLeod, M. (1984). Women against men: An examination of domestic violence based on an analysis of official data and national victimization data. *Justice Quarterly,* pp. 170-193.

Nisonoff, L., & Bitman, I. (1979). Spouse abuse: Incidence and relationship to selected demographic variables. *Victimology: An International Journal, 4*(1), 131-139.

Oswald, I. (1980). Domestic violence by women. *Lancet, 2,* 1253-1254.

Pagelow, M. D. (1981). *Woman battering: Victims and their experiences.* Newbury Park, CA: Sage.

Pagelow, M. D. (1984). *Family violence.* New York: Praeger.

Pleck, E., Pleck, J. H., Grossman, M., & Bart, P. B. (1977-78). The battered data syndrome: A comment on Steinmetz' article. *Victimology: An International Journal, 2,* 680-684.

Salzman, F. (1979). Aggression and gender: A critique of the nature-nurture question for humans. In R. Hubbard & M. Lowe (Eds.), *Genes and gender: Vol. II: Pitfalls in research on sex and gender* (pp. 71-90). New York: Gordian Press.

Saunders, D. G. (1980). The police response to battered women: Predictors of officers' use of arrest, counseling, and minimal action. (Doctoral dissertation, University of Wisconsin-Madison, 1979). *Dissertation Abstracts International, 40,* 6446-A.

Saunders, D. G., & Size, P. B. (1980). *Marital violence and the police: A survey of police officers, victims, and victim advocates.* Unpublished research report to the Wisconsin Council on Criminal Justice, Madison, WI.

Schneider, E. M., & Jordan, S. B. (1978). Representation of women who defend themselves in response to physical or sexual assault. *Family Law Review, 1*(2), 118-132.

Schulman, M. (1979). *A survey of spousal violence against women in Kentucky.* New York: Garland.

Simons, D. E. (1983). An examination of attitudes about violent self-defense behavior exhibited by abused wives. (Doctoral dissertation, University of Wyoming, 1983). *Dissertation Abstracts, 83,* 27753.

Stark-Adamec, C., & Adamec, R. E. (1985). Problems in aggression research: An introduction. *International Journal of Women's Studies, 8*(4), 356-362.

State of Washington v Wanrow, 88 Wash. 2d 221, 559, p. 2d 548 (1977).

Steinmetz, S. K. (1977). *The cycle of violence.* New York: Praeger.

Steinmetz, S. K. (1977-78). The battered husband syndrome. *Victimology: An International Journal, 2*(3-4), 499-509.

Steinmetz, S. K. (1980). Women and violence: Victims and perpetrators. *American Journal of Psychotherapy, 34*(3), 334-350.

Straus, M. A. (1979). Measuring intrafamily conflict and violence: The conflict tactics (CT) scales. *Journal of Marriage and the Family, 41*(1), 75-88.

Straus, M. A. (1980). Victims and aggressors in marital violence. *American Behavioral Scientist, 23*(5), 681-704.

Straus, M. A., & Gelles, R. J. (1986). Societal change and change in family violence from 1975 to 1985 as revealed by two national surveys. *Journal of Marriage and the Family, 48*(3), 465-479.

Straus, M. A., Gelles, R. J., & Steinmetz, S. K. (1980). *Behind closed doors: Violence in the American family.* New York: Doubleday/Anchor.

Totman, J. (1978). *Murderess—A psychosocial study of criminal homicide.* Palo Alto, CA: R & E Associates.

Vanfossen, B. E. (1979). Intersexual violence in Monroe County, New York. *Victimology: An International Journal, 4*(2):299-304.

Walker, A. J., & Thompson, L. (1984). Feminism and family studies. *Journal of Family Issues, 5*(4), 545-570.

Walker, L. E. (1984). *The battered woman syndrome*. New York: Springer.

Wardell, L., Gillespie, D. L., & Leffler, A. (1983). Science and violence against women. In D. Finkelhor, R. J. Gelles, G. T. Hotaling, & M. A. Straus (Eds.), *The dark side of families: Current family violence research* (pp. 69-84). Newbury Park, CA: Sage.

Washburn, C., & Frieze, I. H. (1981). *Methodological issues in studying battered women.* Paper presented at the National Conference for Family Violence Researchers, University of New Hampshire.

Wolfgang, M. E. (1957). Victim-precipitated criminal homicide. *Journal of Criminal Law, Criminology and Police Science, 48*(1), 1-11.

Yllö, K. (1983). Using a feminist approach in quantitative research: A case study. In D. Finkelhor, R. J. Gelles, G. T. Hotaling, & M. A. Straus. (Eds.), *The dark side of families: Current family violence research* (pp. 277-288). Newbury Park, CA: Sage.

5

How Women Define Their Experiences of Violence

LIZ KELLY

In order to live in the world, we must name it. Names are essential for the construction of reality, for without a name it is difficult to accept the existence of an object, an event, a feeling. (Spender, 1980, p. 163)

The power of naming is at least two-fold, naming defines the quality and value of that which is named—and it also denies reality and value to that which is never named, never uttered. That which has no name, that for which we have no words or concepts, is rendered mute and invisible; powerless to inform or transform our consciousness of our experience, our understanding, our vision, powerless to claim its own existence. (Du Bois, 1983, p. 108)

In order to define something a word has to exist with which to name it. As Spender and Du Bois point out, what is not named is invisible and, in a social sense, nonexistent. The name, once known, must be applicable to one's own experience. Although this seems self-evident, neglecting this factor has significant implications for research design, analysis, and conclusions in the domain of woman abuse. Access to a name is the first step in defining experiences of sexual violence. Throughout this chapter the term *sexual violence* is used to refer to all forms of violence women and girls experience from men and boys. One central theme of the research project on which this chapter is based has

AUTHOR'S NOTE: This research was made possible by a postgraduate grant awarded by the Social Science Research Council.

been to explore the similarities and differences among a range of forms of violence. Distinctions between "sexual" and "physical" assaults are considered false and/or arbitrary, both from the perspective of feminist theory (MacKinnon, 1979, 1982) and in terms of how women experience violence and abuse (Kelly, 1988).

Commonly, areas of sexual violence are studied separately in the major areas of battering, incest, or rape. In the course of my research, I developed the concept of a continuum of sexual violence. I wanted to find a means of discussing all forms of sexual violence that reflected the range of forms of abuse and that took into account the complexity of how women defined their own experiences (Kelly, 1987). I use the word continuum to mean a continuous series of elements or events that pass into one another, and are connected by the basic common characteristic that physical, verbal, and sexual coercion and assault are employed by men against women. Within this framework, it is possible to highlight the connections between everyday sexism and acts of criminal violence, which Stanko (1985) has referred to as distinctions between "typical" and "aberrant" male behavior. Within the continuum, the range of behavior women experience as abusive both within and among different forms of sexual violence can be documented. In discussing sexual violence in this way, women are able to locate actions within the continuum that they experience as abusive without necessarily having to name them as a particular form of abuse. It enables researchers to develop wider definitions and new names for forms of sexual violence that more accurately reflect women's experience.

In feminist writing on the patriarchal structure and content of language (see, for example, Daly, 1979; Spender, 1980), writers stress that women's experience is silenced and made invisible by the lack of words with which to name it. A major contribution of feminist social action around sexual violence has been to provide and create new words with which to describe and name our experience. For example, the terms *battered woman* and *sexual harassment* did not exist 20 years ago. Even if a name exists and is known, the way it is understood can vary greatly. For example, feminists have challenged the limited traditional defini-tions of forms of sexual violence by expanding the definition of *rape* to include unwanted and/or forced intercourse between husband and wife and by including psychological abuse and coercive sex in the definition of domestic violence. Limited definitions tend to draw on stereotypes of forms of sexual violence, stressing particular features and ignoring others.

This chapter explores the themes of naming, defining, and redefining sexual violence, using data from an in-depth study of how women experience and cope with sexual violence. After examination of current definitions of sexual violence, the feminist perspective underlying the methodology and analysis is presented. After detailed discussion of the factors affecting how women defined their experiences of sexual violence, implications for research design, intervention, and feminist research and practice are summarized.

The Importance of Definitions

In our culture, the meaning of words such as *rape, battering,* or *incest* are often taken for granted. These terms are often employed uncritically in social science research as analytic categories defined before the research is begun. The reports of women who have been victimized are then recorded with these predetermined categories. This often results in the distortion and even exclusion of instances of sexual violence, as it fails to take account of the complexity of how women define and understand their own experience(s).

Several researchers have recently acknowledged the importance and complexity of this issue, and have begun to change the kinds of questions they ask women. For example, in the past, researchers would ask, "Have you ever been raped?" This question assumed that the woman and the researcher shared a common definition of what counts as rape. However, many women did not define an experience as "rape," although it may be so defined by an outside observer (Finkelhor & Yllö, 1983; Russell, 1982). Now, more open-ended terms are used, such as "have you ever been forced to have sex?" How questions are posed influences the kinds of incidence figures obtained by research. Russell (1984), who found higher than usual incidence figures for rape and sexual abuse in her study, accounted for this finding by suggesting that she had asked broader, more general questions that allowed women to name experiences that would not have been recorded in studies using more restricted terms.

Although many researchers are aware of this fundamental problem, there is still little research to date that examines whether women define certain experiences as violence of a particular sort and/or that explores the definitional parameters by which women label incidents as sexual violence. For example, although there have been a considerable number of investigations of attitudes toward rape (see Pugh, 1983), only a minority of studies explicitly examine the underlying implicit question—

how rape is defined (Schepple & Bart, 1983; Zellman, Goodchilds, Johnson, & Giarusso, 1981). There are almost no studies to date that explore women's definitions of battering, incest, or sexual harassment. Since a number of studies have documented that how acts are defined influences public attitudes, agency practice, and legal decisions (Borkowski, Murch, & Walker, 1983; Holmstrom & Burgess, 1978; L. Radford, 1987), this provides further support for the importance of understanding how women understand and categorize their own experiences.

Feminist Research Practice

My research into sexual violence grew out of many years involvement in a variety of feminist campaigns and projects in the United Kingdom. I have worked in a refuge for battered women for 14 years and was a founding member of a local rape crisis group.

Feminist research based on wider definitions of sexual violence is increasingly documenting the prevalence of violence in women's lives (Hall, 1985; Hanmer & Saunders, 1984; L. Radford, 1987, Russell, 1984). Sexual violence is a common experience for women, and explanations of sexual violence must address social factors, in particular, the issue of power relationships between men and women (Stanko, 1985).

I believe that feminist research is more than research about women's position in society. It is research that is based on the theoretical premise that women are oppressed. It is research with the intention of understanding our oppression in order to end it. Just as there are a number of theories within feminism accounting for women's oppression, so feminist researchers use a variety of methods in their studies. Within my research, I tried to integrate the principles of practice that we have established within women's groups: respect, honesty, empathy with other women, and the sharing of skills or information (Kelly, 1984).

Feminist researchers have a particular relationship to their work. As women, we are part of the group whose experience we are attempting to document, understand and change. Reflexivity, therefore, is both inevitable and integral to feminist research:

> Feminism forces us to locate our own auto-biographies and our experience inside the questions we might ask, so that we continually feel with women we are studying. (McRobbie, 1982, p. 32)

How Women Define Sexual Violence:
An Empirical Study

The goals of my research were: (1) to document the range of sexual violence women experience in their lives, (2) to explore the links between different forms of sexual violence, and (3) to study the long-term impact of rape, incest, and domestic violence. My interest in the process of defining and naming sexual violence developed while analyzing the interview data.

Sample

In-depth interviews were conducted with 60 women, 48 of whom also took part in follow-up interviews. In order to reach a wider spectrum of women than is commonly studied (usually women who report to official or voluntary agencies), women were contacted by a number of methods including articles and letters in newspapers and magazines, and solicitation through radio announcements, talks, and discussions at a range of community women's groups. Thirty women volunteered because they had experienced rape, incest, or battering (10 in each category). Another 30 women were interviewed who did not necessarily identify themselves as survivors of any form of sexual or physical abuse. The predominantly white sample was characterized by women ranging in age, social class, marital status, occupation, and sexual orientation.

Methodology

In designing the research project, I drew on my own experiences and on those of women I knew. The interview guide was carefully developed so that women could report events they experienced as abusive but had not named as a particular form of sexual violence. Interview questions about various forms of sexual violence were organized chronologically, moving through childhood and adolescence to adulthood. Early questions used open-ended terms. Women were asked if they had ever felt pressured to have sex, had ever had a negative sexual experience in childhood or adolescence, or had ever experienced violence in intimate relationships. Later questions referred explicitly to rape, incest, and domestic violence. It was therefore possible to explore factors that affected how women defined their own experiences over time. In data analysis, women's own definitions were respected and terms such as pressurized sex and coercive sex have been used to reflect this.

Each woman interviewed was sent a transcript of her original interview. We then met a second time and discussed, among other issues, her reactions to the interview and to reading the transcript. This interactive aspect of the research methodology enabled women to reflect on what they had said, to add to or to change their original statements, and to explore aspects of their experience in more depth. At times, this resulted in incidents of sexual violence being recorded that would not have been otherwise. The dialogue between me and the women enabled me to understand better the aspects of interviews that were ambiguous and to check my interpretation of what women had said.

I often spent as much time talking to women after the tape recorder was turned off as I spent on the interviews themselves. These conversations included requests for advice and information and questions about the research project as well as reflections on aspects of the interviews. As Oakley (1981) notes, contrary to traditional views on interview technique, these conversations did not compromise my position as a researcher, but aided my understanding and gave me the opportunity to give something back to the women I interviewed. Detailed fieldnotes were taken throughout all phases of the research.

Results

The results will be summarized according to major content areas: (1) how women defined events when they first occurred and whether these definitions changed over time; (2) stereotypes; (3) the coping strategies of forgetting and minimizing; and (4) the process of redefinition.

Defining Sexual Violence

Certain of the detailed questions on rape, incest, and domestic violence referred to how women defined the events when they first occurred and whether these definitions had changed over time. Over 60% of the women did not initially define their experiences as a form of sexual violence. However, 50% of the incidents of physical abuse by a partner were defined as "violence" as the abuse continued. About 70% of the women changed their definitions of their experiences over time, almost always in the direction of relabeling an incident as abuse. Even though women experienced similar acts of assaults against them by men, they often defined these experiences in very different ways. This, coupled with the fact that women were often not sure how to define or label particular events, confirms the importance of the issues of naming and defining.

> I didn't really understand what he was doing. I knew that it was wrong but I didn't understand—I didn't know what sex was so I couldn't call it sex.

> I called it not being very nice (laughs). I knew there was something wrong with it, I knew I didn't like it but I don't think I had a name for it. The older I got, the more I came to see it as abusive. It's only very recently, the last year say, that I see it as incest.

Some of the names that have been applied to domestic violence caused problems for some women. *Wife beating* implies that violence happens only to married women. The terms *beating* and *battering* tended to be understood in terms of severe, frequent physical violence.

> What he did wasn't exactly battering but it was *the threat*. I remember one night I spent the whole night in a state of terror, nothing less than terror *all night*. . . . And that was *worse* to me than getting whacked. . . . That waiting without confrontation is just so frightening.

> Quite a lot of time he wasn't physically violent but there was just this *threat all the time* you see. . . . It was mental cruelty, as there was always the threat of physical violence.

> Mental violence is something you can't pinpoint. I suppose physical violence is there. . . but you can't define mental torture. It comes in very funny ways.

In some situations, women, as girls or as adults, felt abused but were unable to name their experience at the time. Even when a name is known, however, women may not apply it to their own experience.

Certain forms of sexual violence are closer to acceptable "normal" behavior than others. Acts that were extensions of typical male behavior, and so further away from stereotypic definitions of sexual violence, were often difficult for women to define as abuse. For example, many men make assumptions of intimacy with women working in certain jobs, such as bar work or waitressing. It is difficult for women to name behaviors as "sexual harassment" when this same behavior is accepted and expected by customers, employers and, occasionally, female coworkers.

Many instances of sexual abuse and early incidents of incestuous abuse were extensions of affection considered appropriate between adults and children. Women remembered the confusion they felt in such circumstances, not understanding why being kissed or hugged by a male relative or friend made them feel so uncomfortable.

> He'd say "Let's do a jigsaw" and when I went to sit down his hand would be there. I just thought it was ridiculous always having to sit on his hand.

For this woman, and for most of the incest survivors interviewed, the pattern of incestuous abuse changed. For one woman, however, her father's behavior remained an extension of accepted affectionate behavior. It took her much longer than the other incest survivors to define his behavior as abusive.

The way women distinguished between pressurized sex, coercive sex (assaults women described as being "like rape"), and rape clearly highlights the ambiguity of many situations for women. Over 80% of the women interviewed had felt pressured to have sex, often on a number of occasions by different men. Responding to the question about pressure to have sex, many women qualified their answer by saying there was no physical force. Women were often unsure how to define their experience when physical force was not used and when there were no obvious injuries. Moreover, the "seriousness" of the abuse was questioned, often despite the woman's own feelings and reactions. Being coerced to have sex or being raped by men with whom women had previously had consensual sex were extensions of the more common pressure. Knowing the man and the previous nature of the relationship made defining the event as rape more difficult.

In many instances of forced or coerced sex, women submitted because of the perceived threat of violence. They were not physically hurt nor did they resist throughout. Both of these factors influenced how they defined the event afterwards.

> I don't know whether to regard it as an assault or not. Last summer I was hitching to the coast. This man who gave me a lift was chatting and I said I was unemployed and poor and he said "Well, I know one way you can earn some money quickly." He said if I gave him a blow job, he'd pay me five pounds. I didn't want to, but he became very insistent and said "I'll give you ten," took it out of his wallet while steering erratically across the road. His manner frightened me *very much*. I didn't know what would

happen if I kept insisting no. I thought the best thing to do was to accept this arrangement, as it might prevent me from being raped or physically hurt—so that's what I did.

She added during the follow-up interview:

I think it was an assault because I was definitely coerced. . . . My feelings about it are contradictory—on the one hand, I feel that I perhaps had some choice in submitting to it and on the other I was forced.

Stereotypes

Every person has his or her own common sense definition of what constitutes different forms of sexual violence, which are often linked to explanations of why sexual violence happens, who commits it, and which women experience it. Definitions can be limited or broad in their scope. Many of the more limited, "common sense" definitions of forms of sexual violence draw on stereotypes. Stereotypes are highly simplified descriptions that exclude certain factors while stressing others. For many women, accepting these limited definitions and stereotypes results in a disjunction between the reality of their experience and how they are encourged by society to interpret it.

Stereotypic representations of sexual violence suggest that violence is relatively infrequent, takes place in particular circumstances, and is directed at certain types of women by certain types of men. Such stereotypes imply that it is relatively easy to distinguish between what is and what is not sexual violence. But many of the experiences documented in the interviews did not fit the stereotypic definitions, and so the women were often unlikely to name an experience as a particular form of sexual violence at the time. For example, rape is stereotypically defined as sexual assault by a stranger who uses high levels of physical force against a woman he doesn't know (Chandler & Tomey, 1981; Holmstrom & Burgess, 1978). The woman is expected to resist throughout. This stereotype prevented a number of women from defining their experience of forced sex as rape at the time of the assault:

For a while, I didn't even think it was rape since I had let him into the house and I knew him. I had this idea that rape was something that happened to you in an alley.

Well, I suppose I thought that rape was something that happens to you on the street, like with a complete stranger. [ironic laugh]

It wasn't classic textbook—as I then thought rape was.

This limited definition of rape also affected whether women defined sexual assaults by family members as rape:

I thought rape was a violent act and the woman got hurt, physically hurt.... When I look back now I feel, yes, I must have been raped. But not in the way most people mean rape—the public view of rape. I feel I've been raped but it's an acceptable rape.

In a way I suppose what happened with my father was almost always rape, wasn't it? It was always against my wishes—yeah, I've never thought of it like that before.

Because rape is stereotypically defined as a rare experience between a woman and an anonymous assailant, many women who were forced to have sex repeatedly within intimate relationships, or who had been forced to have sex by a number of men, did not define these experiences as "rape." Often, women who had been repeatedly coerced to have sex defined one incident "rape" and the others "forced sex." This linguistic device protected women from acknowledging that they had been raped more than once. The incident labeled rape was usually the one where the man used the most physical force, where the woman resisted throughout, or where the relationship between the woman and man was least close, such as forced sex by an acquaintance or friend rather than a partner. Part of the difficulty in defining assaults by friends, partners, or relatives as rape may be that the rapist is someone for whom the woman has, or once had, positive feelings. The stereotypes of rapists and child molesters seldom fit women's friends, lovers, husbands, or fathers, even when they had committed acts of sexual assault.

In contrast, the "common sense" stereotypes of domestic violence focus on other social and psychological characteristics. "Battered wives" are portrayed as poor, weak, and downtrodden and as nagging women who "deserve" to be hit. Stereotypes of batterers often focus on aggressive personalities or alcohol abuse. Battering is defined as frequent, life threatening violence. These stereotypes seldom fit women's experiences. One woman helped establish a refuge for battered women in her town. Although her husband was beating her at the time, she did not make the conscious connection between her situation and that of the women she was helping:

I just thought that the incidents of violence that I—in order to be a battered woman you had to be really battered. I mean OK, I had a couple of bad incidents, but mostly it was pretty minor, in inverted commas, "violence." I didn't see myself in that category, as a battered woman at all.

Another woman stated:

I feel now that the sort of image of the battered woman being basically ill-educated, inarticulate and poor is totally misconceived. Not nearly enough is written and talked about women who are not beaten up by drunken husbands every week, but who were in my situation.

Coping Strategies:
Forgetting and Minimizing

Anyone who has worked with abused women or done research on sexual violence will have noticed that many women forget experiences of abuse, have vague and sketchy memories of the actual incidents of abuse and may use phrases like "It wasn't that bad, really." Rather than interpret these responses, as some in the mental health community tend to, as evidence of deception, resistance, or manipulation, they must be understood as the result of two common adaptive coping strategies to experiences of victimization: forgetting and minimizing.

Forgetting. It is obvious that in order to define an event one must know that it has happened. Initially, I was surprised when women told me they had forgotten abusive experiences for long periods of time. I stopped being surprised as more and more women discussed this and as I myself remembered previously forgotten personal experiences during the research. We forget experiences in order to cope with an event that we do not understand, cannot name, or that places acute stress on our emotional resources. McCombie (1976) is one of a number of researchers to note that an immediate response of a substantial number of women to rape is to want to forget the experience. Forgetting is one of a range of coping strategies women use in relation to sexual violence.

Forgetting can take several different forms. When we have no words with which to name and understand experiences, memories are likely to be suppressed. The memory can become conscious only when we have the knowledge that enables us to make rational sense of the event(s) and of our reactions. This form of forgetting was particularly common to the women interviewed who reported childhood sexual abuse or rape. Almost 60% of the women who had been raped and 62% of the women who had been incestuously abused forgot their experience for a period of time. Women who had been battered were likely to suppress details of the assaults, but not the whole experience:

> I think half of me having a bad memory is because I don't want—I choose not to remember.

Remembering, for these women, almost always involved some sort of trigger: a book or article, a television program, dreams, giving birth, experiencing another assault, or talking to other women.

> For a long time I didn't think about it [incest]. It hadn't happened. It didn't exist. If I saw him, it would come into my mind for a split second. It wasn't until . . . I can remember the exact day—I was in a group and women were talking about what had happened to them. I was wondering what I could do because I hadn't any experiences like that and suddenly I thought "Oh yes you have."

> I didn't really want to think of it [incest]. It was just part of life that I forgot.

> I told you events, like the miscarriage, but there was other stuff as well. I had been raped by him [her husband] and it came out in a group session. It just came into my head and I started crying and suddenly it all came out.

Many memories were triggered for the women by the interview and/or by reading their transcript. The fact that a number of women had not recalled certain events but remembered them later points to how prevalent the adaptive coping strategy of forgetting is and to the impossibility of accurately assessing incidence through single questions in survey questionnaires.

For some women, another factor contributing to forgetting was not wanting to be defined by self or by others as "victims." The shame and self-blame that many women recall following assaults may contribute to this, as does the stigma and blame that women expected from others. It is interesting that a number of the triggers prompting women to remember involved hearing or reading comments that blamed abused women:

> I *had* to make him understand. It was really important to me and to make him stop talking. Like an idiot, I suddenly said "Well this is what

happened to me" and I totally freaked out. I suddenly thought "Oh my God, this *is* what happened to me!"

Women often forgot incidents that they did not define as "serious" and/or that happened frequently. For example, when discussing street harassment, many women commented on the fact that it was a common experience but they could not remember many specific incidents.

Forgetting was helpful for some women, giving them time to gather strength before coping with the experience and its effects. For other women, however, forgetting had serious consequences. The abusive experience had affected their feelings, behavior, and attitudes toward themselves and others, but they had no way of understanding how. The most extreme example of this was a woman who had been sexually abused by a number of family friends in childhood. She had only begun to remember the abuse when we first met. Since 18, she had been convinced she was "mad," and had tried to injure herself and commit suicide numerous times, resulting in 13 hospitalizations with drug and electroconvulsive therapy. She attributed the recent improvement in her mental health to knowing that her behavior was the result of abuse. She was extremely angry that no one involved in her treatment had attempted to discover the cause of her distress.

Minimizing. The term minimizing refers to the process whereby women tried to limit the importance and impact of incidents that they defined as abusive to some degree. They either minimized the seriousness of the assault in order to minimize its effects or they minimized the effects in order to minimize the assault. In both cases, this required the control and suppression of women's feelings and reactions at the time and over time. For example, if women believed others would not define their experiences as serious, they described and/or publicly responded to the events in ways that were often at odds with their emotional reactions. On the other hand, many women minimized the effects on them in order to cope with ongoing abuse. These must again be seen as adaptive coping strategies.

Minimizing occurred frequently with more common forms of sexual violence, such as sexual harassment. For example, during a first interview, a woman made a flippant remark about sexual harassment being a joke. The meaning of this comment was ambiguous—did she think it was a joke or was she treating it as a joke? In the follow-up interview, it became clear that she chose to define the harassment as not serious in order to limit its effect on her:

I suppose it's my way of coping, my way of interpreting the situation so that they don't get through to me.

J. Radford (1987) notes the frequency with which women respondents in a community incidence study prefaced accounts of street harassment and assault with remarks such as "nothing really happened" or "I was lucky really." She suggests that comparing one's experience to something "worse," such as rape, is a coping strategy that makes one's own experience seem less serious and enables women to continue with their daily lives. By minimizing the event, the fear and threat of possible future assaults is also minimized. Minimizing requires women to deny the reality of their experience at the time, and to define as "not serious" consequences that may, in reality, be lasting and severe.

> Looking back, it wasn't that bad, but for me it was the most awful thing that ever happened.

> It was very confusing to know what to make of it at the time. I had a clash of attitudes—sort of not wanting to make a fuss because, in fact, I had got away quite light, but actually feeling quite damaged.

Getting "away quite light" in this case meant not being raped. This woman had, however, been terrified at the time and recalled experiencing many of the reactions of women immediately after a rape.

Women experiencing physical abuse in intimate relationships also minimized its severity. Very few of the women who had experienced physical violence by their partners only once or infrequently defined these events as domestic violence. Frequency of violence was, in fact, the most important factor influencing how soon a woman defined a man's behavior as abusive. When there were long gaps between incidents, women minimized the violence by focusing on the nonabusive times, and hoping that it would not occur in the future.

> It was really cyclical actually, really incredible. And the odd thing was that in the good periods I could hardly remember the bad times. It was almost as if I was leading two different lives.

> There are long gaps sometimes . . . if it had been continuous battering then I'd just have gone. There were always times of hope.

Taking the severity of the violence seriously, specifically its life threatening nature, prompted many women to leave violent men. For a number of women, it was only in retrospect, after they had left, that they could acknowledge the severity of the violence and its effects on them.

The Process of Redefinition

Definitions of sexual violence are usually perceived as fixed in time. But names and definitions are not static. Women's understandings of what happened to them often change over time. Many factors contribute to this, including the creation of terms (such as "battering" or "marital rape") that allow women to name experiences previously silenced, the personal development of the woman over time, and the availability of a supportive and accepting social network. This process of redefinition is most evident when women have been battered or have suffered incest as children. As women begin to redefine incidents as sexual violence, they often may make connections with other experiences, which are also named as sexual violence.

> The first time he inveigled his way into my bed, I think that could be defined as a kind of rape. I've redefined things like being harassed as well.

> It was partly as a result of it not being so awful that I realized that in some of the situations in which I'd had intercourse with lovers were *not actually* that different.

Over time, women often remember more details of what happened to them, and so redefine events in new ways. At the same time, redefining what they have experienced often enables them to remember more of the abuse. This process can be extremely distressing and painful. But through the process of redefinition, women began to focus on and validate their own feelings and reactions—a crucial aspect of working through the experience of sexual violence. A quote from one incest survivor who began redefining her sexual abuse during our interviews illustrates this process.

> The things that I was unsure about were basically the things that I came out with about the incest thing. I hadn't worked that out at all and it just all came out. It was really revelatory to me because I'd never ... I'd always accepted it, that there was something wrong between me and my father, something indistinguishably wrong about our relationship, but I never verbalized it ever, but it really came out with your questions. It was only through reading it over that I realized what I'd said, and seeing how hard

certain questions were for me to answer and therefore recognizing there were big blocks about certain things. I now know that my father had sexual feelings towards me . . . that the way he was with me, even the violence, was a way of communicating with me sexually . . . but to say that it's incest, I think incest is too much of a decision right now.

It was clear from the interviews that, through the process of redefinition, women were focusing on their own feelings and reactions rather than on stereotypes or limited definitions or the perceptions of others. They were no longer minimizing the severity of the assault(s) or the effects on them. Remembering and redefining are empowering for women in a number of ways. In acknowledging abuse, women are able to look at and find ways of coping with its effects. They are also likely to develop precautionary strategies in order to prevent further abuse. These strategies involve taking more control over their lives and choices. For example, many women placed a positive value on developing a strong belief in their right to say "no" to sex when they didn't want it. The process often involved women shifting blame from themselves to the abusive man, which enabled them to express anger. This anger, and the determination to keep control of one's life, were linked to politicization for several women, who felt that their sympathy for feminism was a result of understanding their own experience.

Conclusions

For women, naming and defining experiences of sexual violence is not a simple process. It may not take place until many years after an abusive experience has occurred. This process, regardless of its timing, is a crucial and empowering one involving claiming one's experiences, coping with its effects.

In research on sexual violence, we should not assume that there are unproblematic definitions of forms of sexual violence. The kinds of questions we ask must facilitate exploration of events that women are unsure how to define but that they experienced as abusive. If we are studying incidence, we must acknowledge the commonness of forgetting and minimizing. We have no way of knowing how many incidents are still buried in memory or that women choose not to tell us about. The incidence figures we produce are likely to be underestimates. The methods we use in research, however, can somewhat decrease the margin of error. An interactive method that encourages women to reflect on their experience in more than one meeting is likely to result in some forgotten experiences being remembered. The increased trust in the researcher and involvement in the research project may also encourage women to discuss incidents they chose not to reveal during the first meeting. In data analysis and research reports, we should be very clear about how we are using definitions. Are we taking women's own definitions seriously? Have we developed analytic categories that solely reflect our own definitions? The concept of a continuum is one way of reflecting women's personal evolving definitions. It is also a framework within which new names and definitions can develop.

This research also has important implications for social action. Male dominance of language and its meanings is undoubtedly responsible for the limited terms and definitions of sexual violence that are currently available. It is in men's interest, as a class and as the perpetrators of sexual violence, to ensure that the definitions of sexual violence are as limited as possible. Language is a further means of controlling women.

A better understanding of how we still lack names with which to define our experiences and of the developmental process of definition is crucial for feminist researchers, service providers, and activists. It has been our work and intervention that has provided new names, widened definitions, and prompted changes in professional practice. Understanding the complexity of women's experience explains why so many survivors of sexual violence remember/name their abuse only many years after it has occurred. It points to the importance of providing supportive contexts where women can explore, name, and redefine what has happened to them.

This research also points to possible directions for preventive action. Many children experience sexual violence before they have words to encode what happened to them, or they lack the vocabulary to describe to others what has occurred. The development of sex education programs that provide children with a proper vocabulary can significantly address this problem. For example, in the United States, prevention programs are being developed that emphasize children's right to control who touches them and how.

But the first step is to develop names and definitions of sexual violence that accurately reflects women's experiences from their own frames of reference. Feminists have made great progress in extending current definitions and providing new names for sexual violence. Much energy has been directed toward legal reform, establishing codes of conduct, and changing professional practice. We need to focus more on reaching women with our analyses. The way we name and understand our experiences is not a static process. It is changing and dynamic. It may be a never-ending process as we understand more about the many subtle ways sexual violence can be experienced. It is essential that we develop a language, names, and definitions, that reflect our growing understanding. Feminist research can make a major contribution in this area.

REFERENCES

Borkowski, M., Murch, M., & Walker, V. (1983). *Marital violence: The community response.* London: Tavistock.

Chandler, S., & Tomey, M. (1981). The decisions and processing of the rape victim through the criminal justice system. *California Sociologist, 4*(2), 156-169.

Daly, M. (1979). *Gyn/Ecology.* London, Women's Press.

Du Bois, B. (1983). Passionate scholarship: Notes on values, knowing and method in feminist social science. In G. Bowles & R. Duelli Klein (Eds.), *Theories of women's studies.* London: Routledge & Kegan Paul.

Finkelhor, D., & Yllö, K. (1983). Rape in marriage: A sociological view. In D. Finkelhor, R. Gelles, G. Hotaling, & M. Straus (Eds.), *The dark side of families.* Newbury Park, CA: Sage.

Hall, R. (1985). *Ask any women.* London: Falling Wall.

Hanmer, J., & Saunders, S. (1984). *Well-founded fear.* London: Hutchinson.

Holmstrom, L., & Burgess, A. (1978). *The victims of rape: Institutional reaction.* New York: John Wiley.

Kelly, L. (1984). Some thoughts on feminist experience in research on sexual violence. In O. Butler (Ed.), *Feminist experience in feminist research: Studies in sexual politics* (Vol. II). Manchester: Department of Sociology, Manchester University.

Kelly, L. (1987). The continuum of sexual violence. In J. Hanmer & M. Maynard (Eds.), *Women, violence and social control.* London: Macmillan.

Kelly, L. (1988). *Surviving sexual violence.* Cambridge: Polity Press.

MacKinnon, C. (1979). *Sexual harassment of working women.* New Haven: Yale University Press.

MacKinnon, C. (1982). Feminism, marxism, method and the state: An agenda for theory. *Signs, 7*(3), 515-544.

McCombie, S. (1976). Characteristics of rape victims as seen in crisis intervention. *Smith College Studies in Social Work, 46,* 137-158.

McRobbie, A. (1982). The politics of feminist research: Between talk and action. *Feminist Review, 12,* 47-57.

Oakley, A. (1981). Interviewing women: A contradiction in terms. In H. Roberts (Ed.), *Doing feminist research* (pp. 30-61). Boston: Routledge & Kegan Paul.

Penfold, P., & Walker, G. (1984). *Women and the psychiatric paradox.* Milton Keynes: Open University Press.

132   Feminist Research

Pugh, M. D. (1983). Contributory fault and rape convictions: Loglinear models for blaming the victim. *Social Psychology Quarterly, 46*(3), 233-242.

Radford, J. (1987). Policing male violence—Policing women. In J. Hanmer & N. Maynard (Eds.), *Women, violence and social control.* London: Macmillan.

Radford, L. (1987). Legalising woman abuse. In J. Hanmer & M. Maynard (Eds.), *Women, violence and social control.* London: Macmillan.

Russell, D. (1982). *Marital rape.* New York: MacMillan.

Russell, D. (1984). *Sexual exploitation.* Newbury Park, CA: Sage.

Schepple, K., & Bart, P. (1983) Through women's eyes: Defining danger in the wake of sexual assault. *Journal of Social Issues, 39*(2), 63-80.

Spender, D. (1980). *Man-made language.* London: Routledge & Kegan Paul.

Stanko, E. (1985). *Intimate intrusions.* London: Routledge & Kegan Paul.

Zellman, G., Goodchilds, J., Johnson, P., & Giarusso, R. (1981). *Teenagers' application of the label "rape" to nonconsensual sex between acquaintances.* Unpublished paper.

6

Why Do Men Batter Their Wives?

JAMES PTACEK

Throughout the past decade of feminist work on violence against women, the testimony of battered women has been indispensable in making public the oppression that had long been hidden from view. With the growth in social services for men who batter, researchers and activists have recently had the opportunity to talk with batterers about their perspective on violence against wives. What can we learn about wife beating from men who batter? Surely, the testimony of batterers cannot be taken at face value. Nevertheless, when placed in the context of a feminist analysis of women's oppression, men who batter have a good deal to contribute. Not only is their discussion richer than what is found in clinical interpretations of their behavior, but, unwittingly, their testimony also presents its own critique far more powerfully than what is contained in most psychological and sociological treatments. That is, not only do they present their violence in a light that illuminates its intentionality and cruelty, but their words also reveal the blind spots in the dominant clinical perspectives. From the unlikeliest of sources, then, comes a challenge to the narrow psychological explanations of wife beating so popular today.

In this chapter I will present transcripts of how men who batter talk about their violence. For this study I conducted interviews with 18 abusive men. Small as this sample is, this study represents one of only a few successful attempts to gather evidence systematically of batterers' perspectives on wife beating. In order to make sense of the accounts presented here, at least three levels of analysis are necessary. First, there is the issue of methods, or in other words the relationship between the researcher (myself) and the men in the study. Questions of what my motivation was in doing this research, how I collected the data, and how I dealt with conflicts that arose during the process of interviewing will be addressed. By providing this background I seek to sort out the problem of bias and its effect on the content of the interviews.

The second level of analysis involves examining some relationships within the batterers' testimony, that is, the patterns and contradictions that are found in the accounts. The question of the role that batterers' rationalizations play in the progression of the violence and abusiveness can then be investigated.

Finally, the third level of investigation concerns the relationship between the batterers' explanations for their violence and those explanations prevalent in the wider society. I shall compare the batterers' accounts with the analysis offered in the clinical literature on wife beating. In addition, some attention will be given to the discourse on battering encountered in the criminal justice system. With this threefold analysis, I hope to provide a proper context for understanding what batterers have to say.

The Study

In order to examine the ways batterers perceive their violence, I conducted in-depth interviews with 18 male clients I recruited through my work with Emerge, a Boston organization that offers counseling for wife beaters. The men's involvement in counseling ranged from a single intake session to 24 weeks in the group counseling program. Only 33% of the sample had completed the full six months of group counseling; 39% had attended three or fewer counseling sessions. While their experiences at Emerge likely affected how they viewed their actions, it is important to note that contact with Emerge was rather limited for a good portion of the men. None of the men was in counseling at the time of the interviews; most had been out of contact with Emerge for over a year. In all but two cases, the man's violence had allegedly stopped.

While this is clearly not a representative sample of batterers in any scientific sense, this group of men is quite diverse as far as demographic data and levels of violence are concerned. The age range is broad, from 22 to 53 years, although most of the men are in their 30s. All but two of the men are White. Only half of the men were officially married during the period of the violence; three men had not even been sharing a common residence with their partner during the time of the abusiveness. The data on education, occupation, and income indicate that the proportion of working-class and middle-class men is about equal. Seven men held at least a college degree; professional, technical, and social service categories account for the employment of eight of the men. One man was unemployed; two men reported income of less than $5,000 for the previous year.

In half the relationships, the men became violent less than a year after the relationship began. Based on their own testimony, the violence involved shoving, slapping, dragging by the hair, throwing objects—such as a plate or an ashtray—punching, kicking, bodily throwing, choking, "beating up," threatening with a knife, and rape. One third of the men reported that their partners sustained broken bones or other substantial physical injuries as a result of the violence. It is my opinion that this is at best a conservative estimate of the violence these men inflicted; underreporting by batterers is frequently noted in the clinical literature (Adams & Penn, 1981; Bograd, 1983; Brisson, 1982; Lund, Larsen, & Schultz, 1982). There was, unfortunately, no way of corroborating the batterers' reports short of calling up the battered women and asking them to talk about the abuse, which in most cases occurred some years ago.

All the interviews were conducted in the Emerge offices. The men were offered eight dollars for their participation. This indicated that they would be doing something for Emerge's benefit, and established that the interview was not formally a counseling session. Half of the men declined the money, usually with the statement that they were happy to give something back to Emerge, since Emerge had helped them. The interviews followed an open-ended, semistructured format. The men were asked to describe the first, last, and most violent episodes; to talk about what happened before, during, and after the episode; and to explain what they were thinking and feeling during all of this.

The value in using the in-depth personal interview to study wife beating lies in its potential for comprehending the batterer's perspective. However, this very virtue raises the possibility of bias, a problem that requires serious attention.

Bias in Field Research

While national surveys and other more "quantitative" methods may not be any less susceptible to bias (Becker, 1970), the in-depth interview and more "qualitative" methods pose particular problems for the interpretation and evaluation of research. The major advantage of this approach is the possibility of developing trust and exploring the respondent's perceptions, feelings, and rationalizations through dialogue. The limitations result from the reliance of the research on one unique "instrument"—the field researcher—who often simultaneously acts as theorist, provocateur, observer, recorder, and interpreter. Because of this singularly personal involvement with the phenomenon being studied, a number of field researchers have emphasized the importance of accounting for the motivation and self-presentation of the researcher in the write-up of the study. This is important in order to enable the reader to gauge the impact of the researcher on the subject of the research. For example, Reinharz (1979, pp. 10-11) states that the process and the biases of the researcher should be made clear:

> Since research is a personal activity, research reports should contain a vivid description of the experience of the researching. In these reports the value positions of the researcher should be faced squarely and addressed fully.

In light of these considerations, I would like to make explicit my motivations for conducting this research. This will be followed by a description of how I presented myself in the research setting, and a discussion of some of the conflicts I experienced in interviewing men who batter.

Motivation of the Researcher

I came to study wife beating as a way of contributing to social action against men's domination of women. Prior to entering graduate school, I became involved with Emerge in Boston. I have continued my affiliation with Emerge while in school, working as a group counselor, public speaker, trainer, and researcher for the organization. As Emerge defines wife beating in political terms and draws its analysis from the women's movement, I am both an activist and a researcher on the issue of violence against wives. As the Dobashes point out, there are not many clear models for how to operate in this nexus:

> Despite all protestation to the contrary, social research and political issues are inevitably related. Yet, social science is largely lacking in models of how to develop scientific work within this context, how to analyze the social and political consequences of the messages inherent in research and

how to participate with community groups and social agencies in the collective creation of social change. (Dobash & Dobash, 1981, p. 7)

The point is that each orientation on the issue of wife beating carries its own limitations and potential for bias, whether one is an activist or an academic, a man or a woman. If the researcher's motivation is clearly stated, the reader will have a fuller context within which to evaluate the research enterprise.

Presentation of Self
in the Research Setting

I presented myself to the 18 respondents as an Emerge counselor, as a researcher, and as a graduate student, in that order of emphasis. Having employed these institutional affiliations in order to secure an interview, it was nonetheless incumbent upon me to minimize my impact on the respondent as much as possible during the interview itself. Leading questions were eliminated from the interview guide. For example, rather than asking directly, "Do you think the violence was justifiable," I assumed that excuses and justifications would arise spontaneously under direct questioning about the violence.

During the interviews, I tried to limit my emotional responses and judgmental affect as much as I could. My intent was to facilitate a narrative rather than continually challenge the men. This interviewing style contrasts with the much more confrontative counseling approach used at Emerge. While the confrontative approach can be an effective strategy in bringing about change in a batterer's behavior, I felt that as an interviewing style this would result in a collection of the most defensive, superficial, and dishonest responses from the men. Such an interviewing posture would maximize my impact on the batterers' testimony, and would minimize their own contribution.

Having said that, it is nevertheless important to recognize that there are moral and political dimensions to this type of "impartial" approach. As Alan Stone says:

Human problems do not come packaged in psychiatric bits and moral bits. It seems that there may be a moral cost even in nonjudgmental listening (Stone, 1984, p. 231).

For *psychiatric* one could easily substitute *sociological*. Does it not, at some level, reaffirm a lack of moral seriousness concerning wife beating to listen to a man describe a bloody assault on a woman, and remain dispassionately composed? Does it not, at some level, reinforce male entitlement to hear a man explain how he broke a woman's ribs because she wasn't sexually "motivated," and then continue questioning as though this account was reasonable?

In all but 2 of the 18 cases, the respondent's physical abusiveness had allegedly stopped. In these two cases and in a third case involving a child, the men reported ongoing if sporadic violence: pushing, restraining, slapping, hair-pulling. During these three interviews, I switched from an interviewer role to a confrontative counselor role after the formal questions had been completed. On one occasion, this led to a heated argument about the "justifications" for assaulting someone; in another case, the respondent's vengeful intent to hurt and the resulting fear in his wife and children were discussed; and in a third instance, the batterer was encouraged to return to Emerge for help (after a four-year lapse). This third individual did contact the Emerge office, and was called by the counseling coordinator, but subsequently failed to reenter counseling.

This more confrontative stance followed the collection of the interview data, and therefore did not "contaminate" the interview. While a brief confrontation will likely have little or no immediate effect on an individual's behavior, it must be remembered that a pattern of tolerance of or indifference toward wife beating is implicated by most sociological theories as a reason for its persistence. At the very least, such confrontation ensures that among these batterers' contacts with various professionals there is at least one place where the violence, in and of itself, is made a serious matter.

Regarding those cases where the violence had allegedly stopped, and where this type of confrontation did not take place, I don't feel I resolved the issue of nonjudgmental listening satisfactorily. In retrospect, a frank, confrontational debriefing could have been structured into the interview format.

Empathy and Politics
in the Interviewing Process

With the doubts discussed around the issue of nonjudgmental listening, I have already begun identifying the conflicts I experienced owing to the demands of being both an empathetic participant in the interviews, and a detached, politically judgmental observer. It is worth examining this tension a bit further because it shaped my relationship to the men I interviewed.

In a sociology term paper written when I first began to work with batterers, I described the conflict between compassion and repulsion that I was feeling:

> It is nonetheless confusing to sit down and talk to men who have beaten their wives, with all of these contradictory feelings turning inside me. I observed two hour-long intakes at Emerge this fall, and both men presented sides of themselves that were immediately likable. Both had beaten the women closest to them . . . I responded to parts of their characters; but when they revealed their violentness I felt myself recoiling, as though I was refusing to touch this part of their nature. ["Or your own?" commented my instructor, in the margin.]
>
> In a traditional setting I would have more barriers to separate me from such men. They would be seen as borderline personality disorders, as suffering from psychological dysfunctioning, as deviant. This would keep me from recognizing the common background we share.

My professor at that time had made a shrewd observation: My repulsion may have arisen in part from a refusal to acknowledge my own potential for violence. While I was clear at the time that psychological labels inhibit the recognition of commonality with a violent client, what I didn't see so clearly was that moral and political judgments can be just as self-serving if I want to avoid confronting my own sexism (I'm the "good guy," they're the "bad guys"). Such an exaggerated dichotomization can also slide over into chivalry or paternalism—notions that women need my protection from "those men." That attitude is typically masculine: Chivalry and paternalism represent the benevolent face of men's domination. The line at Emerge is that all men are on a continuum of violence and controlling behavior; I have learned that this can be conveniently forgotten.

By the time I began interviewing for the study, I had gone through training as a counselor and had been a coleader of a six-month batterers' group. Nonetheless, during the early interviews, I wasn't quite confident that I would be able to establish rapport, or that I could successfully negotiate the tension between political judgment and the empathy that is necessary to build a sufficient level of trust. In field notes from an early interview, I recorded how I first started to feel I could establish trust, ask difficult questions, and keep my tendency to be judgmental from excessively coloring the interaction:

The interview was painful, although I feel good about the rapport and his openness. . . . We pretty much looked each other straight in the eye, in a very real expression of connection, throughout the interview. We clearly trusted each other.

I feel kind of high, like this is exciting, like this is really a way to learn about wife beating. I feel the thrill of a dynamic connection.

I felt I pushed him as far as he would allow concerning specifics about the violence. He was clearly distraught talking about this, at times. I had us both take a break after the most intense "violence questions" to allow us both to gather our energy, take in some air.

During the questions concerning the violence, I felt my face get hot, felt a little nervous and self-conscious. I was concerned about expressing my own discomfort at the difficulty of pressing someone for this gruesome information. I was concerned that he felt accepted and not alienated by my reaction. I believe he felt supported throughout, and I think he probably didn't notice those few moments of my nervousness.

There is other evidence, however, that the men I interviewed did pick up on this tension. There seemed to be a subtext of resistance and a jockeying for power beneath the otherwise friendly manner these individuals displayed in our initial phone conversations. After agreeing to participate, many of the men I talked with failed to show up for their appointment; they then apologized when called back, rescheduled, and failed to show up again; if called back, they would again apologize, reschedule, and on and on, as long as my patience and common sense would allow. On 22 occasions, I waited for someone who never appeared. And if busy signals, no-answers, and "he's not home"'s are counted, over 275 phone calls were made before 18 interviews had been completed.

This process was extremely frustrating. Obviously, this conflicted interaction is due in part to the difficulty of sharing the cruel details of one's past with a stranger, even after having agreed to do so. I think there is also some irresponsibility here on the part of these men, an ambivalence about confronting the consequences of their violence that is also seen in the many men who drop out of the counseling program. Lastly, I think this strain may also indicate their rebellion against my knowledge of their past and my access to resources (power), such that I could send them a letter inviting their participation in the first place.

In a discussion on family violence research, Linda Gordon stated that "a gender analysis is always necessary—nothing, no social relations are free of gender" (Gordon, 1984, p. 80). I have attempted to bring this insight into the description of field relations with the men in this study. Inconclusive as this discussion is, I think it offers a frank characterization of this rapport and addresses some of the conflicts raised by politically motivated field research.

The Findings:
Batterers' Excuses and Justifications

The 18 men interviewed for the study all came for help to Emerge, a counseling program for batterers. Whether they defined the "problem" as their violence or, as is more likely, saving their relationships, the very existence of a program for men who batter established the sense that their violence was wrong. And once they arrived, this sense of wrongness was made explicit by the counselors. On a average of 1.8 years later, these men return and talk with a man, identified as both an Emerge counselor and a researcher, about their violence. The sense that the violence is wrong is institutionalized in the very setting of the interviews. In this context, and to this interviewer, how do these men talk about their abusiveness?

When an individual whose behavior is regarded as socially unacceptable is questioned about such behavior, the individual's response may be called an account (Scott & Lyman, 1968). Accounts represent a complex of anticipated judgment, face-saving, and status negotiation. Scott and Lyman distinguish two types of accounts that serve to neutralize socially disapproved behavior: excuses and justifications. Excuses are those accounts in which the abuser denies full responsibility for his actions. Justifications are those accounts in which the batterer may accept some responsibility but denies or trivializes the wrongness of his violence. These descriptive categorizations will become clearer in their application to the batterers' testimony. In making excuses and justifications, the deviant individual employs "socially approved vocabularies" that are routinized within cultures (Scott & Lyman, 1968, pp. 46, 52). The batterer appeals to standard rationalizations in an attempt to make sense of or to normalize his behavior.

While on the whole, the batterers' accounts consist of more excuses than justifications, most men use both verbal strategies in an attempt to neutralize their behavior. They tend to excuse themselves of full responsibility, and at the same time, they offer justifications for their abusiveness. As a result, their accounts are often internally inconsistent.

This suggests that over the course of a two-hour interview, a variety of strategies were employed to neutralize the violence, regardless of whether they conflicted with one another. This lack of integration will be discussed further as the validity of the batterers' explanations is addressed.

Excuses: Denial of Responsibility

Perhaps the most common way that batterers attempt to excuse their violent behavior is by an appeal to loss of control. Such appeals to a diminished capacity to control their actions take several forms. Partial or complete loss of control is usually spoken of as resulting either from alcohol or drug use or from a buildup of frustrations. The sense here is that physiological or psychological factors lead to a state where awareness or will is impaired, thus diminishing responsibility. Of the 18 men interviewed, 94% (N = 17) employed an account that falls into one or more subcategories: appeals to alcohol or drugs, frustration, and complete loss of control.

Of the sample of 18 batterers, 33% (N = 6) maintain that their self-control was diminished by alcohol or drugs:

> It's taken the edge off my self-control. That's what I will call it, being intoxicated. It's taken my limits off me and let me do things and become disruptive in a way I would not become. I can get angry with people, really violent, stone sober. But the more I was drinking on a day-to-day basis, the more easy that was to come across.

> I've been involved with A. A., and that's why I'm much better. And a lot of—my problems—not all of them, but most of my problems at the time were due to that. And it's just amazing to know that there was a reason for the way I acted.

Asked whether they thought they would be violent with a woman again, it was common for these men to say no, as long as they were able to remain free of alcohol or drug dependency. (Most of them said they had successfully quit.)

To what extent does alcohol cause loss of control over one's behavior? In a study of family violence, Gelles (1974) cites anthropological data that establishes drunken behavior as learned (rather than purely chemically induced) behavior. Drunken comportment varies widely from culture to culture, according to Gelles. Because it is believed to lead to loss of control, people behave as though it actually has that property, and use this "loss of control" to disavow or neutralize deviant behavior such as wife beating. As shall be shown, the contradictions in the batterers' own testimony supports this argument.

A frustration-aggression description of violence is present in the accounts of 67% (N = 12) of the men. As in a previous study (Bograd, 1983), these accounts present temporary loss of control as resulting from an accumulation of internal pressure. This pressure is often described as building with a hydraulic type of inevitability:

> I think I reach a point where I can't tolerate anything anymore, and it's at that time where whatever it is that shouldn't be tolerated in the first place now is a major issue in my life. I do better now. I used to come out at one thing. It didn't matter what it was. It just, you know—I couldn't hold it back anymore. It just came out in a tirade.

> We used to argue about picayune-ass things anyway. And a lot of this was building and building. And I was keeping it all inside. All of the frustration and anger. You're supposed to sit there and take this stuff from you wife. And, like I say, I'd take it for awhile, but then I'd lose my head.

But as Bandura (1973) argues regarding the frustration-aggression hypothesis, aggression is only one of a number of responses to frustration. Other possible responses include dependency, achievement, withdrawal and resignation, psychosomatic illness, drug or alcohol use, and constructive problem-solving. Most of the men in this sample must have responded to frustration in ways other than violence, for they indicate that their violence is very selective. For 39% (N = 7) of these men, their frustration led to violence only in the presence of their wives or lovers; for 33% (N = 6), their frustration led to violence only when they were in the presence of their partners, children, and mothers. In only 28% (N = 5) of these cases were the men violent both within and outside of the family.

In the accounts of 56% (N = 10) of the batterers, descriptions of the violence are presented in terms of being completely out of control:

> When I got violent, it was not because I really wanted to get violent. It was just because it was like an outburst of rage.

> I was a real jerk for almost a year. And anything would set me off. Anything. I was like uncontrollably violent. I would slap her, knock her down, choke her, and call her a slut and a whore.

> I struck her once before, and I guess it made me see something of myself that I didn't like to see, the way I had no control over myself. And I knew that the anger that I had inside me was very hard to control.

> I'd grab, you know, and squeeze a lot. I grabbed her around the neck one time and I think I almost strangled her. But I finally let go, you know. I realized that—I got ahold of myself, realized what I was doing.

> A blowout is where I lose, I just lose everything. I would just blank out, more or less. You know, like there would be a gap in between where I wouldn't actually remember. You know, like all I could remember seeing is like white, little twinkled white, red, like lights. That's all I can remember. That's a blowout.

> It was all booze. I didn't think. I didn't think at all. It was just like a madman. It was temporary insanity. I really, all's I really wanted to do was crush her. There was nothing there but—I wanted to cause pain and mess her looks up.

Of the 10 men claiming such total loss of control, only three of them blamed this on alcohol. Blackouts or partial memory losses were reported by two of the men who claimed they had been intoxicated, but such memory losses were also reported by two men who allegedly had not been drinking.

The second main category of excuses is victim-blaming. As in the case of the loss of control excuses, the wrongness of the violence is more or less accepted; but here, the men deny responsibility by claiming they were "provoked." In a few isolated incidents, the batterers presented their violence as a response to the woman's physical aggressiveness:

> She slapped me across the face hard. It hurt. . . . And that did it. Then I slapped her, and punched her, and kicked her, and knocked her down. I mean, I just let her have it.

More commonly, the batterers assert that their violence was a response to the woman's verbal aggressiveness. Some 44% (N = 8) of the sample blamed the victim in this fashion:

> She was trying to tell me, you know, I'm no fucking good and this and that . . . and she just kept at me, you know. And I couldn't believe it. And finally, I just got real pissed and I said wow, you know. I used to think, you're going to treat me like this? You're going to show me that I'm the scum bag? Whack. Take that. And that was my psychology.

Women can verbally abuse you. They can rip your clothes off, without even touching you, the way women know how to talk, converse. But men don't. Well, they weren't brought up to talk as much as women do, converse as well as women do. So it was a resort to violence, if I couldn't get through to her by words.

It wasn't right for me to slap her. It wasn't unprovoked, you know what I mean? It was almost like she was being an asshole at that particular time. I think for once in her life she realized that, you know, it was her fault.

On some occasions she was the provoker. It didn't call for physical abuse. I was wrong in that. But it did call for something. . . . You know, you're married for that long, if somebody gets antagonistic, you want to defend yourself.

These men seem to regard verbal aggressiveness as equivalent to physical aggressiveness, as if a woman's verbal behavior somehow excuses them of responsibility for their violence. There are serious deficiencies in the men's perspective (Dobash & Dobash, 1979). Even if one takes the extreme position that verbal aggressiveness warrants a physical response, the question becomes: who "provoked" the verbal aggressiveness? Furthermore, the "provocation" argument implies that there is a proper way a wife can address her husband that the husband is empowered to maintain. The above accounts reveal just such a male arrogance: While his retaliatory behavior is acceptable, her verbal excesses are not. The "provocation" excuse solidifies male dominance (Dobash & Dobash, 1979).

Justifications:
Denial of Wrongness

Appeals to loss of control and victim-blaming are common ways by which these men excuse their violence. While excuses represent denial of responsibility, justifications are denials of wrongdoing on the part of the offender.

The first of two categories of justifications is *denial of injury*. According to some clinicians who have worked with men who batter, many batterers neutralize the unacceptability of their behavior by denying or minimizing the injuries battered women suffer (Adams & Penn, 1981; Brisson, 1982; Star, 1983). With this sample, it was not possible to obtain reports from the abused women in order to determine the full extent of minimization. Nonetheless, trivialization of the woman's injuries is apparent in the accounts of 44% (N = 8) of the men.

With some men, this takes the form of a denial that the behavior was violent. With others, the abusers maintain that the woman's fears were exaggerated. And a number of men minimize the nature of the injuries.

A euphemistic redefinition of violent behavior is presented in the accounts of two men:

> I never beat my wife. I responded physically to her.

> Yes, I do believe my physical punishment as a child can contribute to me having a tendency to react violently and think nothing of it. When I say violent, "physically," I think, would be a much more appropriate term.

Looking at the behavior these men report, the first admitted he pushed, grabbed, and slapped his wife, and that she received bruises and injured her knee as a result. The second man admitted to slapping, punching, and grabbing a woman by the hair and dragging her across the floor. One of the many women with whom this second individual was "physical" received a black eye. He was arrested five or six times for assault and battery on men.

Other men claimed that women exaggerated the severity of the violence. This respondent's account is representative:

> These people told her that she had to get all of these orders of protection and stuff like that because I was going to kill her, you know. Well, I wasn't going to kill her. I mean, I'd yell at her, and scream, and stuff like that, and maybe I'd whack her once or twice, you know, but I wasn't going to kill her. That's for sure.

This individual did admit to slapping and punching his wife, giving her a black eye, and throwing and breaking furniture. During one episode, he stated his wife fled the house screaming. Yet when asked if she was frightened of him, he said, "no."

A number of men minimized the extent of the women's injuries by attributing black and blue marks to the ease with which women bruise. This is how three men responded to the question of whether the woman was injured:

> Not really. Pinching does leave bruises. And, I guess, slapping. I guess women bruise easily, too. They bump into a door and they'll bruise.

> Not injured. She bruises easily.

> Yeah, she bruised. Yeah, she bruises easily anyway. If I just squeeze like that, you know, next day she'll get a mark.

The statement that "women bruise easily" goes beyond an observation of comparative anatomy. By admitting that they have bruised a woman, and yet denying that this is very significant, the more internal nonphysical injuries are also denied: the instilling of fear, the humiliation, the degradation, the assault on her identity as a woman.

These other kinds of injury become more visible in this last category of justification. Among the reasons for the violence given by men who batter, there is a pattern of finding fault with the woman for not being good at cooking, for not being sexually responsive, for not being deferential enough to her husband, for not knowing when she is "supposed" to be silent, and for not being faithful. In short, for not being a "good wife." One batterer reported that he threatened his partner with these words: "I should just smack you for the lousy wife you've been." This is the rationale that underlies the explanations in this category. Bograd (1983) titles this category of justifications *failure to fulfill obligations of a good wife.* Of the 18 men interviewed, 78% (N = 14) gave accounts falling into this category. These accounts come from both married and unmarried men. On cooking:

> Until we were married 10 years or so there was no violence or anything. But then after a while, it just became, it just became too much. . . . I don't know if I demanded respect as a person or a husband or anything like that, but I certainly, you know, didn't think I was wrong in asking not to be filled up with fatty foods.

On availability of sex:

> A couple more incidents happened over the next year . . . where I did strike her, and for basically the same reason. I just tried making love, and making love, and she couldn't do it.

> It was over sex, and it happened I guess because I was trying to motivate her. And she didn't seem too motivated.

On not being deferential enough:

> I think a lot of it had to do with my frustration of not being able to handle children. You know, they'd tell me to shut up. "You're not going to tell me to shut up." And then [my wife] would tell me, you know, "Let me handle this." I said, "I'm the man of the house." Then we'd start arguing. That's basically how they used to happen.

> The intent is to have her see it my way. You know, "There's no need for you to think the way you're thinking. And you should see it my way,

there's something wrong with you. You're being abusive to me by not seeing it my way."

That was a way I could win. She would know that she had gone too far in asking me something, in constantly probing, requiring me to answer. So that would let her know how hurt or angry I was feeling.

On not knowing when she is "supposed" to be silent:

I don't think I used to like to be confronted about being high [on heroin], even though I was high. And it would bother me. It bothered me to a point where I would strike out. I was working, but I wasn't making any money. . . . "The baby needs this, and the baby needs that" Jesus Christ what do you want me to do, you know? We were at the table . . . I just picked my plate up and threw it at her.

On not being faithful:

I walked right over and slapped her right across the face. . . . I think it was probably around the time when she was telling me she wanted to see other guys, you know. She was too young to get involved with me or one guy. And I didn't want to hear that.

I was 18. And I was going to be true to somebody, for once, to see what it's like. And it turned out two years later, two and a half years later, she was going out on me. And it totalled me. Because I had made that commitment. It was like a big deal, the first time I was acting like a man and I got it. I got betrayed. And I almost killed her.

These accounts illustrate more than just the way that individual men seek to control individual women. As in the example of "provocation," there is a theme of self-righteousness about the violence that pervades these accounts: "I didn't think that I was wrong"; "she couldn't do it"; "she didn't seem too motivated"; "she had gone too far"; "I got betrayed." But here the sense is not that "she provoked me"; rather, it is a sense that the privileges of male entitlement have been unjustly denied. This is evident in the gendered terms used to express this self-righteousness: "I should just smack you for the *lousy wife* you've been"; "I don't know if I demanded respect as a person or a *husband* or anything like that, but . . ."; "I'm the *man of the house*"; "the first time I was *acting like a man* and I got it." There is sentiment here about the way that women should behave when they're sexually involved with a man, whether married or unmarried.

Adrienne Rich speaks to this sense of male entitlement, or, to use her term, "husband-right" as:

> One specific form of the rights men are presumed to enjoy simply because of their gender: the "right" to the priority of male over female needs, to sexual and emotional services from women, to women's undivided attention in any and all situations. (Rich, 1979, pp. 219-220)

With this assumption of male entitlement, the wrongness of the violence is denied; the batterer sees himself as punishing the woman for her failure to be a good wife. Other investigations have found a similar pattern in the batterer's violence (Bograd, 1983; Coleman, 1980; Dobash & Dobash, 1979; Elbow, 1977; Gelles, 1974). But this assumption of male privilege is not limited to the expectations of men who batter. Feminists have been pointing out for years that this vocabulary of male entitlement has been routinized within the culture at large.

Patterns and Contradictions in the Batterers' Testimony

The definitions of excuses and justifications turn on the denial (or acceptance) of responsibility and wrongness. Most of the men made statements falling into both categories. Within the context of individual interviews, this presented a great deal of inconsistency. For example, one individual who grabbed his wife around the neck said of his violence:

> It's a condition of being out of control.
>
> She's going on and on about how much money we need.... I'll listen to it for awhile, but then, you know, you gotta get up and do something, you know. That's the way I felt, the way to do it was go over and try to shut her up physically.
>
> I'd lose my head.

In the space of a few minutes, this man seems to go from *denying* responsibility, to seemingly *accepting* responsibility while minimizing the wrongness, to *denying* responsibility again. How can this be accounted for? Earlier I discussed the jockeying for power I perceived during the interviews. Scott and Lyman (1968) see accounts as attempts at face-saving or avoiding judgment. In this analysis, the conflicting statements result from the batterers' willingness to apply any number of verbal strategies to the task of making the violence appear normal, regardless of whether the accounts have any internal consistency.

But there is more here than inconsistency: there is contradiction. The batterers' excuses of "loss of control" and "provocation" are undercut by the callousness they displayed about their partners' injuries, and by the goal orientation that appeared in their own words. The above transcripts reveal that these men were motivated by a desire to silence their partners; to punish them for their failure as "good wives"; and to achieve and maintain dominance over these women. Their objectives were accomplished according to the men: The women fell silent; they were taught a lesson; and they were shown who was in control of the relationship, and to what length the batterer would go in maintaining control.

Other goals of the violence are acknowledged as well. Asked directly whether they intended to hurt their wives or lovers when they assaulted them, five men admitted such an intent:

I wanted to hurt somebody. She was the best person, the closest one to me. Nobody else really made any difference.

There are times that I really wanted to kill her.

Yeah. Yeah. Because I didn't stop. I mean I wasn't—she slapped me once, and I hit her, I don't know, maybe 10 to 15 times there, and quite a few times at home.

I think I was trying to hurt her.

I just kept beating her. The police arrested me. I would have killed her.... Yeah. I wanted to kill her.

And beyond an intent to hurt, frightening their wives or lovers was a goal for 67% (N = 12) of the men, as this testimony demonstrates:

A lot of my verbal abuse, in thinking about it now . . . the verbal abuse would be a threat. A threat of violence.

I grabbed her, and said, "I'm going to fucking kill you if you do this again to me."

I put her up against the wall one night and held my fist up cocked and said, I just said, you know, I said, "I'd love to just knock your fucking head off."

There's another form of violence I also remember. Once we had an argument . . . we were in a car . . . I sped up . . . made a quick U-turn, drove recklessly . . . She was terrified. She was terrified, and angry, and really scared. . . . She wanted to get out of the car and walk.

These last three examples are from men who explain their violence by appealing to complete loss of control. However, the hostile manner with which these men terrorized their partners and the warnings of future violence seem more indicative of a deliberate strategy than of an inability to control one's actions.

The batterers' denial of responsibility is further contradicted by other evidence they provided about their behavior. In none of these relationships was the violence completely anomalous to the batterer's other actions toward his wife or lover. In every case, the men's testimony offered other examples of behavior directed at achieving or maintaining dominance. This does not refer merely to subtle controlling behaviors, but to such things as writing threatening letters to the woman, driving her back to her mother's house to make her learn how to cook, forcing sex, threatening the woman if she talks about leaving, tearing the phone off the wall to prevent her from calling the police, and spying on the woman's house and lying in wait to assault her new boyfriend.

Thus a pattern of intentional, goal-oriented violence is established by the batterers' testimony, despite the contradictory denials of responsibility. "Loss of control" and "provocation" cannot explain the violence; they merely serve as excuses, as rationalizations, and as ways of obscuring the benefits (however temporary or enduring) that the violence provides.

Socially Approved
Rationalizations for Violence

Scott and Lyman (1968, p. 46) insist that excuses and justifications are "standardized within cultures," that they are "socially approved vocabularies" for avoiding blame. To complete the analysis of the batterers' accounts, then, it will be necessary to trace the extent to which these rationalizations represent culturally sanctioned strategies for minimizing and denying violence against women.

Appeals to loss of control and victim-blaming are the most common ways that these men sought to escape responsibility for their violence. Having challenged the credibility of these defenses with the batterers' own testimony, the question can be posed: To what degree does the larger society accept these excuses at face value? Evidence from the clinical literature on men who batter and a recent study of battered women and the criminal justice system suggests an answer to this question.

The Clinical Literature
on Men Who Batter

An examination of the books and articles written by social workers, psychologists, psychiatrists, and others working directly with batterers reveals that a good portion of the clinical literature appears to take the excuses of "loss of control" and "provocation" at face value.

Most striking is that batterers and clinicians use similar language to characterize "loss of control." The batterers speak in terms of irrational attacks ("I went berserk"; "I wasn't sane"; "temporary insanity"); uncontrollable aggression ("I had no control over myself"; "it's a condition of being out of control"; "uncontrollably violent"); and explosion metaphors ("I just blew up"; "blowout"; "walking time bomb"; "outburst of rage"; "eruptions"). Like the batterers, many clinicians also describe the violence as irrational or psychopathological. There is reference in clinical discussion of batterers to "paroxysmal rage attacks" and the "pathologies of both partners" (Lion, 1977); "psychiatric abnormality" and the "mentally disturbed nature of the population" (Faulk, 1977); and "irrational aggressive actions" among males who are "passively aggressive," "obsessive-compulsive," "sadistic," "paranoid," and "borderline" (Shainess, 1977). Many of the more recent articles and books are less dramatic in their language, but nonetheless assume irrationality with terms such as "aggressive impulses"; "poor impulse control"; or "impulse to batter" (Deschner, 1984; Garnet & Moss, 1982; Geller, 1982; Geller & Walsh, 1978; Goffman, 1984; Star, 1983).

Like the abusers interviewed for this study, many clinicians also explicitly state that the violence represents "uncontrollable rage" or "uncontrollable aggression" (Deschner, 1984; Geller, 1982; Goffman, 1984; Walker, 1979). And finally, like the batterers, clinicians frequently use explosion metaphors, such as "violent eruption"; "temper outbursts"; or "explosive rage" (Coleman, 1980; Deschner, 1984; Goffman, 1984; Pagelow, 1981; Walker, 1979; Weitzman & Dreen, 1982).

Despite the variety of theoretical perspectives that inform these works, all assume that the batterer loses control over his behavior. This notion—that the batterer's will is somehow overpowered, that his violence lies outside of the realm of choice, that battering occurs during brief irrational episodes—constructs a contemporary profile of the batterer as one who is not necessarily *sick,* but who is rather just *temporarily insane.* Seen from this perspective, the batterer is not abnormal enough to be considered a psychopath and not responsible enough to be considered a criminal. But this notion of loss of control is substantially contradicted by the batterers' own testimony. While the men claim that their violence is beyond rational control, they simultaneously acknowledge that the violence is deliberate and warranted.

Concerning victim-blaming, there is also evidence that clinicians accept batterers' rationalizations for the violence. Despite the tireless efforts of feminists in educating the public on this issue, victim-blaming continues in the clinical literature. It is not uncommon to find wife beating treated as a phenomenon no worse than women's "verbal aggressiveness." For example, Deschner (1984) draws a parallel between a man's physical abuse and what she calls a woman's "verbal persecutions (nagging)" (p. 19). Deschner (p. 20) claims that husbands and wives often

> Alternate between giving and getting punishment. After a period of abuse the wife rises up and scolds her husband or else withdraws from him. After tolerating her negatives for a period, he rises up again in another act of violence. . . . Such marriages, though not enjoyable, can be stable over a long period of time because each partner periodically enjoys the rewards of being on top.

Confusing verbal scolding with violence trivializes physical assault and suggests that wife beating is caused by "nagging," redefined by Dobash and Dobash (1979, p. 133) as "continued discussion once the husband has made up his mind." Another example of equating verbal and physical assaults is:

> Careful exploration of a couple's history with violence may reveal that both spouses have contributed to the escalation of anger with one spouse being the more verbally assaultive while the other is the more physically abusive. This places each partner in the role of both abuser and victim. (Margolin, 1979, p. 16)

In clinical publications, there are additional ways that women are seen as creating their own victimization. For instance, Lion (1977, p. 127) speaks of the battered woman's "provocation" and states that "the victim may evoke violence in a vulnerable person." Faulk (1977, p. 121) describes one type of battered woman as "querulous and demanding." And notions of female masochism are still prevalent (Shainess, 1977).

It appears that a good number of clinicians accept and legitimate the batterer's excuses. Fortunately, there is a growing number of authors who reject the above excuses and justifications for wife beating. For a more detailed review of this literature, see Ptacek (1984) and the chapter by David Adams in this volume.

The Response of the
Criminal Justice System

Before concluding this analysis of the batterers' accounts, a few remarks are in order about the prevalence of these excuses and justifications among the police and in the courts. I have shown how men who batter deny responsibility for their violence by claiming they were provoked by their wives. Similar discussions were found in the clinical literature on batterers. This notion that women who are battered must be guilty of wrongdoing can also be found among court clerks, police officers, and judges. A 1985 study of criminal justice responses to battered women in Massachusetts found numerous cases of such victim-blaming. Developed for the governor's anticrime council, this monitoring report detailed such cases as a police officer calling a battered woman a "bitch"; a police officer saying to a woman of color, "you people get what you deserve"; a judge saying to a woman, "most people get married and do not have illegitimate children. These things don't happen to them"; and a court clerk asking a woman what she did to provoke the abuse (Governor's Battered Women's Working Group, 1985, pp. 1-2).

These incidents cannot be dismissed as merely anecdotal: They were witnessed and documented by shelter workers, victim/witness advocates, lawyers, and other service providers. In a six-month period in 1985, some 250 such complaints were reported, 79 of which were classified as involving biased or racist attitudes toward battered women on the part of the police, judges, or court clerks. One can only suppose that battered women confronting the system without such witnesses often suffer even worse treatment.

The batterers' accounts detailed previously revealed ways that the men denied or minimized the injuries they caused. Such trivialization of the violence is also evident in this criminal justice report. For example, one judge reproached a woman by saying, "There is nothing wrong with you—you're not bruised or hysterical"; on another occasion, a judge suggested to a woman that if her husband didn't drink, gamble, or run around with other women, she had no reason to be in court; a police officer, refusing to hold a batterer in custody, told the abused woman that she was "only given a whack"; and in a different case, police joked around with a batterer with whom they were friends, despite the fact that he had just injured his wife severely enough to require hospitalization (Governor's Battered Women's Working Group, 1985, pp. 8-9).

Such failure to treat violence against women as a crime must be understood as a structural aspect of the criminal justice system (Bowker, 1982; Lerman, 1981; Tong, 1984; United States Commission on Civil Rights, 1982). On the basis of these case studies, it is reasonable to suspect that when these police officers and judges encounter batterers, a mutual validation of victim-blaming and minimization occurs. While reform is proceeding among the various levels of the criminal justice system, an acceptance of batterers' rationalizations for their violence remains commonplace.

Conclusion

Jürgen Habermas (1971, p. 311) speaks to the relationship between individual rationalizations and collective interests:

> From everyday experience we know that ideas serve often enough to furnish our actions with justifying motives in place of the real ones. What is called rationalization at this level is called ideology at the level of collective action.

The excuses and justifications I have detailed are ideological constructs: At the individual level, they obscure the batterer's self-interest in acting violently; at the societal level, they mask the male domination underlying violence against women. Clinical and criminal justice responses to battering are revealed as ideological in the light of their collusion with batterers' rationalizations.

This study of what batterers have to say about wife beating suggests a context in which to pursue further research on this issue. The interrelationship between private rationalizations and public responses recommends using a critical social psychology framework to examine men's violence against women. Such a theoretical framework could place wife beating, rape, incest, and the sexual harassment of women in relation to one another, which offers fertile ground for addressing class-specific forms of male entitlement, male anger, male subjectivity, and misogyny. A critical social psychology could develop and interrelate sociological and psychological analyses without reducing one to the other. By combining what is generally approached in a piecemeal fragmented fashion, the resulting portrait of male domination becomes more difficult to deny.

REFERENCES

Adams, D. C., & Penn, I. (1981, April). *Men in groups: The socialization and resocialization of men who batter.* Paper presented at the annual meeting of the American Orthopsychiatric Association, Boston. (Available from Emerge, 25 Huntington Avenue, Room 323, Boston, MA 02116).

Bandura, A. (1973). *Aggression: A social learning analysis.* Englewood Cliffs, NJ: Prentice Hall.

Becker, H. S. (1970). *Sociological work.* Chicago: Aldine.

Bograd, M. (1983). *Domestic violence: Perceptions of battered women, abusive men, and non-violent men and women.* Unpublished doctoral dissertation, University of Chicago.

Bowker, L. H. (1982). Police services to battered women: Bad or not so bad? *Criminal Justice and Behavior, 9,* 476-494.

Brisson, N. (1982). Helping men who batter women. *Public Welfare, 40,* 28-34.

Coleman, K. H. (1980). Conjugal violence: What 33 men report. *Journal of Marital and Family Therapy, 6,* 107-213.

Deschner, J. P. (1984). *The hitting habit: Anger control for battering couples.* New York: Free Press.

Dobash, R. E., & Dobash, R. (1979). *Violence against wives: A case against the patriarchy.* New York: Free Press.

Dobash, R. E., & Dobash, R. (1981). Social work and social action: The case of wifebattering. *Journal of Family Issues, 2,* 439-470.

Elbow, M. (1977). Theoretical considerations of violent marriages. *Social Casework, 58,* 515-526.

Faulk, M. (1977). Men who assault their wives. In M. Roy (Ed.), *Battered women: Psychosociological study of domestic violence.* New York: Van Nostrand Reinhold.

Garnet, S., & Moss, D. (1982). How to set up a counseling program for self-referred batterers: The AWAIC model. In M. Roy (Ed.), *The abusive partner: An analysis of domestic battering.* New York: Van Nostrand Reinhold.

Geller, J. A. (1982). Conjoint therapy: Staff training and treatment of the abuser and the abused. In M. Roy (Ed.), *The abusive partner: An analysis of domestic battering.* New York: Van Nostrand Reinhold.

Geller, J. A., & Walsh, J. C. (1978). A treatment model for the abused spouse. *Victimology, 2,* 627-632.

Gelles, R. J. (1974). *The violent home: A study of physical aggression between husbands and wives.* Newbury Park, CA: Sage.

Goffman, J. M. (1984). *Batterers anonymous: Self-help counseling for men who batter women.* San Bernardino, CA: B. A. Press.

Gordon, L. (1984). Interview in Mid-Atlantic Radical Historians' Association (Eds.), *Visions of history.* New York: Pantheon.

Governor's Battered Women's Working Group (1985). *Violent crime in the family: enforcement of the Massachusetts Abuse Prevention Law.* Unpublished monograph.

Habermas, J. (1971). *Knowledge and human interests.* Boston: Beacon Press.

Lerman, L. G. (1981). Criminal prosecution of wife beaters. *Response to Violence in the Family, 4,* 1-19.

Lion, J. R. (1977). Clinical aspects of wifebattering. In M. Roy (Ed.), *Battered women: A psychosociological study of domestic violence.* New York: Van Nostrand Reinhold.

Lund, S. H., Larsen, N. E., & Schultz, S. K. (1982). *Exploratory evaluation of the Domestic Abuse Project.* (Available from the Domestic Abuse Project, 2445 Park Avenue South, MN 55404).

Margolin, G. (1979). Conjoint marital therapy to enhance anger management and reduce spouse abuse. *American Journal of Family Therapy, 7,* 13-23.

Pagelow, M. D. (1981). *Woman-battering: Victims and their experiences.* Newbury Park, CA: Sage.

Ptacek, J. (1984, August). *The clinical literature on men who batter: A review and critique.* Paper presented at the second national conference for Family Violence Researchers, Durham, NH. (Available from Emerge, 280 Green Street, Cambridge, MA 02139).

Reinharz, S. (1979). *On becoming a social scientist.* San Francisco: Jossey-Bass.

Rich, A. (1979). *On lies, secrets, and silence: Selected prose 1966-1979.* New York: Norton.

Scott, M. B., & Lyman, S. M. (1968). Accounts. *American Sociological Review, 33,* 46-62.

Shainess, N. (1977). Psychological aspects of wifebattering. In M. Roy (Ed.), *Battered women: A psychosociological study of domestic violence.* New York: Van Nostrand Reinhold.

Star, B. (1983). *Helping the abuser: Intervening effectively in family violence.* New York: Family Service Association of America.

Stone, A. (1984). *Law, psychiatry, and morality: Essays and analysis.* Washington, DC: American Psychiatric Press.

Tong, Rosemarie (1984). *Women, sex, and the law.* Totowa, NJ: Rowman and Allanheld.

U. S. Commission on Civil Rights (1982). *Under the rule of thumb: Battered women and the administration of justice.* Washington, DC: U.S. Government Printing Office.

Walker, L. E. (1979). *The battered woman.* New York: Harper & Row.

Weitzman, J., & Dreen, K. (1982). Wifebeating: A view of the marital dyad. *Social Casework, 63,* 259-265.

7

On the Relationship Between
Wife Beating and Child Abuse

LEE H. BOWKER
MICHELLE ARBITELL
J. RICHARD McFERRON

Family violence refers to a range of behaviors between different family members including incest, wife battering, marital rape, and child physical abuse. In families where the wife is battered by her husband, there is often child abuse as well. Although empirical data illuminating possible links between these various forms of abuse is sparse, researchers, clinicians, and lay people alike hold assumptions about how they are interrelated. A popular assumption is that battered women also abuse their children. In this chapter, based on data from a large research project, we challenge this assumption and suggest instead that children of battered wives are more often beaten by their fathers than by their mothers. Furthermore, we believe that men use force against their wives because of their need to dominate family members, rather than because of individual psychopathology or social stresses. A second goal of this chapter is to discuss some of the difficult questions concerning research in the field of family violence, specifically that of sample selection and research methods. We also address the issue of how the institutionalized

AUTHORS' NOTE: The data used in this chapter were partly collected under grant number 1 RO1MH33649 from the National Institute of Mental Health. Many thanks to Jeffrey Koob and Lorie Maurer for their assistance in data analysis and to Donna Michalak, Trish Mauro, and Kristeen Renke for their aid in the development of this chapter.

structures determining what kinds of research are easily published may work against the dissemination of feminist research on wife abuse, which has important implications for how wife abuse is understood, for clinical interventions and for social policy.

Review of the Literature

Research evidence suggests links between child abuse and wife beating; specifically, that husbands and wives who assault each other tend to hit their children. Straus (1978) found that almost one-third of the families in which there was a violent incident between spouses also reported the presence of child abuse. A total of 58% of the respondents reported using some form of violence against their children during the year prior to their participation in the study, and 16% of the couples also admitted directing violence toward each other at least once during the survey year (Gelles & Straus, 1979). Gelles (1980) also found a direct relationship between spousal violence and child abuse. Of a sample of college students, 16% acknowledged that they knew of at least one incident during their last year at home in which one of their parents had physically abused the other and nearly half of these parents had also used physical force against their children. Finally, the U.S. Department of Health, Education and Welfare (1980) has reported that children from homes where the wife is battered are at very high risk to receive their father's abuse.

The link between wife beating and child abuse may be related to the power inequality between husband and wife as well as that between parents and children. Children in a family often become their father's victims at the same time that he is abusing their mother (National Crime Survey, 1980). Half of the women interviewed in the HEW survey (1980) admitted that their children were physically or psychologically abused. These children frequently witnessed wife beating incidents between their parents. Moore (1975) coined the phrase "yo-yo" children to label how children are often used as pawns in arguments by parents who are unable to discuss any rational solution to their difficulties. Woman battering and child abuse typically occur to spite the wife in these marriages.

In an attempt to establish the actual relationship between child abuse and battering in families, 116 mothers of children "darted" or flagged in a single year for abuse or neglect at a metropolitan hospital were studied by Stark and Flitcraft (1984). A screening mechanism developed to identify battering in a medical population was employed to examine each injury episode in the mothers' adult lives. These examinations revealed that 45% of the abused children had mothers who themselves were being physically abused and another 5% had mothers whose relationships were "full of conflict," although abuse was not verified. Children whose mothers had been battered were more likely to be physically abused and less likely to be "neglected" than children whose mothers had not been battered.

We know that children are often present during wife-beating incidents because of the frequency with which they appear in court as witnesses: Of the 1,014 witnesses who testified in 928 wife assault cases, 50% were children (Dobash, 1977). Witnessing fathers' violence against mothers has an impact on children's attitudes toward the use of physical force. A child who is exposed to violence in the home and who is a victim of parental violence is much more likely than the child raised in a nonviolent home to grow up and use violence against a child or spouse (Gelles, 1979).

The female child seems most likely to become the second victim of the battering husband (Dobash, 1977). Female children may be more likely than male children to intervene in altercations between parents, or when male children do intervene, they may be better at avoiding their own victimization. A more important factor may be that daughters, like their mothers, are more likely than sons to be viewed as "appropriate" victims. The husband uses physical force against women and children as a means of controlling them. Abusers may have attitudes supporting their "basic right" to control children and wives even when it entails using physical force.

Although a few researchers have found correlations between wife beating and child abuse, it is difficult to identify the precise mechanisms through which wife beating leads to child abuse. Dobash (1977) found that, in some child-assault cases, children are not the primary targets. Fathers' violence against children occurs either from thwarted intervention attempts or from blows directed at the wife that accidentally strike nearby children. However, child abuse usually does not occur at the same time as wife abuse. In most marriages, child abuse and wife beating are temporally separate crises.

In sum, the preceding literature does not support a solid conclusion that wife beating is a causal factor in the incidence of child abuse. Nevertheless, this evidence does indicate that child abuse is correlated with the battering of women. Wife beating may function as a major precipitant of child abuse in families. But it is also possible that the violent abuse of children and wife beating proceed from independent causal factors that are usually omitted from studies of child abuse, including the degree of husband-dominance in the family, the husband's experiences with violence in his family of origin, and his global tendencies toward a violent adult life (Bowker, 1982a).

Male Domination and Child Abuse:
An Empirical Study

The present study portrays child abuse as one of the products of male domination of the family based of the following hypotheses:

(1) Children of battered wives are commonly abused by their fathers.
(2) The more severe the wife abuse, the more severe the child abuse.
(3) The higher the degree of husband-dominance in a violent marriage, the more severe the child abuse.
(4) The more extensive the father's experiences with violence in his family of origin, the more likely he is to move from wife abuse to child abuse.

These hypotheses reflect a feminist perspective suggesting that child abuse is one of the ways by which men increase their dominance over family members. This approach differs from other views of child abuse in highlighting the male struggle for interpersonal dominance and deemphasizing psychopathological factors, unpremeditated events, and general family dysfunctions. Child abuse is linked to other forms of male dominance in families, including wife beating, punitive economic deprivation, marital rape, coerced social isolation, incest, psychological brainwashing, and deliberately induced fetal death.

Sample and Method

Using public media to advertise investigation of wife beating, 146 volunteer subjects were recruited in southeastern Wisconsin. In-depth interviews with these subjects generated data on premarital and marital history, violence, and the nature and effectiveness of personal strategies and help-sources used to reduce or end violence.

An article summarizing the results of the Wisconsin study appeared in *Woman's Day* magazine and announced that volunteers were needed to continue research on the subject. Written questionnaires were completed by 87% of the women volunteers, an amazingly high response rate considering that our desire to protect the confidentiality and physical health of the participants precluded the use of follow-up letters or call-backs. Upon receipt of the first 854 questionnaires from battered wives, the senior author constructed a 1,000 case national sample by adding the 146 women from the original Wisconsin study. Although the questionnaire was carefully developed so the data could be integrated with the Wisconsin findings, it contained far fewer variables.

This study used a consumer approach, which has many strengths, although direct observation by trained scientists cannot be counted among them. The data consist of self-reports of battered women and are not supported by other observations by the batterer, helping professionals, law enforcement and judicial officers, or behavioral scientists. The battered wives contributed vignettes that leave little doubt in our minds regarding what occurred, yet we should not mistake these vignettes as scientific reports.

Volunteer samples produced through solicitations are, by definition, nonrepresentative. We have no way of measuring the degree to which population parameters are indicated by our sample statistics. Since some variables were ordinal in character, tau b rather than Pearson's r was used to measure the strength of bivariate relationships. The absence of a randomly selected sample limits the technical usefulness of the reported statistical significance levels. Although providing a clue to the multivariate structure of the data, multiple regression was also used with the same reservations regarding technical statistical assumptions. Its value is heuristic rather than definitive.

Results

Of the 1,000 battered women in the study, 225 did not have children with the batterer. Wife beaters abused children in 70% of the families in which children were present. There is a clear association between wife beating and child abuse in these 543 families, and we suggest that professionals working with battered wives and battering husbands assume that child abuse will accompany wife abuse in approximately 70% of the families in which children are present.

Child abuse was generally less severe than wife abuse in these families. Batterers were five times more likely to beat up thoroughly or use weapons against their wives than to inflict these levels of abuse upon their children. Yet, 41% of the batterers slapped (not to be confused with mere spanking) one or more of their children. Lesser proportions of the batterers kicked, hit, or punched (16%), thoroughly beat up (more severe than kicking, hitting, or punching but excluding weapons—4%), or used weapons (9%) against their children. The following quotes from letters written by the battered women illustrate the range of child abuse that existed in their families:

> (My husband) was drunk and ended up hitting my daughter in the head with a cast aluminum skillet.

> My four-year-old daughter is an abused child. She screams at night in her sleep and has nightmares as a result.

> (My husband) attacked my 13-year-old daughter sexually while I was at work and told her he'd beat her if she told.

> I experienced the fear, anxiety, and horror of being abused and helplessly watched the abuse of my children.

> I have lived with this for 30 years now. (Even) my grandson is a victim of abuse. It has left him blind. And to think I stayed for the sake of the children.

We turn now to variables that appear to mediate the relationship between wife beating and child abuse in the sample. All of the relationships discussed below are limited to the husband's abuse of his own biological children born to the battered wife (referred to as spousal children). Families in which there were no such children were excluded from the sample. In the discussion that follows, all relationships mentioned are statistically significant at less than .001 level.

There was no difference in child abuse by race, religion, or frequency of church attendance. Child abuse was associated with higher educational achievement and family income, but lower occupational status. It was directly related to the number of children the parents had together and the total household size, which reflects exposure to the risk of abuse. The more children there are in a family, the more likely one of them is abused. The prevalence of child abuse increases from 51% with one child to 92% with four or more children.

Previous exposure of the parents to violence was a minor factor in child abuse. The strongest relationship (tau b = .12) was between the husband's own physical abuse by his parents and his abusing his own children. This correlation would probably be far higher if the sample included nonviolent families. The husband's previous experiences with violence were stronger predictors of the severity of wife beating than they were of his abusing both wife and children.

The quality of the violent marriage was also related to child abuse. Abuse was more likely to be present where there were frequent separations (including trips to battered women's shelters), the wife's low marital satisfaction apart from the violence, and high husband dominance (measured in terms of the husband getting his way in spousal disputes) in the most recent year together. In Table 7.1, we see that the wife's ability to protect her children from her husband's abuse is partially a function of husband dominance in the most recent year together. Child abuse was most likely to occur where problems were generally solved to suit the batterer during the couple's most recent year together, less likely in egalitarian marriages, and much less likely when the wife generally won arguments.

The worse the wife beating, the worse the child abuse. The strongest correlations in this area were between child abuse and severity of wife beating, frequency of wife beating, and frequency of marital rape. The marital rape relationship is summarized in Table 7.2. The absence of child abuse was more than four times as likely when the wife was never raped by her husband as it was in marriages within which she was raped more than a hundred times. An important finding is that the rise of weapons involvement in child abuse correlates with increasing frequency of marital rape. A standard multiple regression analysis conducted for heuristic purposes with all of the variables above confirmed that exposure (number of children, length of marriage) and violence against wives (frequency of wife beating and marital rape) are far more important than any of the background characteristics of husbands and wives in predicting the presence of child abuse in these violent families.

We asked whether the presence of child abuse in the violent marriages influenced the battered wives to seek different forms of help than would otherwise have been the case, and whether the effectiveness of these forms of help was any different in multiple victim families than in families where the wife was the only victim. The use of all help-sources was higher where child abuse was present than where it was absent, which constitutes strong evidence of the wife's efforts to protect her children. The effectiveness of these help-sources was generally inversely related to child abuse.

TABLE 7.1

Relationship Between Husband Dominance
in the Most Recent Year Together and
Abuse of Spousal Children (in percentages)

Level of Child Abuse	Problems Generally Solved:		
	To Suit Batterer	About Equal	To Suit Wife[a]
None	30.1	40.5	61.6
Slapping	38.3	39.9	25.0
Kicking, biting, punching	17.8	12.1	4.5
Thoroughly beaten up	5.5	2.9	2.7
Weapons involvement	8.3	4.6	6.3
N	472	173	112

NOTE: Tau b = .20, statistically significant at less than .001.
a. Column percentages do not total 100 owing to standard rounding procedures.

Discussion of Research Results

All four of the hypotheses with which we began this study are substantiated by the data. Children of battered wives are very likely to be battered by their fathers. The severity of the wife beating is predictive of the severity of child abuse. Husband-dominance is also a predictor of child abuse. Wife beating is more likely to be accompanied by child abuse in families where the husband was beaten by his parents, although the evidence in support of this hypothesis is weaker than the evidence for the other three hypotheses.

Although 70% appears to be a high figure for the proportion of wife beaters who physically abuse their children, this may still underestimate the true correspondence between these two forms of male domestic violence. First, we noticed that many of the women we interviewed in Wisconsin were extremely reticent to talk about child abuse even though they did not hesitate to relate the most intimate details of their own abuse, degradation, and torture. Second, the women were able to report only the child abuse they knew about. They may not have been aware of many other incidents of their husbands' abuse of the children. Finally, there are many categories of child abuse that were not included in the study, including child sexual abuse, child neglect, and the torture and killing of pets.

TABLE 7.2

Relationship Between Frequency of Marital Rape
and Abuse of Spousal Children (in percentages)

| Level of Child Abuse | Frequency of Marital Rape Incidents | | | | |
	None	1-5	6-15	16-100	Over 100
None	50.8	46.7	14.5	20.0	12.2
Slapping	32.8	28.9	51.3	38.7	41.5
Kicking, biting, punching	10.2	11.1	17.1	29.3	23.2
Thoroughly beaten up	2.8	5.2	3.9	1.3	11.0
Weapons involvement	3.4	8.1	13.2	10.7	12.2
N	354	135	76	75	82

NOTE: Tau b = .28, statistically significant at less than .001.
a. Column percentages do not total 100 owing to standard rounding procedures.

The most intriguing finding is the positive bivariate relationship between husband dominance in the most recent year together and spousal child abuse. This is consistent with earlier publications (Bowker, 1986; Bowker & Maurer, 1985) presenting evidence in support of a theory that identifies the major cause of wife beating as the husband's attempts to maintain familial dominance. In this theory, violent and previolent men have high needs to dominate their wives and children. They achieve and maintain the level of dominance they consider appropriate by a variety of oppressive strategies, including wife beating, child abuse, marital rape, psychological abuse, punitive economic deprivation, and coerced social isolation. We do not know very much about the interaction of these dominance-enhancing strategies with each other or about how they combine to increase the level of family dominance by men. The single measure of husband dominance used in the *Woman's Day* study was not sufficiently refined to permit us to examine this subject in depth.

Is child abuse by fathers merely a result of poor parental self-control, stress at work and at home, poverty, or similar factors? Such theories may be appropriate for understanding child abuse by mothers. However, there is growing evidence that child abuse by fathers is cut from a rather different cloth. We believe, based on our research and on recent theoretical developments, that researchers and practitioners should give more consideration to feminist analysis and the possibility that different mechanisms are at work in paternal and maternal child abuse.

Feminism and Social Science Research:
An Examination of the Research Methods

This research on wife battering employed fairly standard social science survey methods. Feminist theoreticians have critiqued traditional social science methods on the grounds that such methods can perpetuate male-defined knowledge, cannot adequately illuminate women's experiences, can create an undesirable power relationship between researcher and "subject," and may result in data that is interpreted in ways detrimental to battered women. On the other hand, replicable standard research methods and statistical analyses can provide a solid base of empirical data that meets current criteria of what constitutes scientific knowledge. These issues will be addressed through examining the sample selection for the present research and the decision to employ quantitative statistical methods.

Readers may ask why no attempt was made to randomize the sample, why there was a switch from in-depth interviews in the Wisconsin study to written questionnaires in the *Woman's Day* study, or why there has been such a quantitative emphasis in reports based on data from both studies. Isn't quantitative research inconsistent with feminist ethics? Doesn't it demean and dehumanize those who participate in the research while simultaneously creating fictional social entities that are not part of the experience or consciousness of the participants?

Every piece of social survey research contains dozens of biases, including those arising from sampling methodology, differential response rates, questionnaire design, coding and data entry conventions, the author's choice of materials for inclusion in the analysis as well as for publication, and the author's interpretation of the findings. Randomization, assuming that it is properly designed and carried out without complication or compromises, deals only with sampling biases. Controlling sampling biases allows us to generalize from samples to populations with known probabilities of error. Male-dominated social science research tends to emphasize random sampling and quantitative analysis while deemphasizing most of the other methodological factors that make sociology an inexact science. Randomization is appropriate as a way of obtaining answers to some questions, but may not be necessary in obtaining answers to many other important questions particularly in the exploratory stages of research.

In the case of wife-beating research, four of the most important questions concern epidemiology, dynamics, etiology, and cessation. Epidemiology requires randomization to provide incidence estimates of victimization (for example, see Straus, Gelles, & Steinmetz, 1980). The high cost of random sampling usually forces researchers to balance the budget by decreasing the complexity of the information sought. Studying the dynamics of wife beating requires a more phenomenological approach, such as using in-depth interviews. Social interaction among spouses is so subtle that it is extremely difficult to understand shifts in power balance, negotiations, and other forms of interaction with standard questionnaire techniques.

External factors also constrain the direction of research on battered women and their families. A proposal to obtain a larger sample of women and men failed to secure grant funding, partly because of the great expense of carrying out in-depth interviews with large samples. Although the *Woman's Day* announcement allowed us to increase inexpensively the number of women in the sample to 1,000, we needed to decrease dramatically the number of variables studied in order to construct a viable written questionnaire. The switch from interviews to questionnaires was in response to funding limitations rather than to scientific, programmatic, or ethical reasons. This reveals how gatekeepers on evaluation panels of funding agencies can unwittingly control the growth of knowledge about battered women and strongly influence the methodology and goals of current research.

Does highly statistical research demean research participants? When combined with intrusive interviewing techniques based on random sampling, it creates a methodological package that can cause considerable unwanted pain for participants. However, when combined with true voluntary participation, women who object to the methodology can simply fail to contact the researcher or neglect to respond to a mailed questionnaire. There is a more general sense in which statistical analysis can be seen as demeaning all research participants by abstracting elements from their testimony and reconceptualizing these elements into variables and concepts that would be unrecognizable and alien to the average research participant. It is in this sense that quantitative research is sometimes seen as less feminist than qualitative research, in which the humanity of research participants is carried forward through the research process into the published reports of the research.

Despite these concerns with statistical research and random sample survey techniques, quantitative research methodologies are not necessarily inferior to qualitative methodologies with respect to the promotion of feminist causes. Officials with responsibility for making and implementing policy, as well as other decision makers, are much more influenced by statistics and large samples than they are by case studies and small samples. Employing a quantitative methodology in feminist research can give researchers legitimacy and enable them to have an impact on decision makers, thus improving the situation of both study participants and women in general.

Publishing Feminist Research: A Personal Note by Lee Bowker

Difficult though it may be to accomplish sensitive research on battered women and to attempt carefully to resolve the complex questions regarding research design and methodology, an even greater difficulty is how to publish feminist research in order to disseminate knowledge that shapes attitudes toward battered women, social policy, and clinical and legal interventions. Although articles submitted for publication are supposedly assessed by neutral objective standards, my experience suggests that there are biased practices that serve to limit, if not obstruct, the publication of explicitly feminist articles on wife abuse.

My experiences in publishing feminist research over the years shed much light on the way in which "gatekeeping" occurs in social science publishing. My scholarly career is unusual in that I have published in many different fields, so I can compare how I am treated as a feminist author with how I am treated as an academic liberal writing about nonfeminist topics. This contrast is heightened by the fact that I have an androgynous first name. When I write a feminist piece, I am often assumed to be a woman (see Frieze, 1985); I am taken to be a man when I write about other subjects.

Table 7.3 summarizes my publishing experiences in the 13 years since I completed my doctorate. I did not keep rejection notices on articles published prior to 1980, so I have had to depend on memory for an approximate count of rejections of articles that were later published elsewhere. All but half-a-dozen rejected manuscripts were eventually published in another scholarly outlet, which makes the editorial reasons for earlier rejections particularly interesting as raw data on gatekeeping in the social sciences. Table 7.3 includes manuscripts currently in press and rejections suffered by articles that have subsequently been resubmitted and are currently under review by other journals. The table does not count resubmissions to the same journal with requested revisions. In every case except one, these revised drafts were eventually accepted for publication by the editor who requested the revisions.

The most striking thing about my publication experience is the difference in acceptance rates between feminist and nonfeminist submissions (Bowker, 1982a, 1982b, 1982c, 1983, 1986; Bowker & Maurer, 1985). The difference would be enough to sink most young professors writing feminist publications at an average rate and applying for tenure after five or six years. It is my impression that most feminist teacher-scholars are facing either tenure or promotion decisions in the near future. Feminist full professors are rare and feminist associate professors are uncommon. Furthermore, early rejections may discourage some teacher-scholars from feminist writing, or at least diminish their productivity substantially. If I had not resubmitted any manuscript that had been rejected, my writing in criminology, corrections, gerontology, drug abuse, or higher education would hardly have been affected. In contrast, one of my four feminist books would have died, and more than a third of the feminist articles would never have been published.

I have "marketed" my feminist articles (in which I tried to expose and so reduce some aspect of women's oppression by men) in two different ways. The first strategy was designed to achieve quick acceptances by sending articles directly to journals I thought most likely to publish them. For women's issues, this meant either a feminist journal or a highly specialized journal in an applied professional field. The second strategy was more playful, testing the gatekeepers by deliberately submitting articles to journals I thought unlikely to publish them. I would prepare a file in advance with one or two gatekeeper tests followed by a target journal and then do the run until one of the journals accepted the article. Of the gatekeeper journals I tested, only the *Journal of Criminal Justice* published one of my feminist manuscripts.

The case of the *Journal of Criminal Justice* is the exception that proves the rule. The editor received more negative comments on my article than were received and transmitted to me by many gatekeeper journals that rejected my submissions, yet he refused to give up on it. Defining it as an important contribution to the field, he worked with me through several subsequent drafts until the manuscript met his standards for publication, as well as the reasonable criticisms of his reviewers. He had enough sense to dismiss inappropriate criticisms based on sexism and other systematic reviewer biases. His motives were presumably

TABLE 7.3
Publication Experience of Lee H. Bowker

	Total Publications	Subject Area Feminist Publications	Nonfeminist Publications
Published articles, chapters, etc.	69	22	47
Approximate number of rejections	27	19	8
Approximate total submissions	96	41	55
Approximate acceptance rate (percentage)	72	54	85
Published books, monographs	16	4	12
Book publication difficulties	few	variable	almost none

NOTE: $\overline{X} = 11.752$, significant at less than .001, for the articles and chapters.

pure, for we were not acquainted. However, I suspect that this is how favored manuscripts are routinely nurtured, improved, and published through the operation of the "Old Boy Network." In my experience, editors are flexible in adapting my nonfeminist work to their needs, but this flexibility is often replaced with rigidity and inability to see any promise in my feminist work.

From my experiences with gatekeeper journals, I think I have found the answer to the question, "What is the correct methodology for carrying out feminist research?" It is "Whatever methodology you didn't use." The same methodology in my feminist articles has been criticized by one journal's reviewers as too quantitative and by another journal's reviewers as not quantitative enough. Reviewers who are quick to reject a manuscript (because the sample is too small or too large but nonrandom, or representative but of a specialized population) often do so without considering the relationship between the sampling methodology and the goals of the feminist research.

Is it possible for a feminist study on wife abuse with 1,000 subjects on a not previously studied topic of considerable significance to be rejected out of hand because the sample is nonrandom? Program officers at the National Institute of Mental Health do not think so, and have been extremely supportive of my wife-beating research. In contrast, journal reviewers often make comments such as, "The biased nature of the sample means the study doesn't tell anything worth knowing." Reviewers in gatekeeper journals tend to be offended by any hint of feminist criticism in the text of a manuscript. My favorite expression of this sentiment is the following quote:

> In general, my impression of this manuscript is that it fails the most basic tests of scientific communication. Its writing style is often confused and illogical; it wavers between science and advocacy; and, in its present form, would not be suitable for [this publication] or any other professional or scientific journal.

Think of the impact of such gatekeeper judgments on the scholarly self-images of young feminist writers struggling to establish national reputations and to achieve tenure!

Dale Spender (1981) described the gatekeeping system and its effects on feminist research. Too often, we can only guess about how the system works to exclude feminist research. By a lucky slip, I became privy to the tactics of a gatekeeper in action. The child abuse article that forms the main part of this chapter was submitted to a journal early in 1985. The editor wrote to indicate that his two reviewers had "very divergent opinions" and that a third opinion would be necessary. His pledge to me was, "I will give you a decision as soon as the next review has been complete [sic]." Two months later, he closed the file with a letter in which he said:

> The third reviewer [sic] comments are now available. These, plus those of reviewers one and two are enclosed for your feedback. I am not able to accept your chapter for publication. The views expressed in these enclosures reflect my concerns as well.

This sounds perfectly fine, and I would have known nothing further except that the editor (or his secretary, most probably) slipped and enclosed, by mistake, a copy of the real third review and an illegitimate, secret fourth review. Reviewer number one wrote, "Potentially a very interesting article about possible relationships between wife battering and child abuse" and recommended publication if a few changes were made in the manuscript. Reviewer number two gave a more typical, antifeminist review:

> This chapter presents an elaborate scientific analysis of a very unscientific study. It is a study of the perceptions of women, who volunteer for a study of women who feel that they are abused by their husbands.

The real third reviewer liked the article, concluding:

> This is an excellent and timely piece of research which adds significantly
> to the child abuse etiology puzzle. Should be of great impact clinically,
> and caution wife abuse treatment sources re: testing the children.

By the rules of editing and by his own statement, the editor should have
accepted the article upon the receipt of review number three. He instead
sent the manuscript to a fourth reviewer along with copies of the
comments written by the first two reviewers. The fourth reviewer was
misled into thinking he or she was the third reviewer and was on good
terms with the editor, who is addressed by his first name at the beginning
of the review. The conclusions of this reviewer are as follows:

> I think both reviewers picked up the major weakness of this chapter,
> namely that it is based on volunteers responsing [*sic*] to an article about
> the relationship between wife beating and abuse that appeared in a lay
> magazine. This method of recruiting participants to the study would
> select women with coexistence of these factors, and therefore the chapter
> has no real clinical or scientific value other than to present the question of
> how much child abuse and wife beating coexist. I primarily agree with
> reviewer #2 who felt the chapter failed in terms of science and should not
> be published.

Having finally solicited the negative review he already agreed with, the
editor felt safe in rejecting the manuscript with the words I quoted
earlier. The evidence suggests that the editor knew reviewer number four
well enough to be fairly sure about his or her opinion on the article. I
suspect that had he been wrong, and the fourth opinion turned out to be
as positive as the third, there would have been a fifth review instead of an
article accepted for publication.

I have had many strange things like this happen to my feminist
manuscripts, but almost never to manuscripts I have submitted on
nonfeminist topics. Taking all these experiences into account, I have
come to the conclusion that there are many gatekeepers in the world of
scholarship whose professionalism is insufficient to keep their antifeminist attitudes in check.

REFERENCES

Bowker, L. H. (1982a). *Beating wife-beating*. Lexington, MA: D. C. Heath.
Bowker, L. H. (1982b). Police services to battered women: Bad or not so bad? *Criminal
Justice and Behavior, 9,* 476-494.

Bowker, L. H. (1982c). Battered women and the clergy: An evaluation. *Journal of Pastoral Care, 36,* 226-234.

Bowker, L. H. (1986). *Ending the violence.* Holmes Beach, FL: Learning Publications.

Bowker, L. H., & Maurer, L. (1985). The importance of sheltering in the lives of battered wives. *Response to the Victimization of Women and Children, 8,* 2-11.

Dobash, R. E. (1977). *The relationship between violence directed at women and violence directed at children within the family setting.* London: House of Commons, Select Committee on Violence in the Family.

Frieze, I. (1985). Understanding violence in the family. *Contemporary Sociology, 14,* 156-157.

Gelles, R. J. (1979). The myth of battered husbands and new facts about family violence. *Ms.,* Vol. 8, pp. 65-72.

Gelles, R. J. (1980). The violent family. In S. K. McNall (Ed.), *Critical issues in sociology.* New York: Holt, Rinehart, & Winston.

Gelles, R. J., & Straus, M. A. (1979). Violence in the American family. *Journal of Social Issues, 35,* 15-38.

Moore, J. G. (1975). Yo-yo children: Victims of matrimonial violence. *Child Welfare, 54,* 557-566.

National Crime Survey. (1980). *Intimate victims: A study of violence among friends and relatives.* Washington, DC: U.S. Government Printing Office.

Spender, D. (1981). The gatekeepers: A feminist critique of academic publishing. In H. Roberts (Ed.), *Doing feminist research.* London: Routledge & Kegan Paul.

Stark, E., & Flitcraft, A. (1984). *Child abuse and the battering of women: Are they related and how?* Paper presented at the National Family Violence Conference, Durham, NH.

Straus, M. A. (1978). *Family patterns and child abuse in a nationally representative American sample.* Paper presented at the Second International Congress of Child Abuse and Neglect, London.

Straus, M. A., Gelles, R., & Steinmetz, S. (1980). *Behind closed doors: Violence in the American family.* Garden City, NY: Doubleday.

U.S. Department of Health, Education and Welfare. (1980). *Domestic violence, service delivery assessment.* Washington, DC: U.S. Government Printing Office.

PART III

Rethinking Clinical Approaches

8

Treatment Models of Men Who Batter

A Profeminist Analysis

DAVID ADAMS

Shifting the Paradigm

Counselor: What do you think causes you to hit your wife?

Client: Insecurity. I guess it goes way back. . . . My father was a drinker too. He wasn't just a drinker; he was a mean drunk. Once during Thanksgiving he got mad and threw the whole damned bird on the floor. . . . He'd whack my mother for no reason really. . . . I left home when I was 17, got married but it only lasted two months. She was pregnant of course. I've always been insecure with women.

Counselor: This is helping me to understand why you're insecure but not why you hit your wife.

Client: Sometimes I take things the wrong way. . . . I overreact I guess you could say, because of my insecurity. My shrink said I was like a time bomb waiting to go off. She (client's wife) might say something and I don't react at the time, but then the next day or maybe a few hours later I get to really thinking about that and I get really bull shit.

Counselor: A lot of people feel insecure but they are not violent. What I'm interested in finding out is how do you make the decision to hit your wife—and to break the law—even if you are feeling insecure?

Client: I never really thought of it that way, as a decision.

Counselor: But you were talking just now as if your violence is the direct result of your insecurity, or of something she says or does.

Client: Yeah, you're right, I do. But I'm still thinking about what you said about the decision. I honestly have to say that I never thought of it that way before. I mean, I'm really dumbfounded! I'm going to have to really think about that.

Counselor: What are you waiting for?
Client: What do you mean?
Counselor: I mean are you waiting to stop feeling insecure before you stop being violent?
Client: Yeah, I guess that's what I've been waiting for.

This dialogue was part of an intake session at Emerge. The client, Jack, came to Emerge following three years of therapy that included both individual and couple sessions with his wife. In this session, Jack's model for understanding his own violence is being challenged. Jack's former therapist had interpreted Jack's violent and abusive behavior as being related to his drinking, to unresolved feelings stemming from an emotionally deprived upbringing, and to poor communication patterns between Jack and his wife. Though some progress had been made in reducing Jack's level of drinking and in helping him to become more introspective, he continued to have "temper tantrums" during which he would grab, shake, slap, or kick his wife.

Jack's past therapy experience reveals a problem that is all too common when therapists and other potential interveners encounter men who batter. The problem is that the battering behavior is not identified as a primary treatment issue but rather as a symptom of some larger (usually underlying) problem. The result of this misnaming of the problem is that the batterer is given the message that his nonviolence is negotiable—depending on his ability or motivation to better himself, develop insight, or improve his (or his wife's) communication skills. The tacit message is that he will likely continue to grab, shake, slap, and kick his wife *until* he makes changes in these other areas. Such messages are analogous to the ones alcoholics often receive from therapists who are naïve to the alcoholic's use of denial, rationalization, and excuses to maintain drinking (Johnson, 1980). Unlike alcohol work, however, therapeutic misinterpretations of battering behavior are not confined to those therapists who are clinically inexperienced or unspecialized. In fact, current clinical work with men who batter is characterized by various specialized approaches that routinely give contradictory and nontherapeutic messages to men about why they batter and what they (or their partners) must do to stop it. From a feminist perspective, some of these approaches *collude* with batterers by not making their violence the primary issue or by implicitly legitimizing men's excuses for violence.

Schechter (1982) has observed that how individuals and helping institutions understand wife abuse greatly influences which change strategies—both clinical and nonclinical—they will use to combat it. In reviewing five different clinical approaches to wife abuse, I will emphasize how each model's primary techniques and methodology reflect quite different assumptions about and explanations for the battering of women. By further applying a feminist analysis to each model, I will show how some of these approaches collude with batterers by using techniques that do not adequately address the violence or by adopting modalities that compromise the man's responsibility for change.

The clinical approaches to be analyzed include the insight, ventilation, interaction, cognitive-behavioral, and profeminist models. Though many batterers' programs and individual therapists who work with batterers consider themselves eclectic since they use a variety of techniques, my impression is that most programs are guided by one model more than the others. The analysis of each model will begin with a brief overview of its causal explanations, proceed with a description of its preferred methods and modalities, and conclude with a feminist critique of its assumptions and practices. The feminist perspective is rendered more concrete in my description of the profeminist model in the final section.

Insight Model

The insight model is the traditional approach to understanding violence. Though there are many variations within this framework, the broad theme is that certain intrapsychic problems give rise to violent behavior. The list of intrapsychic problems is long: poor impulse control, low frustration tolerance, fear of intimacy, fear of abandonment, dependency, underlying depression, and impaired ego functioning resulting from developmental trauma. In clinical literature, men who batter are also described in terms of the following personality types: obsessive-compulsive (Oates, 1979; Shainess, 1977), paranoid (Faulk, 1977), borderline personality (Deschner, 1984), passive-aggressive (Shainess, 1977), and as pathological (Faulk, 1977; Lion, 1977). Arguing against unitary explanations, however, some authors have constructed personality typologies to account for the different combinations of psychological factors that presumably motivate each "type" of batterer. Elbow (1977) provides three types of "personality clusters," for instance, while Faulk (1977) gives five, and Oates (1979) lists eight.

A common assumption to all insight-oriented approaches to the man who batters is that impaired ego functioning (e.g., poor self-concept, emotional dependency) leads him to overreact to real or imagined threats in a violent manner. Impaired ego function and emotional deficits are believed to be the result of earlier developmental problems such as rejection by one or both parents, overdependency on mother, fear of father, failure to relate well with peers, and so on. Insight therapy seeks to help the abusive man become more aware of how he has been affected by past experiences so that he can learn to respond more appropriately to present relationships. It is assumed that once the abusive man resolves his past injuries and develops the ability to be more introspective, his feelings about himself will improve and he will no longer experience the need to abuse or diminish others. The following description of the AWAIC batterers' program in New York is representative of this perspective:

> Unlike the stereotypic image of the cruel, sadistic, macho male, batterers engaged in treatment at AWAIC have been bright, articulate men with deep underlying shallowness, severely impaired egos, and unresolved conflicts between the desperate need for the mate [sic] and the anger this brings. Their lack of impulse control and inability to deal with anxiety particularly when their limited sense of self is attacked, results in the release of aggression. . . . The main task of therapy becomes assisting the batterer in beginning to feel and cope with the depression that accompanies any frustrating experience. . . . The emphasis is on reconstructing the impaired ego and working through the early developmental conflicts. (Carnet & Moss, 1982, pp. 267-276)

Implicit in this approach is the notion that men who batter have a very fragile sense of self that must be therapeutically bolstered before they can be expected to give up violent and other "overcompensating" behaviors. This conception of abusive men derives in large part from sex role identity theory that holds that exaggerated, hypermasculine behaviors are rooted in men's unconscious anxiety about the "psychologically feminine" parts of their personalities (Biller & Borstelman, 1967; Winick, 1968). Myers (1983), for instance, states that feelings of "emasculation and passivity" occur in abusive husbands who have been abandoned by their wives. He argues for an "invitational, nonthreatening" therapeutic approach in which the goals include "catharsis, resocialization, redefining masculinity, overcoming intimacy fears, regaining sexual self-esteem, and enhancing fathering and coparenting skills."

Though there is considerable merit to all of the above as general goals for men, none specifically address men's violence against women. The psychodynamic emphasis of the hypermasculinity hypothesis has been criticized by Pleck (1981) because it is unheeding of how men are *socially* sanctioned to develop misogynistic values and controlling behaviors. The feminist critique of the insight approach does not dismiss the value of insight as an important dimension of change, but it does question clinical practice that devotes initial emphasis to psychodynamic interpretations when the abusive behavior is ongoing. Purely psychological explanations of battering are seductive. It seems intuitively correct, for instance, to say that a man is violent *because* he is emotionally insecure or impulsive, but what new information do these reasons really give us? In referring to clinical interpretations of child abuse, Gelles (1973) observes that *descriptions* of violent behavior are sometimes used by clinicians as *explanations* for violent behavior. Ptacek (1984) points out this same tendency when terms such as *loss of control, poor impulse control, low frustration tolerance,* and *paroxysmal rage* are used to explain wife beating. Only slightly less misleading are such terms as *low self-esteem, emotional dependency,* and *fear of intimacy* that may well describe certain emotional factors that are present for some men who batter but hardly explain the violence. The fallacy of such explanations is revealed by the fact that many men who are insecure, emotionally dependent, and afraid of intimacy *do not* batter their wives.

So strong is the tendency for therapists to "look inward" in their attempts to understand violence that they sometimes ignore the obvious. For instance, one survey of 59 battering prevention programs found that 90% cited "increased self-esteem" as one of their primary treatment goals while only 14% listed "having the abuser take responsibility for his violence" as an important goal (Pirog-Good & Stets-Kealey, 1985). By becoming preoccupied by the presumed psychological *etiology* of battering, insight-oriented therapists also fail to recognize the utility, or purposeful nature, of violent and controlling behavior. That the batterer's violence fosters fear, self-blame, and submission in the victim must not be seen as merely coincidental to physical abuse, according to feminists. Rather, these effects are viewed as the fundamental reasons for the violence—regardless of whatever other problems the batterer may have.

Though it may be argued that problems like insecurity, dependency, or unmet childhood needs may contribute to some men using violence to solve problems, working directly on these issues will not necessarily lead the batterer to stop being violent *since he continues to gain compliance and other benefits from his violence.* Ironically, when underlying problems like insecurity are made the central focus of treatment, not only does therapy fail to confront the violence but it also fails to confront the more immediate causes of the insecurity. Violence increases the man's feelings of insecurity since it also increases the risk that his wife will leave or grow distant from him. He typically reacts to this with more violence. Thus, violence (much like alcohol or drug abuse) is self-perpetuating unless it is directly confronted. It cannot be interpreted away. Because of this, more tangible results can be derived from confronting men's excuses for their violence while at the same time helping to increase the costs and consequences for continued violence. The specifics of this approach will be explained in greater detail in later sections.

A final criticism of insight-oriented approaches pertains to the assumption that interventions should be as nonthreatening as possible. Because men who batter are believed to have a "fragile sense of self" and to be highly defensive, supportive validation is seen as paramount to helping them drop their defensive facades and become open to change. Though supportive validation is undeniably an important curative factor in therapy (Yalom, 1975), an overemphasis on providing support and empathy to abusive men can also reinforce their pattern of finding excuses for their violence and for projecting blame onto their partners. Supportive validation becomes overaccommodation and implicit collusion whenever it is not accompanied by a persistent focus on the violence and a challenging of the man's excuses for violence. When the threat and danger of violence is ongoing, therapists cannot afford to get stuck on other issues or to wait for the client to develop insight. Taking the time to create a safe environment for the batterer can sometimes mean perpetuating an unsafe environment for his partner.

Ventilation Model

During the 1960s, the suppression of anger was "discovered" by popular psychologists as a common cause of such disparate problems as depression, peptic ulcers, heart disease, sexual impotence, and violence. As antidotes to the outmoded conventions and "stifling civility" of earlier eras, new approaches like Gestalt therapy, Synanon, primal therapy, psychodrama, and encounter groups sprang up with promises of teaching a more honest, "gut level" form of communication. Particularly the expression of anger was central to overcoming emotional repression and unblocking communication (Bach & Wyden, 1968; Rubin, 1970). Openly expressing anger and resentments was thought to ensure against storing up hostile aggression until its potentially explosive discharge, or against its conversion to other symptoms such as physical complaints, depression, and "passive-aggressive" behavior (Bach & Goldberg, 1974; Rubin, 1970).

Because violence is seen as symptomatic to the core problem of emotional repression, proponents of the ventilation model have not provided specialized interventions for violent individuals. Rather, violent husbands and their wives are usually included in heterogeneous groups of couples or individuals that address repressed feelings and dishonest communication. When spouse-abuse is specifically cited by ventilation therapists in the clinical literature, it is usually to compare it to other forms of miscommunication or "game playing." In most cases distinctions between violent and nonviolent clients—and between perpetrators and victims—are deemphasized or blurred. An example of this blurring can be found in the following account of spouse abuse (Goldberg 1983):

> Powerful romantic feelings are frequently only a step away from painful explosions of rage, and the same defensiveness that produces romantic ardor also sets the psychological stage for such explosions. . . . [Spouse violence] is rooted in the intertwining of powerful needs with feelings of being trapped and the hunger for freedom.

> Those who would turn the tragedy of spouse violence into an issue of sexism, politics, or morality; who perpetuate myths about the brutalizing male and the "helpless" female . . . who define "victims" and "victimizers" do great damage to the process of growth and self-awareness for both men and women. (pp. 41-42)

In the ventilation approach to batterers and nonbatterers, participants are encouraged to "level with one another" while they are also taught to "fight fairly." In some cases, acts of "mock fighting" (e.g., pillow punching, hitting one another with styrofoam clubs) are practiced in order to facilitate the release of pent-up aggression (Howard, 1970). In defense of this, Shostrom (1967, p. 176) asserts that "hurting is a necessary part of a (marital) relationship."

The belief that verbal aggression diminishes the likelihood of physical aggression has not been confirmed by research (Berkowitz, 1973; Straus, 1974; Tavris, 1982). In his survey of the "conflict tactics" used by 385 randomly surveyed families, for instance, Straus (1974) found that verbal aggression is strongly associated with escalating levels of verbal and physical aggression. Tavris (1982) similarly reports that the ventilation of anger—far from helping individuals become less angry—tends to "become addictive to the user." In empirical research on gender differences in the discharge of anger, Hokanson (1970) concludes that catharsis is a reaction to anger, "which is more often learned and practiced by men than by women." Still other researchers have found that, rather than facilitating greater understanding between intimates, angry outbursts tend to foster resentment and to increase the likelihood of retribution (Berkowitz, 1973; Novaco, 1975).

These findings sharply contradict the ventilation therapists' claim that verbal aggression acts as a kind of preventive safety value against physical aggression. Their injunction to "fight fairly" while venting hostile feelings provides a dangerous contradictory message to clients about the acceptability of violent behavior. Evidence of this ambiguous message is revealed in the following explanation by Bach and Wyden (1968) in *The Intimate Enemy,* the widely read book about fair fighting techniques for couples:

> Our fight training outlaws physical violence, although we recognize that there are times when roughness can be pleasurable and sexually stimulating. On the other hand, . . . the exchange of spanks, blows, and slaps between consenting adults is more civilized than the camouflaged or silent hostilities of ostensibly well-behaved fight-evaders who are "above it all." (p. 116)

Men who batter their wives do not need permission from experts to continue to vent their anger with little regard for its consequences to others. Pence (1985) comments that abusive men are already "experts at venting their anger" and that they often justify their angry outbursts on the grounds of being honest about their feelings. From a feminist therapeutic standpoint, more benefits are derived from questioning men's often distorted interpretations of their partner's actions than from encouraging them to express more fully the anger that these interpretations inspire (Adams & Penn, 1981). What one becomes angry about and how one expresses that anger are greatly influenced by both culture and gender (Allen & Haccoun, 1976; Tavris, 1982). Men more often than women view the open expression of anger and hostility as constructive and "liberating." But because women more often place self-expression within the broader context of care and responsibility to others, they are less likely to regard angry outbursts as constructive (Baker-Miller, 1986; Surrey, Kaplan & Jordan, 1985). Ventilation therapy (Ehrenreich, 1983) and the broader "human potential movement" have been criticized for promoting sexist and egocentric standards of growth and freedom. When growth is seen as antagonistic to concern for others and when responsibility is equated with guilt or with a "fear of taking risks," the psychology of self-liberation encourages a narcissistic flight from commitment (Ehrenreich, 1983; Lasch, 1979).

How one chooses to communicate one's thoughts, feelings, and reactions matters a great deal—and clearly, some choices are more responsible than others. As it has been applied to men who batter, ventilation therapy dangerously distorts men's understanding of growth and emotional maturity by selectively promoting certain forms of self-expression without confronting the violence.

Interaction Model

The interaction model is similar to the ventilation approach since treating both the abuser and the abused is considered essential for improving marital communication, resolving conflict, and ending violence. Consequently, couples are either seen together in conjoint therapy or are included in specialized groups with other "violent couples." But interaction therapists generally do not consider ventilation to be an appropriate method of ending violence.

Proponents of the interaction model philosophically justify their use of couples counseling as the treatment of choice by drawing from the family systems literature. Neidig (1984), for instance, supports his assertion that battering is primarily an "interpersonal transaction" (as opposed to one in which the batterer is solely responsible for his violence) by citing the following well-known family systems formulation:

> To assert that person A's behavior causes B's behavior is to ignore the effect of B's behavior in A's subsequent reaction; it is in fact to distort the chronology of events by punctuating certain relations in bold relief while obscuring others. (Watzlawick, Beavin, & Jackson, 1967, p. 11)

According to the interactionist perspective, battering is not characterized as one partner attempting to control or dominate the other but by the couple's combined communicational deficits and the attempts of both partners to coerce and otherwise incite the other. The following description for example, casts battering as an essentially circular transaction between husband and wife (Deschner, 1984, p. 83):

> Consort battering [*sic*] fits very well into the model of coercive exchanges building up to aggression by one party and forced submission by the other partner. . . . It hardly matters whether the husband or the wife initiated the first unpleasant event, for they both respond by trying to control the other person via escalation of negative remarks and threats, until one of them loses control and resorts to physical force to make the other one submit.

Since the violence itself is seen as but one aspect of an ongoing dysfunctional pattern that has rather arbitrary beginning, middle, and end points, it is presumed to have a nonlinear circular causality. Consequently, therapeutic interventions can and should address all parts of the interactive pattern, and not merely focus on the violent actions or choices of one partner. The goal of therapy is for each partner to identify and change how he or she contributes to the circular problem. For instance, the woman's withholding of sex, failure to state her own needs adequately, angry accusations, "nagging," or overinvolvement with the children may be considered just as significant contributing factors as the man's outbursts of temper, possessiveness, lack of responsibility for the children, and attempts to dominate. Because each partner is further believed to play overly rigid roles within the relationship, interaction therapists are quite hesitant to assign blame for the violence to one partner or the other. Fixed labels like "abuser" and "abused" are accordingly rejected in favor of the presumably more neutral label of "abusive couples."

It is this tendency of couples counselors to equalize responsibility for violence between the man and the woman that has been at the heart of the feminist criticism of the interaction model. Couples counseling gives ambiguous and contradictory messages to the abuser about how much responsibility he should take for ending his violence (Adams, 1984; Bograd, 1984; Edelson, 1985; Ganley, 1981; Schechter, 1982). Geller (1982), a proponent of couples counseling, provides evidence of this ambiguity. While stating that "it cannot be emphasized enough that the violent behavior is the sole responsibility of the violent partner," she contradicts this in a subsequent case example by reporting, "the couple was able to work together to get the violence under control." *His* violence has been turned into *the* (and in other cases *their*) violence, even though there is no indication that the woman has been violent. Geller appears to propose a shared responsibility for the husband's violent outbursts by advising him to take a cooling off period (by going into another room) whenever he develops the impulse to become violent during arguments, while also instructing the wife to "suspend" her arguments (by not continuing to push her points or followng him into the other room) until he has cooled down. Strongly implied in the assigning of such parallel tasks, however, is the message that the woman is partially responsible for the husband's subsequent violence should she fail to recognize his nonverbal cues accurately and desist from further argument. By assigning the wife the task of helping her husband to bring his violence under control, the therapist is giving a mixed message to both partners about how much "sole responsibility" the husband should really take for his violence, and whether he should continue to expect certain changes on her part before he makes a commitment to nonviolence.

Not only do interactive approaches blur the distinctions between violent and nonviolent behavior, but they also give a tacit message that battering is an understandable, though unfortunate, response to behavior on the victim's part that the batterer deems "controlling" or "provocative." Most clinicians who work with batterers are aware of the men's attempts to excuse or justify their violence by projecting blame onto their partners (Adams & Penn, 1981; Ganley, 1981). A crucial element in this defensive pattern is the man's ability to define his partner's behavior in a self-serving manner. This seems quite similar to the well-recognized tendency of the rapist or incest offender to deny or minimize responsibility for his actions by saying that the victim was "seductive" or that "she led me on" (Groth, 1979; Herman, 1981). In reporting their research, which shows that virtually any behavior on the part of the battered woman is likely to be deemed "provocative" by her husband, Dobash and Dobash (1983, p. 59) call attention to the sexist assumptions that underlie the myth of provocation:

> The notion of provocation is insidious because what is really being said is that the woman has no real right to negotiate with her husband about issues such as how the money is spent, the time he spends away from home, the amount of assistance he might give with household tasks, or

about her freedom to go to work, engage in her own hobbies or interests if such negotiations irritate or offend him.

If the woman continues to negotiate beyond the point where the man has said the argument is over, he reserves the option of labeling her continued talk as "provocative" or "nagging." Therapists who are not sensitive to sexist dynamics and the unequal balance of power in the relationship often buy into the man's characterizations of his wife's actions rather than attempting to understand them more from the woman's perspective (Bograd, 1985; Hare-Mustin, 1980). Understanding the woman's "nagging" from a less male-defined perspective, for instance, may reveal that the woman is repeating herself because he does not listen to her. When the woman's "precipitating" behavior becomes the object of focus and when men's definitions of their wives' actions go unquestioned, therapists implicitly reinforce men's attempts to divert attention away from their own choices. To focus on what the woman can do to prevent her husband's anger not only compromises the woman's right to express her own anger, but denies the man's basic responsibility to express his feelings and reactions in a nonviolent manner.

Besides clouding the issue of who is responsible for the violence, couples counselling places the battered women in an impossible bind. Though she is expected to be open about her feelings, air her grievances, and report her husband's violence, to do any of these things places her in grave danger of continued violence. Many battered women report that past family therapy sessions were followed by violent episodes. The threat of continued violence leads battered women to communicate their feelings and concerns in an indirect manner, which is often misinterpreted by couples counselors as noncompliance (Ganley, 1981).

Interaction therapists violate their own logic by being only selectively attentive to violence as an overriding influence in the marital interaction. Poor communication is seen by interaction therapists as a contributing factor, rather than as an inevitable *effect* of violence. Most therapeutic interventions are accordingly directed at improving the couple's communication. Critics of this approach do not deny that there is a communication problem, but they do deny that it can be rectified so long as the violence, or the threat of violence, persists (Ganley, 1981; Schechter, 1982; Walker, 1984). But violence creates fear and distrust in both partners, which in turn determines how each will respond and communicate with the other. For the woman, fear of his violence prevents her from communicating her own wishes and feelings in a direct or consistent manner. For the man, violence gains compliance but also perpetuates his fears of her independence and anger about her noncompliance, which reinforces his attempts to control her. The woman cannot stop being afraid so long as the threat of violence is present. So long as this is so, neither can trust or openly communicate with each other.

Cognitive-Behavioral and Psychoeducational Models

In contrast to the three previous models, the cognitive-behavioral approach to battering makes violence the primary focus of treatment. Moreover, because violence is seen as having a dominating influence on marital interaction, abusive husbands are seen separately in specialized groups or in individual therapy to increase the opportunity for men to focus on their own behavior.

Since violence is a learned behavior, nonviolence can similarly be learned, according to the cognitive-behavioral model (Edelson, Miller, & Stone, 1983; Ganley, 1981; Sonkin & Durphy, 1982). This belief derives from social learning theory that sees problem behaviors such as violence as socially learned and self-reinforcing (Bandura, 1977). The following self-reinforcing aspects of battering are identified by Sonkin, Martin, & Walker (1985, p. 47):

> First, the reduction of bodily tension makes the violence a means to reduce stress or anxiety. . . . Second, violence does put a temporary end to an uncomfortable situation, even though the long-term consequences continue to propagate the discomfort. Third, the violence will often create an immobility in the woman which can be viewed by the batterer as complicity. The violence becomes a way of controlling and incapacitating his partner to the extent that he is less threatened by her independence and her possibly leaving him.

Recognizing these functional aspects of the violence, the psycho-educational therapist points out the damaging and ultimately self-defeating consequences of violence and teaches alternative behaviors. Since battering behavior is also seen reflecting certain social skill deficits, interpersonal skills training is provided as an important element in helping men abstain from violence. The following set of skills, for example, are cited by one batterers' program as central to nonviolent conflict resolution:

> The ability to clearly identify and state the parameters of a problem situation, to identify and express his own feelings about what is happening, to be able to identify and state his partner's point of view, to offer solutions from which he and his partner may benefit and to negotiate a final compromise . . . and the ability to temporarily extricate himself (take a "time-out") from highly stressful situations. (Edelson et al., 1983, p. 7)

Though sharing a philosophy that identifies skills-learning as fundamental to change, psychoeducational programs vary in terms of *which* alternate skills are emphasized, such as systematic relaxation training (Edelson et al., 1983; Purdy & Nickle, 1981; Sonkin & Durphy, 1982) or assertion training. The teaching of assertion skills to abusive husbands is based on the observation of cognitive-behaviorists that aggressive individuals often lack appropriate self-assertion skills (Novaco, 1978; Rimm, 1977). Lange and Jakubowski (1976), for instance, observed that some aggressive individuals confuse assertiveness with passivity or "being wimpy," while others justify their aggression on the grounds that they are being properly assertive. Sonkin and Durphy (1982) note that abusive husbands often alternate between failing to ask for help or affection from their wives and then demanding it in a hostile manner.

Self-observation, the ability for men to monitor their own external and internal responses when interacting with others, is cited as an important skill by many psychoeducationally oriented programs. One common technique used to teach this skill is assigning men to keep journals (often referred to as "anger logs") in which their thoughts, feelings, and physical sensations during tense situations are recorded. The rationale for this exercise is that it helps men to identify their own physical, emotional, and cognitive cues or "triggers" to violence (Sonkin & Durphy, 1982). Ganley (1981) reports that most men's violence is preceded by irrational and anger-arousing "self-talk" that distorts their perceptions of their partner's actions and leads them to overreact. A strong tenet of cognitive-behavioral approaches is that these irrational and rigid thought patterns must be challenged in order for abusive men to learn more flexible and accommodating responses to conflict situations. The rational-emotive framework of Albert Ellis (1970) has inspired this application of "cognitive restructuring" techniques to men who batter

(Edelson et al., 1983). Such techniques are thought to work best in a group counseling context since peer groups afford men many opportunities to recognize each other's rigid response patterns and to devise alternative ways of thinking and acting.

Besides differences in which social skills are emphasized and how they are taught, psychoeducational programs also vary in how explicitly they address battering as an abuse of power issue or confront the sexist expectations of their clients. At one end of the continuum, some programs explicitly define battering as controlling and sexist behavior, while others avoid discussion of sexism altogether. Those psychoeducational programs that do not address issues of sexism tend to view battering more generally as a skills-deficits or a stress management problem than as a sexist control problem. Their emphasis on skills-deficits is reflected by their use of such terms as "anger-management," "conflict-containment," "stress-control," or "men and anger" to publicize their counseling groups. The majority of interventions are aimed at helping abusers better manage their anger, cope with stress, and to improve communication skills.

From a feminist standpoint, there are several problems with this orientation. The major weakness is that when interventions are too broadly aimed at reducing stress or improving interpersonal skills, the important power and control dimensions of wife abuse are minimized or ignored. Unless gender politics are considered, approaches that point to external stress or poor coping skills cannot explain why women are often the sole targets of men's abuse (Schechter, 1982). Nor can they adequately account for the evidence that many men who lack basic interpersonal and stress-coping skills do not beat their wives.

Closer attention to gender politics reveals that how men cope with stress, communicate feelings, and attempt to resolve conflicts is situation specific. It depends as much on the gender and status of the person(s) with whom he is interacting as much as it does on his social skill level. For instance, some research has shown that men are better listeners when interacting with male coworkers and other male peers than when with female coworkers or their spouses (Henley, 1977; Spender, 1980). How and where men use assertion (versus aggression) skills is similarly selective. Abusive men's interactions with police officers, bosses, neighbors, and coworkers often reveal that they are able to respond in a conciliatory or assertive manner when they perceive such responses to be in their best interests. It may well be that men choose not to use these same skills when responding to their wives for the same reason—because they perceive it to be in their best interests. These apparent contradictions between the abusive husband's at-home and away-from-home behavior are more consistent when we look at them from the standpoint of what he perceives to be to his maximum benefit, considering the balance of power between himself and the other. Rather than reflecting a coping skills deficit, the violent husband's selectively abusive behavior indicates an established set of control skills.

Education and practice on self-assertion and other alternate skills will not necessarily induce batterers to stop using their control skills unless such work is also accompanied by strengthened social and legal sanctions against continued violence, along with specific attention to the inherent sexist expectations (Adams, 1988; Pence, 1985). The timing of therapeutic interventions is vital. Though social skills training should be included at some point in treatment as a long term prevention of recidivism, achieving a nonnegotiable abstinence from violence must be the initial focus of treatment.

The cognitive-behavioral model has provided many useful insights and interventions for battering behavior. It has identified some of the self-reinforcing aspects of violence and also recognized the need for stronger social and legal consequences. This approach is weakest when its practitioners fail to adequately integrate a political understanding of battering that identifies and confronts its sexist underpinnings.

Profeminist Model

Wife beating is controlling behavior that serves to create and maintain an imbalance of power between the battering man and the battered woman (Martin, 1981; Schechter, 1982). This is the feminist insight that informs the profeminist approach to batterers. Because power and control are seen as the fundamental issues, therapeutic interventions directly challenge the abusive man's attempts to control his partner through the use of physical force, verbal and nonverbal intimidation, and psychological abuse. Compared to other models, the profeminist model defines violence more broadly as any act that causes the victim to do something she does not want to do, prevents her from doing something she wants to do, or causes her to be afraid. Violence need not involve physical contact with the victim, since intimidating acts, such as punching walls, verbal threats, and psychological abuse, can achieve the same results. Pyschological abuse includes behavior that directly undermines the self-determination or self-esteem of the other person (Ganley, 1981). These acts are particularly powerful when combined with physical violence since covert controls serve to subliminally remind the victim of the potential for repeated violence (Adams, 1984; Arendt, 1961). Yelling, swearing, sulking, and angry accusations, for instance, are not as frightening or directly undermining as when they are "reinforced" by periodic or even occasional violence.

By analyzing the abusive man's actions in terms of their controlling effects as opposed to his stated intentions, the profeminist model has to learn more about why such behavior persists—even after men have learned new skills or insights. For example, the withholding of praise and other kinds of positive attention are found to be a particularly effective means of control (Henley, 1986). By making his expressions of positive attention rare and contingent on his wife's "good" behavior the abusive husband puts his wife in the position of striving harder to gain his approval. Since it is accompanied by routine verbal criticism and physical "punishment," the man's withholding approval puts him in a parental role in relation to his wife. In providing little attention beyond his anger and disapproval, he retains the power to validate (or invalidate) her, the authority to give (and take back) permission for her actions.

Though the profeminist model, like the psychoeducational model, recognizes the need to provide basic education to batterers about caretaking and communication skills, the profeminist model sees it as just as essential to challenge the sexist expectations and controlling behaviors that often inhibit men's motivation to learn and to apply such skills consistently in a noncontrolling manner. While the focus of early treatment is on the identification and elimination of violent and controlling behaviors, later interventions focus more on sexist expectations and attitudes. Each of these stages of treatment deserve elaboration.

Many profeminist batterers' programs provide counseling groups for men in which initial interventions are devoted primarily to the protection of the battered woman. Men are expected to make "safety plans" that minimize the possibility for continued violence (C. Norberg, RAVEN, St. Louis, MO, personal communication, 1986). Safety plans include respecting the woman's fears and stated limits about the relationship, fully complying with restraining and vacate orders, eliminating drug or alcohol use if it has accompanied violent behavior, and ceasing any pressure or intimidation tactics intended to change his partner's plans or to deny her contact with others. Separate contact with the battered woman is also made by the local battered woman's program or by the batterer's program to apprise her of legal protection options as well as of support, advocacy, and emergency shelter services. She is also validated in her perception of not being responsible for her husband's violence and encouraged to ensure her own safety as much as possible.

Beyond safety planning, early interventions also include confronting the many ways that men attempt to deny or share responsibility for their violence. These include minimizing the violence, projecting blame onto partners, claiming loss of control, blaming alcohol or drugs, or citing internal or external stress as causes of violence (Adams & Penn, 1981). Group members at Emerge are expected to list their common reasons for violence and to recognize how each denies responsibility. The claim of "loss of control," for example, is challenged on the basis that men are quite selective in how and to whom they are violent (Adams & McCormick, 1982; Ptacek, 1984). This is indicated by the fact that some men grab but never strike their wives, some slap but never punch, while others punch but do not use weapons. That a man demonstrates some control over his behavior indicates that he has as much control as he wants to exert in that situation.

Because of the tendency for abusive men to replace physical violence with more subtle forms of abuse, profeminist therapists also identify and challenge the men's other control patterns. These involve his attempts to intimidate or pressure his partner into changing her plans or ending any doubts that she may have about the relationship or his ability to change. Such pressure tactics typically include the withholding of financial support, making accusations or threats of infidelity, issuing ultimatums or deadlines for her to "make up her mind," using the children as allies against her, and accusing her of not appreciating his efforts to change.

Emerge has found that abusive men engage in "bargaining behavior" with their wives and their counselors over *how much* and *how soon* they will give up their abusive and controlling behaviors (Adams, 1988). Usually, men want a "quick fix" to their conflict with their wives. Any initial changes they do make tend to be both cosmetic (for appearances only) and provisional (dependent on immediate recognition and concessions from their wives). Batterers engaged in profeminist counseling programs are given a choice to comply with their treatment and safety plans or be terminated with notification to their partners. Partners of men who fail to comply with treatment are encouraged to pursue legal protection and consequences if they have not already done so. Terminated clients who have been court-mandated into counseling are remanded for violation of probation (Pence, 1985).

One important technique that is used by several programs to help men to become more accountable for their control patterns is assigning them to keep "control logs." Emerge, for example, instructs men to monitor themselves using a written checklist of violent and controlling behaviors. Education is also provided about the damaging and controlling effects of each of the behaviors on the checklist. The Domestic Abuse Intervention Program in Duluth uses video taped portrayals of these violent and controlling behaviors in order to sensitize men further to their own control patterns. Such exercises not only promote more accountability for men's behavior, but also create a keener awareness of the contradictions between the men's stated intentions (e.g., "I just wanted to get her to listen to me") and the actual consequences of their actions (frightening her, pushing her away).

Once the batterer has demonstrated a willingness to abstain from violent and controlling behaviors, more attention is directed at the attitudes, expectations, and feelings that have accompanied such behavior. The men's attitudes and expectations toward their wives usually indicate an *intent to devalue* and denigrate rather than an intent to understand their wives. This is evident in the ways that men report interactions with their partners. Rather than reporting what his wife actually said, the abusive man will *characterize* her words and actions in a mocking, trivializing, or otherwise denigrating manner. Comments like "she went on and on about nothing," "she was in a bitchy mood," and "there was no pleasing her" are examples of these characterizations. Even when pressed by group counselors to relate the specific content of the interaction men cannot recall their wives' actual words or specific complaints, again indicating an intent to devalue and dismiss her concerns rather than an *intent to understand them.*

The devaluation process is seen by profeminist therapists as a fundamental part of the abuse and oppression of women (Adams, 1988; K. Carlin, Director of Men Stopping Violence, Atlanta, personal communication, 1985). Devaluation often serves as an ideological justification for violence since it creates and strengthens negative attitudes (Adorno, Frenkel-Brunswik, Levinson, & Sanford, 1950). Those who are physically abused are usually those who are not taken seriously (Memmi, 1965). Negative attitudes and stereotypes also create opportunities for society to "blame victims" of oppression rather than look at the oppression itself (Ryan, 1972).

Profeminist counselors take an active role in interrupting the devaluation process as it occurs within counseling groups. Alternative and more validating ways of interpreting their partner's words and actions are elicited. At the same time, the contradiction between the men's desire for their wives to feel closer to them and their continuing attempts to dismiss or trivialize their wives' concerns is highlighted. The men are asked "how *can* she feel closer or want to remain with you so long as you criticize and control her?"

Those men who do make changes progress through distinct stages in giving up their attempts of controlling their partners (Adams, 1988). These stages correspond to the five stages of grief described by Kubler-Ross (1975). In the initial stages, the batterer alternates between *denial* (that he is responsible for his violence and that he cannot control the ways she feels, acts, or thinks), *anger* (for his wife calling attention to his violence as a problem), and *bargaining* (to retain some elements of control). *Depression and confusion* characterize the fourth stage since many men do not know how to feel or act if they cannot be in control. It is important for counselors to let men be confused and at the same time interpret it as a positive step toward growth. As the man tries to understand his wife rather than control her, his giving up controlling behavior also enables him to feel and think differently about himself. Once violence is publicly identified, the disparity that the batterer has typically maintained between his public image and his private reality becomes increasingly problematic. His choice is to seek allies in attempting to maintain his public image (at her expense) or face up to the need for change.

Acceptance that he cannot control the ways others act or feel is the final stage of change for the batterer. It is at this point that men become more self-motivated to examine sexist expectations and confront their own controlling behaviors. Because many men at this stage want to expect more of themselves, individual therapy or an ongoing support group may be helpful. Without this, there is a strong likelihood that men may slide back into more familiar patterns. Referrals for couples counseling may also be appropriate in those cases where *both* partners are interested in working on the relationship, and the threat of violence has been eliminated. It is not indicated in cases where the wife cannot bring up her complaints or anger without being fearful of an abusive response on his part. Whether the abusive man progresses to the acceptance stage depends a great deal on the kinds of legal, social, and therapeutic interventions that he encounters along the way. Those that allow men to focus on issues other than their violence, or that permit men to bargain about what controlling behaviors are acceptable alternatives, collude with batterers in their resistance to change.

Though the timing of counseling interventions is important, it is naïve to assume that counseling alone will be effective. Legal sanctions against battering are essential and counseling programs must not simply help men to circumvent the legal consequences of their past or continued violence. Recognizing this danger, court-mandated programs in Minneapolis, Duluth, Seattle, Denver, San Francisco, and Atlanta have played key roles in bringing about proarrest policies in the criminal justice system (Brygger & Edelson, 1985; Ganley, 1981; Paymar & Pence, 1985). By placing convicted batterers on probation and staying their sentences until successful completion of group counseling, abusive men are required to be socially accountable.

Conclusions

This analysis of five clinical models has shown how differing causal assumptions about wife beating give rise to different treatment modalities and techniques. Though particular techniques are not mutually exclusive, the preferred modality, emphasis, and timing of interventions give differing messages to men about allocating responsibility for their violence and about what preconditions to nonviolence (if any) are expected. Those approaches that advocate a shared responsibility between husbands and wives do so at the expense of the battered woman's right to expect changes without jeopardizing her own safety. Therapists who try to trade insights, fair fighting, or reasons for men's nonviolence are missing what one ex-batterer describes as the whole point of his violence—that *might makes right*. Persistently challenging that right is the most fundamental responsibility for therapists and others.

REFERENCES

Adams, D. (1988). Stages of anti-sexist awareness and change for men who batter. In L. Dickstein & C. Nadelson (Eds.), *Family violence*. Washington, DC: Appi Press.

Adams, D. (1985). *Assertion-training for abusive husbands: A review of theory and practice*. (Available from: Emerge, 280 Green St. Cambridge, MA 02139)

Adams, D., & McCormick, A. (1982). Men unlearning violence: A group approach. In M. Roy (Ed.), *The abusive partner: An analysis of domestic battering*. New York: Van Nostrand Reinhold.

Adams, D., & Penn, I. (1981). *The socialization and resocialization of men: Counseling groups for men who batter.* Paper presented at the annual convention of the American Orthopsychiatric Convention, New York. (Available through Emerge)

Adorno, T., Frenkel-Brunswik, E., Levinson, D., & Sanford, R. (1950). *The authoritarian personality.* New York: Harper.

Allen, J., & Haccoun, D. (1976). Sex differences in emotionality: A multi-dimensional approach. *Human Relations 29,* 711-722.

Arendt, H. (1961). *Between past and future.* New York: Viking.

Bach, G., & Wyden, P. (1968). *The intimate enemy: How to fight fair in love and marriage.* New York: Avon.

Baker-Miller, J. (1986). *Toward a new psychology of women.* Boston: Beacon Press.

Bandura, A. (1977). *Social learning theory.* Englewood Cliffs, NJ: Prentice-Hall.

Berkowitz, L. (1973). The case for bottling up rage. *Psychology Today,* Vol. 7, pp. 24-31.

Biller, H., & Borstelmann, L. (1967). Masculine development: An integrative review. *Merrill-Palmer Quarterly, 13,* 253-294.

Bograd, M. (1984). Family systems approaches to wife battering: A feminist critique. *American Journal of Orthopsychiatry, 54,* 558-568.

Bograd, M. (1985). *Women and family therapy: Thoughts on theory and practice.* Paper presented at the annual meeting of the American Orthopsychiatric Association, Toronto.

Brygger, M., & Edelson, J. (1985). *The domestic abuse project: A multi-systems intervention.* (Available from: Domestic Abuse Intervention Project, 206 West Fourth St., Duluth, MN 55806).

Deschner, J. (1984). *The hitting habit: Anger control for battering couples.* New York: Free Press.

Dobash, E., & Dobash, E. (1983). Unmasking the provocation excuse. *Aegis, 37,* 57-68.

Edelson, J. (1985). Violence is the issue: A critique to Neidig's assumption. *Victimology, 9, 5.*

Edelson, Miller, & Stone (1983). *Counseling men who batter: Group leader's handbook.* Available through the Men's Coalition Against Battering, P.O. Box 6447, Albany NY 12206.

Ehrenreich, B. (1983). *The hearts of men.* Garden City, NY: Anchor/Doubleday.

Elbow, M. (1977). Theoretical considerations of violent marriages. *Social Casework 58,* 515-526.

Ellis, A. (1970). *The essence of rational psychotherapy: A comprehensive approach to treatment.* New York: Institute for Rational Living.

Faulk, M. (1977). Men who assault their wives. In M. Roy (Ed.) *Battered women: A psycho-sociological study of domestic violence.*

Ganley, A. (1981). *Court-mandated counseling for men who batter: A three day workshop for mental health professionals.* Manual available from the Center for Women's Policy Studies, Washington, DC).

Garnet, S. & Moss, D. (1982). How to set up a counseling program for self-referred batterers: The AWAIC model. In M. Roy (Ed.) *The abusive partner: An analysis of domestic battering.* New York: Van Nostrand Reinhold.

Geller, J. (1982). Conjoint therapy: Staff training and treatment of the abuser and the abused. In M. Roy (Ed.), *The abusive partner: An analysis of domestic battering.* New York: Van Nostrand Reinhold.

Gelles, R. (1973). Child abuse as psychopathology: A sociological critique and reformulation. *American Journal of Orthopsychiatry, 43,* 611-621.

Goldberg, H. (1983). *The new male-female relationship.* New York: Signet.

Groth, N. (1979). *Men who rape: The psychology of the offender.* New York: Plenum.

Hare-Mustin, R. (1980). Family therapy may be dangerous for your health. *Professional Psychology, 11,* 935-938.

Henley, N. (1986). *Body politics: Power, sex and nonverbal communication.* Englewood Cliffs, NJ: Prentice-Hall.

Herman, J. (1981). *Father-daughter incest.* Cambridge, MA: Harvard University Press.

Hokanson, J. (1970). Psychophysiological evaluation of the catharsis hypothesis. In E. Megargee & J. Hokanson (Eds.), *The dynamics of aggression.* New York: Harper & Row.

Howard, J. (1970). *Please touch: A guided tour of the human potential movement.* New York: Harper & Row.

Johnson, V. (1980). *I'll quit tomorrow: A practical guide to alcoholism treatment.* New York: Harper & Row.

Kubler-Ross, E. (1975). *Death: The final stage of growth.* New York: Prentice-Hall.

Lange, A., & Jakubowski, P. (1976). *Responsible assertive behavior: Cognitive-behavioral procedures for trainers.* Champaigne, IL: Research Press.

Lasch, C. (1979). *The culture of narcissism.* New York: Warner Books.

Lion, J. (1977). Clinical aspects of wifebattering. In M. Roy (Ed.), *Battered women: A psycho-sociological study of domestic violence.* New York: Van Nostrand Reinhold.

Martin, D. (1981). *Battered wives.* San Francisco: Volcano Press.

Memmi, A. (1965). *The colonizer and the colonized.* Boston: Beacon Press.

Myers, M. (1983). *Angry, abandoned husbands—assessment and treatment.* (Available from the Department of Psychiatry, Shaughnessy Hospital, 4500 Oak St., Vancouver, BC V6H 3N1).

Neidig, P. (1984). Women's shelters, men's collectives and other issues in the field of spouse abuse. *Victimology 9,* 483-489.

Novaco, R. (1975). *Anger control.* Lexington, MA: Lexington Books.

Novaco, R. (1978). Anger and coping with stress: Cognitive-behavior interventions. In J. Foreyt & D. Rathjen (Eds.), *Cognitive behavior therapy: Research and applications.* New York: Plenum Press.

Oates, M. (1979). A classification of child abuse and its relation to treatment prognosis. *Child Abuse and Neglect, 3,* 907-915.

Paymar, M., & Pence, E. (1985). *Facilitator's guide to an educational curriculum for court mandated men who batter.* (Available from the Domestic Abuse Intervention Project, 206 West Fourth St., Duluth, MN 55806)

Pence, E. (1985). *The justice system's response to domestic assault cases: A guide for policy development.* (Available from the Domestic Abuse Prevention Project, 206 West Fourth St., Duluth, MN 55806)

Pirog-Good, M., & Stets-Kealey, J. (1985). Male batterers and battering prevention programs: A national survey. *Response, 8,* 8-12.

Pleck, J. (1981). *The myth of masculinity.* Cambridge: MIT Press.

Ptacek, J. (1984, August). *The clinical literature on men who batter: A review and critique.* Paper presented at the second national conference for Family Violence Researchers, Durham, NH.

Purdy, F., & Nickle, N. (1981). Practice principles for working with groups of men who batter. *Social Work with Groups 4,* 111-112.

Rimm, D. (1977). Treatment of anti-social aggression. In G. Harris (Ed.), *The group treatment of human problems: A social learning approach*. New York: Grune & Stratton.

Rubin, T. (1970). *The angry book*. New York: Collier.

Ryan, W. (1972). *Blaming the victim*. New York: Vintage.

Schechter, S. (1982). *Women and male violence: The visions and struggles of the battered women's movement*. Boston: South End Press.

Shainess, N. (1977). Psychological aspects of wifebeating. In M. Roy (Ed.), *Battered women: A psycho-sociological study of domestic violence*. New York: Van Nostrand Reinhold.

Shostrom, E. (1967). *Man, the manipulator*. New York: Abingdon Press.

Sonkin, D., & Durphy, M. (1982). *Learning to live without violence: A handbook for men*. San Francisco: Volcano.

Sonkin, D., Martin, D., & Walker, L. (1985). *The male batterer: A treatment approach*. New York: Springer.

Spender, D. (1980). *Man-made language*. London: Routledge & Kegan Paul.

Straus, M. (1974). Leveling, civility and violence in the family. *Journal of Marriage and the Family 36*, 13-39.

Surrey, J., Kaplan, A., & Jordon, J. (1985). *Women and empathy*. (Available from the Stone Center, Wellesley College, Wellesley College, MA 02181)

Tavris, C. (1982). *Anger: The misunderstood emotion*. New York: Simon and Schuster.

Walker, L. (1984). *The battered woman syndrome*. New York: Springer.

Watzlawick, P., Beavin, J., & Jackson, D. (1967). *Pragmatics of human communication*. New York: Norton.

Winick, C. (1968). *The new people: Desexualization in American life*. New York: Pegasus.

Yalom, I. (1975). *The theory and practice of group psychotherapy*. New York: Basic Books.

9

Battered or Schizophrenic?

Psychological Tests Can't Tell

LYNNE BRAVO ROSEWATER

Behavioral science has been criticized for misogyny and a priori victim blaming (Wardell, Gillespie, & Leffler, 1983). These problems are apparent to me in my work as a clinician, especially in the area of woman abuse. Repeatedly I have seen professionals fail to distinguish the symptoms of victims of violence from the symptoms of the sufferers of mental illness or to understand their interplay (Rosewater, 1985b). This failure is especially evident in the American Psychiatric Association's new diagnosis of self-defeating personality disorder, which was originally called masochistic personality disorder (Rosewater, 1987).

In blatant victim blaming fashion, two common errors are made: the extreme fearfulness (paranoia) and confusion created by repeatedly experiencing violence are misdiagnosed as psychiatric symptoms, and / or the woman is diagnosed as having a character disorder, which is seen as a *predisposition* for the violence that occurs. Thus the victimized woman is viewed either as "crazy," with her tales dismissed as ravings, or as inadequate and provoking the violence in her life. Either way, she is clearly a loser in the mental health care delivery system.

Incorrect diagnosis leads to the question of whether any diagnosis ought to be used at all. The "bible" for the mental health delivery service is the *Diagnostic and Statistical Manual of Mental Disorders (DSM-III)*. Kaplan (1983), in a feminist critique of the diagnostic procedures of the DSM-III, raises a critical issue: "Masculine-based assumptions about what behaviors are healthy and what behaviors are crazy were codified in DSM-II and are now codified in DSM-III, and thus influence and will continue to influence treatment rates" (p. 788). Kaplan also addresses the profound dilemma, faced by mental health professionals, namely how to judge "when society should be labeled as 'unjust' and when an individual should be labeled as 'crazy' " (p. 789).

As a feminist therapist, I have advocated focusing on the implications of any diagnostic label: treating the *source* of the problem, not merely the *symptoms* (Rosewater, 1984). Nonetheless, in our current mental health system, DSM-III is a fact of life and a basis for frequent misdiagnosis of battered women. (If any diagnosis is appropriate at all, the one that most accurately describes the dynamics of battered women is posttraumatic stress disorder.)

Combating misdiagnosis *is* a feminist issue. Hence I have argued that personality assessments can and ought to be interpreted in a feminist fashion. Like the Supreme Court justices, we must use a basis of standardization, but, like them, we must also use our own judgment and discrimination, which are influenced by existing cultural values (Rosewater, 1985a). In addition, feminist interpretation also involves sharing the test results with the client and incorporating her feedback as part of the test results.

The test for which I have developed feminist interpretations and used in my research is the Minnesota Multiphasic Personality Inventory (MMPI), which is the most widely used personality assessment in the country. Such an interpretation strengthens our ability to be effective advocates—an indispensable part of feminism.

The MMPI

The MMPI is a personality inventory consisting of 566[1] self-reference true and false questions. According to Hathaway and McKinney (1967), who first published the MMPI in 1943, "Subjects sixteen years of age or older with at least six years of successful schooling can be expected to complete the MMPI without difficulty" (p. 9). The test, based on a sixth grade reading level (Hanes, 1953), usually takes an hour to an hour and a half to complete. Originally the MMPI was developed to be an objective aid in determining diagnostic assessment and severity of psychological symptoms. As used today, the MMPI is described by

Hathaway and McKinney (1967) as "designed to provide an objective assessment of some of the major personality characteristics that affect personal and social adjustment" (p. 7).

The MMPI consists of 10 clinical scales, each of which assesses a different aspect of behavioral functioning: Scale 1 measures somatizing, the converting of psychological distress into physical symptoms; Scale 2 measures depression; Scale 3 measures repression, the tendency to "sit on" one's feelings and keep them inner rather than outer directed; Scale 4 measures anger, both with others and with ourselves; Scale 5 measures stereotypic masculine or feminine behavior, indicating how closely an individual conforms to such stereotypes; Scale 6 measures fearfulness or paranoia; Scale 7 measures anxiety; Scale 8 measures confusion in thought processes and feelings of being overwhelmed; Scale 9 measures the activity level of an individual, the tendency to be slow or fast paced; and Scale 0 measures introversion/extroversion, how comfortable or uncomfortable an individual is with others. All of the Clinical Scales (except 1 and 7) have subscales (the Harris-Lingoes subscales for Scales 2, 3, 6, 8, and 9 and the Serkownek subscales for Scales 5 and 0) that break down the behavior measured into more exact descriptors. For example, Scale 2, which measures depression, is broken into five subgroups that measure different aspects of depressive affect: feeling sad, being slowed down, not feeling well physically, not thinking clearly, and ruminating.

There are also four Validity Scales that detect devious test-taking attitudes: the number of questions left unanswered (?), how favorably one presents him/herself (L), how confused one presents oneself (F) and how defensively one presents oneself (K).

In addition to the Clinical and Validity Scales, there are numerous Research Scales, six of which were used in this research. These six research scales measure anxiety (A), repression (R), ego strength (ES)—how well an individual feels able to cope, overcontrolled hostility (O-H), the tendency to be abusive with alcohol or drugs (McAndrews Alcoholic Index, Mc/Al) and acceptance of passivity (AP).

Raw scores on the scales of the MMPI are converted to T-scores having a mean of 50 and a standard deviation of 10. Scores over a T-score of 70 are considered statistically significant, because they are two standard deviations above the mean. The MMPI scales are listed in a special coded score listing the highest to lowest clinical scales. An MMPI profile is usually the first three (highest three) of these clinical scales, which is known as the 3-point code type. A composite MMPI profile is one that averages the profiles of members of a common group, like male alcoholics or chronic schizophrenic women (see, for example, Lanyon, 1968).

Using the MMPI with Battered Women

One criticism of research done with women is that there is patriarchal bias in the ways in which questions about women are posed (Westcott, 1979). Domestic violence research has also been criticized for its tendency to "isolate as deviant not only wife-beating, but also beaten wives" (Wardell et al., 1983, p. 71). My research sought to change basic assumptions. Rather than asking, "Are battered women crazy?," I was exploring *what* battered women looked like, so that whatever data emerged for battered women could be used to inform other mental health workers about characteristics that battered women showed on the MMPI.

Much of the literature on domestic violence is consistent with a feminist analysis with its focus on the power disparity in a patriarchal culture and the resultant physical and sexual victimization of women (Dobash & Dobash, 1977; Freeman, 1977; Martin, 1976, 1977; Smith & Caplan, 1980; Straus, 1974, 1980; Walker, 1979, 1984). Wardell et al. (1983), however, are strongly critical of much of the literature on battered women, saying "underneath the new analyses and good intentions flourish the same misogynist assumptions the literature believes it attacks" (p. 70). They claim that the sole focus on the battered woman and the assumption that battered women differ from "officially un-battered women" is another kind of sexism that contains "an a priori assumption of victim-blaming" (pp. 77-78).

This kind of misogynist thinking is exemplified in the two previous studies using the MMPI to study battered women. Palau (1981, Note 1) chose to use the Masochism Scale in her preliminary research. Such choice reflects, in my opinion, Palau's inexperience with the MMPI and her stereotyped image of battered women. More recently, Gellman, Hoffman, Jones, and Stone (1984), having administered the MMPI to a control group of 10 battered women and a control group of 10 nonbattered women, concluded, "Women in abusive relationships manifest, to some extent, disordered personalities. Consequently, they must be treated in conjunction with the abuser to bring about changes in the relationship" (p. 603). These authors (two of whom are women) imply that pathology produces battered women, rather than understanding that violence produces pathology. Such research is an excellent illustration of a priori victim blaming (Wardell et al., 1983).

Another kind of victimization of battered women, which is not addressed much in the literature, is the relationship between violence and alleged mental illness. I have argued (Rosewater, 1985b) that DSM-III's behavioral descriptors for schizophrenic disorders and borderline personality disorders match the characteristics found for battered women. It is likely that many battered women have been and continue to be misdiagnosed. Further, the relationship between violence and the development of mental illness needs to be studied. Carmen, Rieker, and Mills (1984) have tried to look retrospectively at the relationship between psychiatric illness and victims of violence. They conclude that the complexity of the victim to patient process needs to be further examined, with the major focus in treatment being to help victims become survivors.

My research sought to determine if an MMPI profile existed for battered women. In addition, this research sought to determine whether the composite profile for psychotic women also fits battered women, since there are many commonalities between battered women and psychotic women: confusion, fearfulness, and feeling overwhelmed (Roy, 1978, Davidson, 1978). Because there is previous research to indicate that Blacks score differently on some MMPI scales (Baughman & Dalstrom, 1972; Erdberg, 1970; Gynther, Laschar, & Dalstrom, 1978; Harrison & Kass, 1968), this research also sought to explore whether the commonality of battering is a more important variable than is race.

Methodology

Subjects

The subjects consisted of 118 battered women, all but 12 in currently abusive situations. These women, 58 white, 54 black, and 4 Hispanic, ranged in age from 17 to 53. The subjects consisted of four groups: Group I (N = 50), battered women from Women Together (a battered woman's shelter); Group II (N = 29), battered women from the Family Violence Program (aimed at early intervention with domestic violence cases); Group III (N = 27), battered women from the Witness Victim Service Center (aimed at victim advocacy); and Group IV (N = 12), formerly battered women who had been clients of these agencies.

I met with over half of these women for a minimum of 30 minutes each. Almost all the women were afraid that they were "crazy"; they were amazed that I understood what was happening in their lives. What was most outstanding was these women's alienation—from themselves and from others—and their pessimism about getting their lives together.

As a researcher, a clinician, and a woman, I left those sessions feeling frustrated. One woman especially touched me: She was one of the few formerly battered women. She had been shot by her husband six times, four bullets aimed at her, the last two at her young son, whose body she shielded with her own. The man was given *six months* in jail. She divorced him, had a restraining order, and had moved to another county. A few weeks before our interview she had seen her ex-husband on her property and called the police, who replied, "We can't help you. He hasn't done anything yet." When I asked the woman what she was going to do, she replied bitterly, "I bought a gun. Nobody's going to take care of me. If he comes back, I'm going to use my gun."

Additional Data

In addition to the demographic information, the following information about the subjects was also collected: amount of time in the relationship, amount of time battered, severity rating of the battering (on a scale of 1-7), injury outcome, act itself, and frequency of battering. Included on this sheet was the Injury Severity Rating (adapted from Frieze, Knoble, Zomir, & Washington, 1980). Frieze et al. devised this 7-point rating scale to reflect the need to measure the severity of violence by the amount of psychological trauma as well as physical trauma. This psychological trauma is dependent on the level of violence in the batterer's overt behavior, which they labeled *Violent Action,* as differentiated from the level of physical damage done to the woman, which they labeled *Violent Hurt.* The higher the rating (on a 1- to 7-point rating scale), the more severe or constant the behavior. My original intention was to combine the Violent Action and Violent Hurt ratings into one overall rating, figuring that the amount of violence used and the amount of damage done would be congruent. I soon found, however, that there was not always a consistent relationship between the amount of force used and the amount of damage done. For instance, a man could hold a woman at gun point for hours (a high Violent Action), but actually cause no physical damage (a low Violent Hurt). On the other hand a man could shove a woman (a low Violent Action) and she could strike her head on a table and suffer a severe concussion (a high Violent Hurt). It was decided, therefore, to use both rating scales, and to use each one as a separate variable in the data treatment.

In addition to the Injury Severity Rating, I devised a 6-point scale to describe the frequency of battering, with a higher number being indicative of greater frequency (with a range of "less than every 2 years" to "more than once a week").

Procedure

On intake at Women Together, the Family Violence Program and the Witness Victim Service Center, women were requested to take the Minnesota Multiphasic Personality Inventory. They were given a cover sheet explaining why they were being asked to take the test; no woman was required to take the test nor denied any services if she refused. Formerly battered women (at least a year of no battering) were recruited if they made contact with the agency during the time of the research. While attempts were made to contact other formerly battered women, the necessity of keeping their whereabouts hidden made it exceptionally difficult to find women in this category.

A one-way ANOVA was run across groups on all 72 variables to check the viability of a "battered women" profile in various settings. A correlation study of the variables was done to determine if the length of time battered, the frequency of the battering, the amount of the violent action, or the amount of violent hurt affected the elevation of the MMPI profiles.

You Should Have Done It Better

The biggest criticism that has been made of my research is that I did not have a control group. However, because the MMPI is a normed test, I do not believe I needed a control group. The purpose of my research was to see if a pattern emerged for battered women on the MMPI and to see if there was a correlation between clinical scale elevation and the abuse variables (length of time battered, frequency of the battering, and severity of the battering). This correlational study was an attempt to determine the linkage between experiencing violence and the behavioral consequences of violence.

I have also been criticized for using a composite MMPI profile. The argument against such composite profiles is that in averaging the scales, the true nature of the diversity of the profiles is lost. There is, however, a precedent for using MMPI composite profiles. Lanyon (1968) presents 297 mean profiles of wide ranging diagnostic and behavior groups. Further, because of my concern about women not feeling coerced about taking the MMPI, I did not ask the agencies to keep track of the women who chose not to take the test. In retrospect, this statistic would have proven a useful one to have. I believe that it is difficult for those not involved with working with violence to understand that safety first is always a priority. Were I to replicate this research I would have a simple data sheet that would list why someone did not take the test.

An additional criticism of my research is that its sole focus on battered women makes it sexist (Wardell et al., 1983). While I agree with Wardell and her associates that the assumption that battered women are different from "officially un-battered women" is sexist, I believe there is a strong need for research such as my own to dispel misogynist myths and to enlighten the mental health profession about the dangers of misdiagnosis (Rosewater, 1985b). Wardell et al. focus on *what* research is done; I would focus on *how* that research is used.

An MMPI Profile for Battered Women

This research sought to find if there was a "battered woman's MMPI profile." A one way ANOVA was used to determine the mean score for each MMPI scale used. As can be seen from Table 9.1 (which presents the mean and standard deviation for all MMPI scales used and the supplementary variables), the highest mean score (all mean scores are MMPI T-scores) for Groups I, II, and III is Scale 4, which measures anger. The second highest mean score for Groups I and II is Scale 8, which measures confusion, while the second highest mean score for Group II is Scale 6, which measures fearfulness or paranoia. The third highest mean score for Groups I and II is Scale 6, and the third highest mean score for Group III is Scale 8.

MMPI results are usually presented as a 3-point profile (the highest three scales in descending order). The MMPI code type for Groups I and II is 486, and the code type for Group III is 468. These code types, for practical interpretation purposes, are the same (see Figure 9.1 for the Currently Battered Women Composite Profile).

The 468 profile as a general type has been described by Lachar (1973) as follows:

TABLE 9.1
MMPI Means and SD: All Groups

	Group I		Group II		Group III		Group IV	
	$\overline{X}$	SD	$\overline{X}$	SD	$\overline{X}$	SD	$\overline{X}$	SD
Age	20.16	6.23	28.70	7.55	31.00	7.05	34.08	10.86
Violent action	4.68	1.30	4.31	1.39	4.66	1.44	5.25	1.42
Violent hurt	4.68	0.95	4.58	1.18	4.40	1.44	5.16	1.19
? (Cannot-say)	50.04	0.28	50.41	2.22	50.03	0.19	50.00	0
Scale L	52.06	6.93	50.20	7.82	51.55	7.86	51.08	7.62
Scale F	68.18	12.79	67.03	14.49	64.29	13.48	60.58	12.36
Scale K	47.08	7.72	48.44	6.92	48.88	10.80	51.91	8.73
Scale A	59.16	9.29	59.20	9.90	56.48	11.64	54.33	13.28
Scale R	47.14	9.51	48.96	9.12	48.77	9.26	49.08	8.59
Scale ES	38.70	9.53	41.89	12.32	43.25	13.18	44.75	8.71
Scale 1	61.46	14.49	63.06	12.17	62.59	16.97	59.25	5.16
Scale 2*	66.46	13.32	70.48	13.46	66.00	17.24	56.75	10.09
Scale 3	64.36	12.45	68.20	10.54	68.18	14.82	62.50	8.15
Scale 4	72.84	11.60	73.20	12.17	71.77	11.51	65.83	15.33
Scale 5	49.50	8.28	49.79	9.34	47.33	7.65	45.33	8.71
Scale 6	69.94	11.36	71.96	12.75	69.29	13.54	61.91	16.27
Scale 7	65.56	9.76	66.79	11.83	63.40	11.84	58.00	11.49
Scale 8	70.34	13.66	72.24	14.03	68.88	14.48	68.41	14.64
Scale 9	68.08	11.04	63.31	10.47	63.44	9.77	62.66	11.98
Scale 0	59.82	8.82	59.93	9.77	58.37	13.41	55.75	10.73

*Difference across groups significant at .05 level.

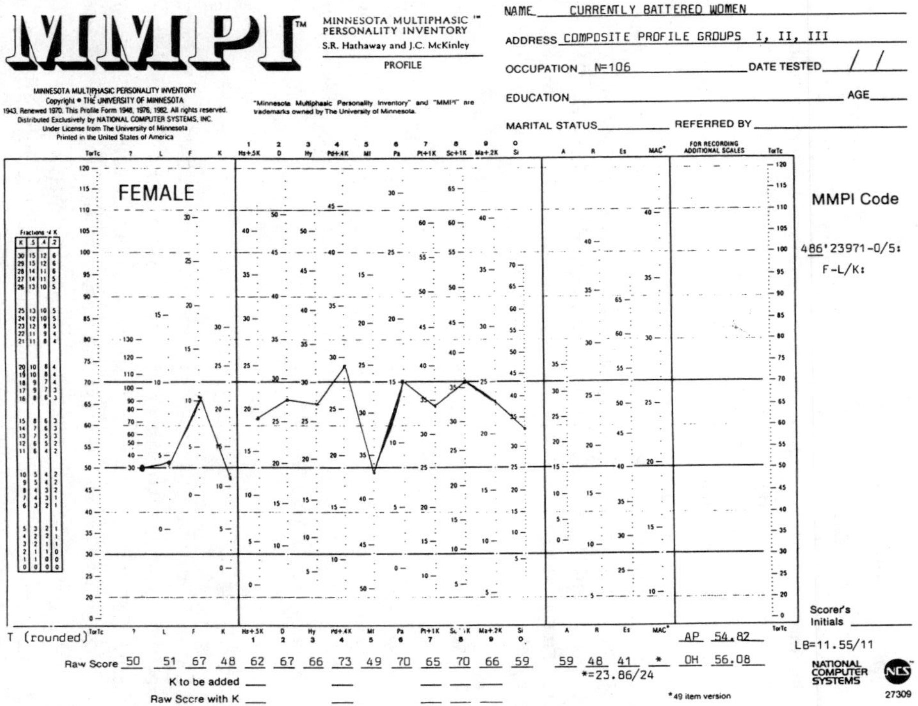

Figure 9.1 Currently Battered Women Composite Profile

This profile suggests a chronic emotional disturbance, most likely a character disorder or paranoid type of schizophrenia. Patients with such profile types are described as being evasive and defensive about admitting psychological conflicts and as being generally hostile, irritable and suspicious in their relationships with other people. They are easily hurt by criticism and tend to suffer from ideas of reference. However, their typically extrapunitive ways of dealing with frustration do not prevent them from being quite tense, nervous and anxious. They can be very demanding, in a narcissistic and egocentric way, for attention, affection and sympathy from others. Inner conflicts about sexuality are often present and are likely to be responsible, among others, for their characteristically poor marital adjustment.

Psychiatric treatment of any kind does not seem to help these patients very much, and the interviews are made difficult by the patient's tendency to rationalize and be argumentative, and by their deep-seated resentfulness to authority and to anything that can be construed as a demand. Their range of response to disagreeable therapeutic measures goes from passive resistance to aggressive dependency and open defiance and hostility (p. 82).

I present this description, *not because I believe it applies to the battered women's profiles collected in this research,* but because I think it is important to present how a standard clinical interpretation might be made about such women as were subjects of this study, *which judgment would be clinically inappropriate.*

Interpreting the Profile

The 3-point mean MMPI profile found for currently battered women indicates that battered women are angry. However this anger, rather than being directed outward, is retroflected and directed inward, as shown by the fact that the highest subscale elevation for Scale 4 was self-alienation. In addition, battered women are confused, overwhelmed by the violence in their lives. This confusion is manifested by difficulty in thinking clearly and in getting mobilized. Further, battered women are fearful. The highest subscale of Scale 6 for all three groups is Ideas of External Influence, which measures the belief that "someone is out to get me."

Scales on the MMPI can be significantly low as well as significantly high. Two scales were exceptionally low for the currently battered women tested: those that measure intactness (K), how strong an individual feels internally, and ego strength (ES), how well an individual feels able to cope, indicating that battered women feel internally weak and pessimistic about their ability to cope.

The currently battered women did not score as typically passive, nor did they have high mean scores on the scale that measures acceptance of passivity. Of the 106 currently battered woman, 56 had significant elevation on the MacAndrews Alcoholic Index, indicating that chemical abuse is a salient concern for currently battered women.

Group II also had a significant mean elevation on Scale 2, which measures depression. While none of the groups of currently battered women had expected elevations on Scale 3, which measures repression, as Palau (1981) has found in preliminary research, there was elevation on the subscale of Lassitude-Malaise, which measures a depressive component of slowing down.

The battered woman's profile indicates a reactive behavior set to being a victim of violence, which includes anger, confusion, fearfulness, weakness, and a sense of pessimism.

The MMPI Profile for
Formerly Battered Women

Formerly battered women (Group IV) had a three-point MMPI mean profile of 849. Formerly battered women tend to have similar configurations (especially on the subscales) but lower elevations than the currently battered women. The greatest difference between formerly battered women and currently battered women seems to be less alienation and less feeling of inferiority. Formerly battered women described themselves as more passive than did the currently battered women, but, like currently battered women, were less willing to be as passive as they described themselves. While formerly battered women feel more intact than currently battered women, they share the feeling of pessimism about being able to cope, but to a lesser degree. Of the 12 formerly battered women, 5 had significant elevation on the MacAndrew's Alcoholic Index. Overall, 51.69% of all the battered women in the study had the potential to be chemically abusive, as measured by the usual criteria.

Impact of Race on Research Results

Race proved to be a relatively unimportant variable in terms of defining differences in this sample. Although research (Erdberg, 1970) has indicated that Blacks and Whites have significant differences on

Scales F, K, 4, and 8, none of these differences were found between Black and White battered women in this study. The only significant differences that were found were cultural. Black women in the sample were tougher, less passive, less willing to be passive, and more abusive with alcohol and/or drugs, all externalizing behaviors, while White women were more critical, more introverted, more passive, and more willing to be passive, all internalizing behaviors. In a society that is both sexist and racist, Black women are understandably tougher, but still vulnerable to sexual stereotypes and the resulting victimization.

Correlation Among Variables

Because this research aimed to see if any key variables affected the elevation or configuration of the MMPI profiles, a Pearson Correlation was run for each of the four groups separately and together. The five variables that were examined were age, violent action ratings, violent hurt ratings, amount of time battered, and frequency of battering.

The variable that has the most impact on clinical scale and subscale elevations is the frequency of battering. The higher frequency of battering has a positive correlation with elevations on the scales that measure somatizing and repression, as well as the scales that measure depression, paranoia, anxiety, confusion, and withdrawal. The fact that all but one of the subscales for both Scale 2, which measures depression, and Scale 8, which measures confusion, are positively correlated with the frequency of the battering demonstrates that battered women feel depressed and overwhelmed. In that process they develop somatic symptoms. In addition, battered women are fearful, with that fear escalating as the frequency of the beating rises. This is demonstrated by Scale 6, which measures fearfulness, being correlated at the .01 level of significance and the subscale Ideas of External Influence at the .001 level of significance.

Distinguishing the
Battered Woman's Profile
From a Chronic Schizophrenic Profile

I compared a composite mean profile of the women in the battered women study (N = 118) with a "cookbook" chronic (female) schizophrenic profile (N = 133) from Lanyon (1968). Since only the clinical and validity scales are used in Lanyon's book, it was not possible to compare differences in research scales or any of the subscales. Because of the similarities between these two profiles, it is essential that the clinician keep in mind that *these two profiles may be indistinguishable;* thus the clinician must determine if what appears to be a schizophrenic woman is not, in fact, a battered woman by checking to see if her fearfulness and confusion are related to some current domestic violence in her life. It is also possible that a woman is schizophrenic *and* battered. It is likely that some women previously diagnosed as schizophrenic may have been better identified as battered women.

What the MMPI measured for the currently battered women were reactive states, not character traits, of battered women. The elevation on anger is a natural reaction to brutalization. In a society that does not give permission to women to express their anger directly, it is not surprising that battered women tend to retroflect their anger and develop feelings of alienation. This sense of alienation is culturally cultivated by the expectation that it is a woman's responsibility to "take care of her man." Women who experience violence from their men feel that somehow they have failed. Batterers heighten this sense of failure by blaming the women for their violence ("I wouldn't have hit you if . . .").

Elevation on the clinical scale that measures confusion on the MMPI indicates that an individual is feeling overwhelmed. The currently battered women in my research sample felt overwhelmed. The subscale elevation indicates that the violence in their lives affects their ability to think clearly and drains their energy. Confusion is a consequence of, not a precursor to, violence.

It is not surprising that the currently battered women in my research sample had elevations on the scale that measures paranoia/fearfulness. The fearfulness developed by battered women is also reactive and appropriate. Paranoia is clinically a measure of fearfulness without basis. Battered women, however, have good reason to be fearful. The fact that the level of fearfulness rises in correlation to the frequency of battering indicates that the violence causes the paranoia, not that paranoia causes violence.

The kind of victim-blaming that says that women are passive recipients of violence is belied by the finding that the women did not score as stereotypically feminine (passive), nor did they have high mean scores on acceptance of passivity. In other words, these women neither described themselves as passive, nor were they willing to be passive.

The pessimism currently battered women feel about their ability to cope and about their inner strength are also consequences of violence.

Despite the active attempts they make to protect themselves, their inability to be safe creates that sense of hopelessness. Browne (1987), in a study of battered women who killed, found that of seven variables that predicted lethality, all but one of these was based on the batterer's behavior.

Conclusion

This present study found both that violence intensifies psychological dysfunction and that battered women appear similar to schizophrenic women on a major clinical diagnostic tool. Battered women are also frequently misdiagnosed as borderline personality disorders (Rosewater, 1985b). Research on domestic violence needs to explore the impact of violence on mental health. Clearly the traits measured for currently battered women on the MMPI are reactive states, not character traits. We need to question how psychiatric labels are being applied to victims of violence, further victimizing them. Sadly, this process highlights the failure of the mental health profession to understand that illness lies less in the individual than in the society.

NOTE

1. The MMPI actually consists of 550 items, 16 of which are repeated. The repetition of the 16 items was to ensure the accuracy of computer scoring, when such scoring was first introduced.

REFERENCES

American Psychological Association. (1980). *Diagnostic and statistical manual of mental disorders* (3rd ed.). Washington, DC: Author.

Baughman, E. E., & Dalstrom, W. G. (1972). Racial differences on the MMPI. In S. S. Guterman (Ed.), *Black psychotherapy model: Personality patterns of Black Americans*. Berkeley: Glendessary.

Browne, A. (1987). *When battered women kill*. New York: Free Press.

Carmen, E. H., Reiker, P. P., & Mills, T. (1984). Victims of violence and psychiatric illness. *American Journal of Psychiatry, 141*(3), 378-383.

Davidson, T. (1978). *Conjugal crime: Understanding and changing the wifebeating pattern*. New York: Ballantine.

Dobash, R. E., & Dobash, R. P. (1977). Love, honour and obey: Institutional ideologies and the struggle for battered women. *Contemporary Crisis, 1*(4), 403-415.

Erdberg, S. P. (1970). MMPI differences associated with sex, race, and residence in a southern sample. (Doctoral dissertation, University of Alabama, 1969). *Dissertation Abstracts International,* (University Microfilms No. 340 5236B)

Freeman, M. D. (1977). Le vice anglais?—Wife battering in English and American law. *Family Law Quarterly, 11*(3), 199-251.

Frieze, I.H., Knoble, J., Zomir, G., & Washburn, C. (1980, March). *Types of battered women.* Paper presented at the annual research conference of the Association of Women in Psychology, Santa Monica, CA.

Gellman, M. T., Hoffman, R. A., Jones, M., & Stone, M. (1984). Abused and non-abused women: MMPI profile differences. *Personnel and Guidance Journal, 62,* 601-604.

Gynther, M. D., Lachar, D., & Dahlstrom, W. G. (1978). Are special norms for minorities needed? Development of an MMPI F scale for Blacks. *Journal of Consulting and Clinical Psychology, 46*(6), 1403-1408.

Hanes, B. (1953). Reading ease and MMPI results. *Journal of Clinical Psychology, 15,* 350-353.

Harrison, R. J., & Kass, E. H. (1968). Differences between Negro and White pregnant women on the MMPI. *Journal of Consulting Psychology, 10,* 262-270.

Hathaway, S. R., & McKinney, J. C. (1967). *Minnesota multiphasic personality inventory manual.* New York: Psychological Corporation.

Kaplan, M. (1983). A woman's view of DSM-III. *American Psychologist, 38*(7), 786-792.

Lachar, D. (1973). *The MMPI: Clinical assessment and automated interpretation.* Los Angeles: Western Psychological Services.

Lanyon, R. I. (1968). *A handbook of MMPI group profiles.* Minneapolis: University of Minnesota Press.

Martin, D. (1976). *Battered wives.* New York: Pocket Books.

Martin, D. (1977). Society's vindication of the wife-beater. *Bulletin of the American Academy of Psychiatry and the Law, 5*(4), 391-401.

Palau, N. (1981, August). *Battered women: A homogeneous group? Theoretical considerations and MMPI data interpretation (preliminary findings).* Paper presented at the annual meeting of the American Psychological Association, Los Angeles.

Rosewater, L. B. (1982). *The development of an MMPI profile for battered women.* Unpublished doctoral dissertation, Union Graduate School.

Rosewater, L. B. (1984). Feminist therapy: Implications for practitioners. In L. E. Walker (Ed.), *Women and mental health policy.* Newbury Park, CA: Sage.

Rosewater, L. B. (1985a). Feminist interpretations of traditional testing. In L. E. Rosewater & L. E. Walker (Eds.), *Handbook of feminist therapy: Women's issues in psychotherapy.* New York: Springer.

Rosewater, L. B. (1985b). Schizophrenic, borderline or battered? In L. B. Rosewater & L. E. Walker (Eds.), *Handbook of feminist therapy: Women's issues in psychotherapy.* New York: Springer.

Rosewater, L. B. (1987). A critical analysis of the proposed self-defeating personality disorder. *Journal of Personality Disorders 1*(2), 190-195.

Roy, M. (1978). *Battered women: A psychosociological study.* New York: Van Nostrand Reinhold.

Ryan, W. (1976). *Blaming the victim.* New York: Vintage.

Smith, S. M., & Caplan, H. (1980). Some aspects of violence in families. *International Journal of Family Psychiatry, 1*(2), 153-166.

Straus, M. A. (1974). Cultural and social organizational influences on violence between family members. In R. Price and D. Barried (Eds.), *Configurations: Biological and cultural factors in sexuality and family life.* New York: Lexington.

Straus, M. A. (1980). Victims and aggressors in marital violence. *American Behavioral Scientist, 23*(5), 681-704.

Walker, L. E. (1979). *The battered woman.* New York: Harper & Row.

Walker, L. E. (1984). *The battered woman's syndrome.* New York: Springer.

Wardell, L., Gillespie, D., & Leffler, A. (1983). Science and violence against women. In D. Finkelhor, R. J. Gelles, G. T. Hotaling, & M. J. Straus (Eds.), *The dark side of families.* Newbury Park, CA: Sage.

Westcott, M. (1979). Feminist criticism of the social sciences. *Harvard Educational Review, 49*(4), 422-430.

10

Survivors of Terror

Battered Women, Hostages, and the Stockholm Syndrome

DEE L. R. GRAHAM
EDNA RAWLINGS
NELLY RIMINI

An American male hostage in the 1985 TWA skyjacking was overheard saying at the end of the crisis, "I will be coming back to Lebanon. Hamiye [one of the jailers] is like a brother to me"(Watson et al., 1985). Why did Birgitta Lundblad, the Swedish bank teller, who had been held hostage for six days, visit one of her captors while he was in jail following the bank holdup? Why do many battered women "love" the men who batter them, finding it difficult to leave them? Why do battered women often defend their husbands, even after they have received severe beatings? Why do battered women often "forget" or minimize the life-threatening nature of the abuse they have suffered?

Although the experiences of hostages and battered women are seen as very different phenomena, in this chapter, we suggest that the psychological reactions of battered women can best be explained as a result of their experiences of being trapped in a situation that is very similar to that of hostages. Traditional psychological theories have suggested that battered women love and remain with the men who batter them because

AUTHORS' NOTE: The authors wish to thank Dr. Roberta Rigsby for her editorial assistance.

217

of female masochism. We suggest that their experiences can be better understood through the model of the Stockholm Syndrome, which has been developed to account for the paradoxical psychological responses of hostages to their captors (Dutton & Painter, 1981; Finkelhor & Yllö, 1985; Hilberman, 1980). In particular, when threatened with death by a captor who is also kind in some ways, hostages develop a fondness for the captor and an antipathy toward authorities working for their release. The captor may also develop a fondness for the hostages.

This model furthers a feminist analysis of battered women. First, it is a situation-centered as opposed to a person-centered approach. The model shows how the psychological characteristics observed in battered women resemble those of hostages, suggesting that these characteristics are the *result* of being in a life-threatening relationship rather than the *cause* of being in the relationship. Second, the model uses a power analysis that shows how extreme power imbalances between an abusive husband and battered wife, as between captor and hostage, can lead to strong emotional bonding.

However, the model does not explain why battered women are found primarily in the hostage position and men in the terrorist or captor position. The literature which suggests that women are socialized to be victims and males to be aggressors may be relevant to this issue. However, this literature has a "blame the victim" flavor as it suggests that the conditions for women's oppression are provided by internalized psychological traits rather than by the social context of women's lives. For this reason, we will use a feminist political analysis (Miller, 1976; Polk, 1981) in our examination of why women and not men are the primary victims of battering.

In order to detail carefully the relevance of the literature on hostages for understanding the experiences and psychological reactions of battered women, we will detail the conditions for the development of the Stockholm Syndrome, its underlying psychological mechanisms, and the principles of behavior for hostage survival. After highlighting similarities and differences between the situations of battered women and hostages, we will briefly discuss implications for treatment.

Conditions for the Development
of the Stockholm Syndrome

Four conditions give rise to the development of the Stockholm Syndrome:

(1) a person threatens to kill another and is perceived as having the capability to do so;
(2) the other cannot escape, so her or his life depends on the threatening person;
(3) the threatened person is isolated from outsiders so that the only other perspective available to her or him is that of the threatening person; and
(4) the threatening person is perceived as showing some degree of kindness to the one being threatened.

While these conditions typify circumstances surrounding the development of the Stockholm Syndrome for male hostages, there is an additional element of terror for female hostages with male captors: rape. Rape appears to be as common among women hostages (Barthel, 1981; Hearst & Moscow, 1982) as it is uncommon among men hostages (Elbrick, 1974; Fly, 1973; Pepper, 1978). There is always the threat of rape, even if it does not actually occur (Dortzbach & Dortzbach, 1975; Lang, 1974; Smith, 1985; an exception is Koob, 1982). The threat or occurrence of rape, especially, causes female hostages to become "numb" or "mindless" (Hearst & Moscow, 1982; Lovelace & McGrady, 1980). The women's bodies, servitude, emotions, and minds are the ransom paid for continued physical existence (Barthel, 1981; Lovelace & McGrady, 1980; McNulty, 1980). Moreover, even under coercion, romantic attachments may develop between male captors and female hostages (Moorehead, 1980). This should not be surprising since "normal" heterosexuality involves eroticizing dominance and the use of force (Dworkin, 1983; MacKinnon, 1983).

**Psychological Mechanisms
Underlying the Stockholm Syndrome**

While the social conditions under which the Stockholm Syndrome occurs are fairly well known, its psychological mechanisms are not well understood. The syndrome clearly involves the defense mechanism "identification with the aggressor," in which the victim incorporates the world view of the aggressor, as both hostages and battered women demonstrate.

To account for the emergence of the Stockholm Syndrome in victims of violent crimes who have prolonged contact with the criminal, Symonds (1982) identifies four stages of victimization. First is disbelief and denial. Second, reality sets in and psychological mechanisms emerge that operate together to produce the Stockholm Syndrome: traumatic psychological infantilism and pathological transference. Third, traumatic depression and posttraumatic stress disorders are experienced following release from captivity. Fourth, the trauma is resolved and integrated into the person's future behavior and lifestyle.

Generally, victims of violence do not exhibit uncontrolled panic behavior but develop a condition Symonds refers to as "frozen fright," a hysterical, dissociative phenomenon characterized by numbness or paralysis of affect. In this state, motor and cognitive behaviors appear normal. All of the victim's energy is focused on survival. She or he concentrates on the terrorist or abuser. Superficial compliance is observed. The condition of traumatic psychological infantilism causes the victim to cling to the very person who is endangering her or his life. A victim comes to recognize that the terrorist or abuser has the power of life or death over her or him. That recognition, coupled with the awareness that the terrorist has let her or him live, produces a profound attitude change. She or he comes to see the terrorist as a "good guy," which requires denying the life-endangering aspect of the terrorist or abuser. This is *pathological transference* (Symonds, 1982). McClure (1978) has identified this as a kind of "shell-shock" that affects the critical faculties of hostages and produces a conversion reaction. Symonds contends that captives are aware of the captor's predatory use of their suffering, and this awareness produces a "constipated rage." However, they suppress this rage while in captivity for survival reasons. Pathological transference may persist after the ordeal has ended. If so, the victim fears that any expression of negative behavior toward the former captor or abuser may result in terrible retribution. Though physically free of the captor, the victim is not psychologically free.

Dutton and Painter (1981) provide a psychological explanation that specifically addresses the battering situation. *Traumatic bonding* refers to strong emotional ties that develop between two people in a relationship where one person intermittently abuses and/or threatens the other. For traumatic bonding to occur, there must be a *power imbalance* in the relationship. Battering relationships are extreme versions of the traditional marriage relationship characterized by male dominance and female subordination (Walker, 1979). The subordinate wife in a battering relationship feels helpless and consequently develops unrealistically low self-esteem plus anxiety and depression. The dominant husband develops unrealistically inflated self-esteem and is dependent on the subordinate to maintain the feelings of power and self-aggrandizement. The dependency of the latter is masked until the relationship is disrupted in some way. Each partner comes to require the other to satisfy needs developed as a consequence of the power imbalance. Another essential aspect of traumatic bonding is *intermittent violence* alternating with warm, friendly, kind behavior. In such a situation, when there are no alternative relationships available, the victim will bond to the warmer, positive side of the abuser. The kind behaviors of the abuser temporarily terminate the aversive arousal state of the victim that the abuser has produced.

The advantages of the traumatic bonding theory are that it takes into account reciprocity between victim and abuser, and it evokes specific learning mechanisms. The significance of the differences in social context, duration of the abusive relationship, and extent of the violence for hostages and battered women is not completely understood at this time.

Principles of Behavior
for Hostage Survival

Through descriptions of skyjacking, barricade-hostages, and kidnap-imprisonment, McClure (1978) has sought "to formulate, from a wide variety of operational experience in hostage defense and hostage survival, a set of principles of behavior that might help future victims" (p. 21). Kidnap-imprisonment is the hostage situation most like that of the battered wife because it is long-term, although abused wives usually suffer for longer periods, and involves hostages being kidnapped and maintained singly. McClure suggests that it is critical for hostage survival in kidnap-imprisonment situations that victims respond to their captors' hostility by showing themselves to be individuals rather than symbols of a class or system. McClure (1978) warns that "the answer for the hostages is not to be completely passive and compliant toward the captor; this can be almost as serious an error in some cases as being too belligerent" (p. 42). Captors will respond with contempt if the hostages appear fawning or obsequious.

Further, McClure cautions that the hostage must control the extent of his identification with his captor, walking another fine line: "The problem with spontaneous identification under stress is that the hostages lose their sense of proportion and can become satellites of the person who threatens their life" (p. 43). McClure warns against the development of negative transference, or "the development of antipathy and even aggressive hostility by the hostages toward their captors," noting that "the result has always meant hardship for the hostage" (p. 42). The reasons are that, "such hostility liberates the captors from any guilt they might have felt in seizing the victim, . . . it justifies and intensifies any feeling of hate which the captors may attach to the hostage, . . . [and] it may also wound the ego of a basically insecure captor, prompting direct retaliation" (p. 42).

What works for hostages is similar to what works for battered wives. McClure's message to potential hostages is strikingly similar to the messages young women receive on relating to young men. In a sense, McClure is teaching femininity and avoidance of a concomitant problem, loss of sense of self. But in the case of battered women, these behaviors are often described by mental health professionals and legal personnel as masochistically motivated and as traits battered women possess apart from the context of their abuse. In contrast, the same behaviors engaged in by hostages are seen as situation-typical rather than trait-typical. Yet, it is probably more difficult for the battered woman (as opposed to the hostage) to avoid becoming a satellite of her captor because of the greater physical abuse meted out to her, the longer duration of her ordeal, her lack of outside support, an emotional attachment to her victimizer prior to the beginning of the abuse, and societal messages telling her that her situation is acceptable.

Similarities Between Hostages and Battered Women

Jean Baker Miller's (1976) discussion of characteristics of relationships marked by permanent inequality is relevant to the situations of hostages and battered women alike. As Miller notes, permanently unequal relationships are legitimized as "normal" and thus obscured. Further, she notes, "dominants are usually convinced that the way things are is right and good, not only for them but especially for the subordinates. All morality confirms this view, and all social structure sustains it" (p. 9). Thus the domination of the United States over less powerful countries is normalized, as is the domination of men over women. Terrorist acts against U.S. citizens by persons from less powerful countries are viewed as outrageous, but terrorist acts by men against women are viewed as "normal human relationships." It is within this context that similarities and differences between "political" hostages and battered women are viewed.

Similarities are grouped under six categories: (1) victimizers' sex; (2) victimizers' domination strategies; (3) victims as symbolic targets; (4) victims' active strategies for survival, (5) counterproductive victim responses; and (6) victims' survival as success.

Victimizers' sex. The victimizers of both battered women and hostages are usually male, in keeping with the male sex role.

Victimizers' domination strategies. Victimizers and wife batterers undermine psychological supports by physically removing victims from the presence of outsiders and by concealing from victims that outsiders are concerned for their welfare (Fly, 1973), because outsiders are enemies (Associated Press, 1984; Barthel, 1981; Bugliosi & Gentry, 1974; Hearst & Moscow, 1982; Lang, 1974) or at least not friends (Lovelace & McGrady, 1980). These strategies render victims even more helpless and dependent on their victimizers. Victimizers of hostages and battered women assert control and guarantee submission by threats of violence, which do sometimes end in death. At the same time, many hostages (Barthel, 1981; Dickey, 1985; Watson et al., 1985) and most battered women report that the kidnappers or batterers will show some kindness (Biderman, 1964; Walker, 1979). In contrast to battered women, McClure (1978) notes, "in most cases of hostage imprisonment by political terrorists, there is no attempt to abuse the victim beyond occasional taunting or teasing" (p. 31). But with female hostages and battered women alike, domination strategies also include sexual abuse.

Victim as symbolic target. Men as a group blame women as a group. Women are blamed for not keeping families together; for being too nurturing, too dominating, or too cold; for not being sexual enough; or for being too sexual. Women are blamed for being victims of lower pay, rape, and incest. Both the hostage and battered woman are symbolic targets for their abusers' frustrations, as they are held responsible for circumstances in the victimizer's life. In both wife abuse and hostage-taking, one goal is to send a message to all members of a group that no one in the group is safe, that any member of the group could become such a target at any time.

Victims' active strategies for survival. In relationships marked by permanent inequality, subordinates have to concentrate on survival, which requires avoiding direct, honest reaction to destructive treatment by dominants (Miller, 1976). Subordinates become highly attuned to the pleasure and displeasure reactions of dominants. As a result, they know much about dominants and less about themselves. They come to believe in their own inferiority and to imitate dominants. Miller also notes that "subordinates are described (by dominants) in terms of, and encouraged to develop, personal psychological characteristics that are pleasing to the dominant group. These characteristics form a certain familiar cluster: submissiveness, passivity, docility, dependency, lack of initiative, inability to act, to decide, to think, and the like. In general, this cluster includes qualities more characteristic of children than adults—immaturity, weakness, and helplessness. If subordinates adopt these characteristics they are considered well-adjusted" (p. 7).

Adoption of these submissive postures is an instinctive response to a life-threatening situation from which the victim cannot escape. It is a survival strategy that develops even when the victim cannot understand how the dominants label and encourage these behaviors. In other words, battered women and hostages are not passive. Both hostages and battered women actively develop strategies for staying alive. These include denial; attentiveness to the victimizer's wants; fondness for the victimizer, accompanied by fear; fear of interference by authorities; and adoption of the victimizer's perspective.

Both battered women and hostages use denial to get through their ordeals. Ferraro (1983) identifies several techniques of rationalization that battered women's shelters residents report having used to help them endure violence at home: the assumption that the batterer is a good man whose actions stem from problems that she can help him solve; denial that the batterer is responsible for the abuse, which instead is attributed to external forces; denial that abuse ever occurred; belief that she is the instigator of the abuse and thus deserves the punishment; denial that she would be able to survive without the batterer's support (emotional and/or practical); and belief that marriage and/or following the beliefs of her religion, which may tell her to obey her husband, are more important than her health.

Ochberg (1978) notes that "hostages successfully deny the danger engineered by the terrorists. Having separated this from awareness, they are overwhelmingly grateful to the terrorist for giving them life. They focus on the captor's kindnesses, and not his acts of brutality" (p. 162). According to McClure (1978), victims recognize that they must not antagonize their captors, though they normally would disapprove of them as criminals. To avoid feeling hypocritical, the victims subconsciously resolve their feelings by making "a sudden discovery: The armed captor is not really a villain at all; she or he is misunderstood. With this rationalization, the victims can be genuinely compassionate— thus serving their own vital interests—and be totally untroubled by any guilt feeling of the hypocrite" (pp. 40-41).

Both hostages and battered women feel fear as well as love, compassion, and empathy toward a captor who has shown them any kindness. In the case of battered women, the battering cycle described by Walker (1979) predicts that a build-up of tension in the batterer leads to outbursts of violence followed by tension reduction and often intense expressions of remorse and love. Following a beating, the battered woman is not only in physical pain but is feeling emotionally helpless and needy. The person most readily available to provide succor and support is the batterer. Thus she learns to depend on him to ease the emotional distress he has created. In the hostage situation, after the initial outburst of violence involved in hostage taking or kidnapping, the hostage is feeling frightened and vulnerable. Any acts of kindness by the captors will help ease the emotional distress they have created and will set the stage for emotional dependency of the hostage on the captors.

Hostages and battered women take on the perspective of their victimizers as a result of the power imbalance in the relationship and their isolation from alternative points of view and support for their own perspective. The message may be "driven in" through repetition. Battered women and hostages fear interference by authorities, an attitude promoted by captors. For battered women, resentment of interference can extend to family, friends, and neighbors as well as to police. They are scared that interference will amplify and bring on additional beatings. Among hostages, police intervention is feared because it could lead to a shoot out in which they could be killed (Fly, 1973). This fear, coupled with isolation, leads hostages to feel that their captors, rather than the police, have their best interest at heart (Lang, 1974).

Counterproductive victim responses. A number of counterproductive victim responses are observed among battered women and hostages: (1) denial of terror, anger and the perception of their victimizers as omnipotent people help to keep victims psychologically attached to their victimizers even after the latter have died, (2) high anxiety functions to keep victims from seeing available options, and (3) psychophysical stress responses develop (Hilberman, 1980; Ochberg, 1978).

Victims' survival as success. Hostages and battered women have succeeded, if they survive their captivity. This viewpoint is more often taken in the case of the hostage than in the case of the battered woman.

Since the latter is perceived as willingly subjecting herself to violence, she is seen as masochistic and thus a failure, even if she should find a way to escape her ordeal. As a hostage, Patty Hearst had public support until it appeared that she "chose" her captivity, at which time the public and the authorities (police, FBI) demanded her arrest for her involvement in illegal SLA activities.

Dissimilarities Between
Hostages and Battered Women

Although there are many similarities between battered women and hostages, there are important differences in their situations that also need to be elucidated and better understood. These dissimilarities reflect the politics of battering. Many women are in relationships with men who oppress and abuse them because of a patriarchal system that sanctions men's use of physical force against women as a means of keeping women as a class subordinate to men. The abusive context of many marriages contributes to the development of the Stockholm Syndrome in many battered women. But battered women differ from hostages in certain important respects: the victim's sex; the nature of the victim-victimizer relationship; and the presence of public concern.

Victim's sex. The typical hostage is male, while the typical battered spouse is female.

Victim-victimizer relationship. Several aspects of this relationship differ: the voluntary versus involuntary nature of the initial relationship for the victim, the time that the attachment began relative to the time that victimization began, the length of the period of victimization, the extent of violence inflicted on the victim, whether the victim versus others negotiate for her or his release, and whether the abuser gains or loses bargaining power by abusing his victim.

Marriage is allegedly a voluntary relationship with an intimate, while hostage-taking is an involuntary, coercive relationship with a stranger. While battered women usually love their batterers prior to the time that the abuse begins, hostages develop their attachments to their captors *after* their abuse begins. Battered women experience abuse in the context of a committed relationship whereas hostages suffer abuse at the hands of strangers. This difference suggests that in subsequent relationships, battered women, more than hostages, would have a difficult time trusting that they can choose intimate partners who will not abuse them.

Finkelhor and Yllö's (1985) findings indicate that rape by one's husband was experienced as worse than rape by a stranger because the women came to doubt their judgment in choosing intimate partners, had to live with their rapists, and felt unable to talk with others about the rapes and to get outside support. For analogous reasons, one would expect women to experience being held hostage by a spouse as worse than being held hostage by a stranger.

The ordeal of battered women often lasts for decades while hostages' ordeals are usually a matter of days, weeks, or, at most, months. Ochberg (1978) notes that it takes three to four days of captivity for the Stockholm Syndrome to emerge in hostages; after that, duration is not relevant. While most hostages are not themselves the victims of physical violence (McClure, 1978), battered women are and their physical abuse usually goes on for years, even decades. Thus it would seem that fear engendered by abuse is longer lasting and greater for battered women than for hostages.

A person may be taken hostage and maintained in captivity singly or in a group. The battered wife is maintained in isolation or with her children. The knowledge that others also are being abused could buffer the personalization, self-blame, and loss of self-esteem that occurs with victimization. The presence of other adults in the same situation would seem to diminish the psychological power of the victimizer to control the perspective-taking of the victim.

Outside concern. In the case of hostages, unlike that of battered women, outsiders are likely to negotiate and possibly win their release. In addition, media coverage of the hostages' plight serves to maintain a concerned, sympathetic public. While outside parties negotiate with terrorists, battered women negotiate with their batterers on their own behalf. Hostage negotiations are viewed as "high drama" (McClure, 1978), while the plight of battered women is viewed as a private affair involving personal choice. Hostages usually are released from their captivity by their hostage-takers or are rescued by the state. A battered woman, on the other hand, must find a way to leave her captivity more or less on her own.

Terrorists want broad media coverage of their kidnapping, threats, and violence. As a result, hostages may know that outsiders are negotiating for their release and that a concerned, interested public has not forgotten them, which improves their morale (Lang, 1974). Negotiation for their release does not depend on their proving they are the targets of physical violence nor that they did not desire or provoke it. On the other hand, unless battered women can prove that their batterers have subjected them to life-threatening violence, outsiders are often unwilling to intervene in family life to protect the women. Even when abuse is documented, friends, family, priests, counselors, and social service professionals often urge the battered woman to stay with her batterer.

So while the public and authorities are sympathetic to the plight of hostages, there is often little sympathy for battered women. Both governments and the public see hostages as victims with little control over their situations, though this was not the perception for Patty Hearst (1982), Linda Lovelace (1980), or Hope Masters (Barthel, 1981). Only those considered to be "political prisoners" are seen as blameless victims. From a feminist perspective, all female hostages and battered women are political prisoners. Battering, which includes physical and sexual violence, is a political act since it reinforces the existing power structure of male dominance (Barry, 1979).

In stark contrast to the sympathetic attitudes toward hostages are the "blame the victim" attitudes directed at battered women. Gentemann (1984) found that 20% of her randomly selected respondents reported in telephone interviews that a woman usually causes the beatings she receives. Those holding this belief were more likely to feel that wife abuse is justified than were those who rejected the belief. Women believing in traditional sex roles were more likely to justify a man beating his wife than were women with egalitarian sex role attitudes.

Governments attempt to capture hostage-takers and punish them. Batterers are rarely punished, even for decades of abuse, unless the woman or one of her children is killed. In fact, battered women who kill their batterers in self defense are usually the ones who are punished. In contrast, hostages who kill their hostage-takers are viewed as heroes.

Both battered women and hostages continue to feel emotionally attached to their victimizers long after they have separated. This attachment seems to be a combination of fear of and compassion for their victimizers. The way this continuing attachment is manifested differs for the two groups, however. Hostages are known to visit their captors while the latter are in prison (Lang, 1974) and to refuse to testify against them. Battered women often will drop charges against their batterers and return to them after leaving. Battered women who return often report doing so out of fear that they will be killed by their husbands if they do not. They also return based upon a belief that the batterer has reformed or that they can help him to reform. Hostages report fearing that their captors, even those who have been jailed, will return to capture them again (Lang, 1974). A battered woman often is hounded by her abuser for years after leaving him. This is not known to occur after hostage-imprisonment, however. Thus it is the behavior of the victimizer of battered women—not the battered women themselves—that often prevents the relationship from ending long after separation has occurred.

Directions for Further Research and Treatment Implications

Several elements of the Stockholm Syndrome as it applies to battered women that need to be further explored are: the role of rape in the development of the Stockholm Syndrome in female hostages and battered women; possible sex differences in the development of Stockholm Syndrome; possible psychological effects of differences in duration of captivity and actual versus threatened violence; reasons why hostages who bond with their captors are less likely to suffer physical harm, while this condition does not appear to protect battered women from continued abuse; posttraumatic stress disorders in hostages and battered women; and factors that enable women to leave battering relationships.

Although further research is necessary, what we now know about the parallels between battered women and hostages exhibiting the Stockholm Syndrome have treatment implications for the battered woman. Most importantly, awareness of the Stockholm Syndrome helps a battered woman to avoid blaming herself and to change her behavior once she is out of the violent situation.

Almost all researchers who study battered women report low self-esteem among them (see Walker, 1979, 1985). Low self-esteem also is seen in many hostages and thus appears to be the result, rather than the cause, of being helpless in an abusive situation (Dutton & Painter, 1981). Helping the battered woman to normalize her experience by viewing it within the context of the Stockholm Syndrome and to see her behavior as an adaptive way of surviving can help her recover her sense of power and her positive self-esteem. Helping her label her "hostage self" and "competent self" can also help.

Because of the strong emotional ties to the abusers that were forged under duress, victims often support the interests of the abusers at their own expense. To enable a battered woman to leave the life-endangering battering situation, it is essential to break the symbiotic bond between the battered woman and her abusive partner (Hilberman, 1980) after helping her create strong bonds with nurturing, non-abusive others. Understanding that such an intense addictive bond exists, the clinician can be more understanding of why it is difficult for the woman to leave the batterer and why she often returns. By framing her situation in the context of the Stockholm Syndrome and explaining some of the psychological mechanisms underlying it (e.g., traumatic bonding), the feminist therapist gives the battered woman an alternative perspective from which to view her plight. This may help her let go of the relationship at an emotional level. Reframing also gives the clinician an alternative to "masochism" as an explanation.

Dutton and Painter (1981) report that the loss of the relationship produces distress in battered women, and this pulls them back into the relationship. Helping the battered woman anticipate this reaction and exploring alternative means of dealing with this distress may prevent the puzzling relapses seen in battered women who have left the batterer and seem to be making good progress. Acknowledging the loss of the significant emotional relationship and giving the woman permission to mourn that loss also may be important in the letting-go process. In addition to letting go of the relationship emotionally, the battered woman needs to undergo an individuation process of seeing herself and her needs as separate from those of the batterer. She may need to develop different skills and coping mechanisms to survive outside of the relationship.

Additional issues that need to be addressed in therapy, with the battered woman include: repairing the lack of trust and fear of intimacy brought on by suffering abuse from the person she expected would love and protect her; repairing her lost sense of self by helping her to recognize her own feelings and perspectives and identify warning signs that her self, or voice, is not being supported by others; integrating negative and positive aspects of the abuser, since she cannot leave the abuser as long as she denies his violence and focuses solely on his positive side; breaking down her isolation as well as helping her to understand how the abuser used isolation to ensure her bonding to him; mastering her feelings of terror so she doesn't experience intrusive ideation, which is characteristic of posttraumatic stress disorder; and giving her a safe way to vent her rage to prevent it from being expressed psychosomatically.

The strong denial mechanisms observed in hostages and battered women are adaptive and help them survive their traumatic situations.

On the negative side, this denial, which is so intense that it can result in serious distortions in reality (Ferraro, 1983), covers the anger and intense rage produced by situations of helplessness and powerlessness. If this anger and rage erupt while the victim is at the mercy of the abuser, it could further escalate violence, resulting in more severe injury or death (Huston, 1984). When the hostage or battered woman is out of danger, this anger and rage need to be brought to awareness, expressed in a safe way, and integrated so that healing can occur.

Having the battered woman relive in fantasy some of her more painful experiences within the context of a safe therapeutic relationship can provide catharsis, desensitization, and integration. After repeatedly going through her painful memories and allowing all the suppressed emotions to emerge, the battered woman can be encouraged to imagine different responses that might not have been realistic or adaptive in the actual situation. It is not important that the fantasy be realistic, but that it be sufficiently vivid to evoke strong feelings, which can enhance feelings of mastery, control, and self-esteem in the victims following the fantasy experience.

Conclusion

In this chapter, we have demonstrated similarities in situations of hostages and battered women. Both groups are likely to develop the Stockholm Syndrome, a positive psychological bond with their captors or abusers and an antipathy toward outsiders working to win their release. Comparisons of the similarities and differences between these groups revealed greater empathy and societal support for hostages who, in contrast to battered women, seem to suffer less actual physical abuse and whose ordeals are more likely to be short term. Treatment implications for viewing the battered woman as a hostage exhibiting Stockholm Syndrome were explored. For therapists, seeing the battered woman as manifesting Stockholm Syndrome may help them be more understanding of why it is difficult for the woman to leave the batterer and why she often returns. For the battered woman, understanding the dynamics of the Stockholm Syndrome gives her an alternative perspective that may help her let go of the battering relationship at a cognitive and emotional level and prevent relapses.

From a feminist perspective, identifying the development of Stockholm Syndrome in battered women calls attention to their hostage status, a contextual condition that has been ignored in a sexist system that blames women for their own victimization. Even feminist analyses (e.g., Bayes, 1981; Smith, 1984) often fall into the conceptual trap of attributing the causes and maintenance of battering to men's and women's internalized sex-role traits. In fact, it may be that feminine traits are the result of Stockholm Syndrome—the conditions of which, to some degree, exist for all women in a patriarchal society. Whether or not women personally experience violence, the threat of violence is ubiquitous in their lives (Dworkin, 1983; Leidig, 1981; Polk, 1981; Rich, 1980). In a sense, then, all women are hostages to male terrorism (Barry, 1979; Brownmiller, 1975). The problem in wife abuse is not women's behavior but male violence. The defect that leads to wife abuse exists not in women but in patriarchal society.

REFERENCES

Associated Press. (1982, November 22). "Sex slave" says she was beaten, shocked. *Cincinnati Enquirer*, p. 13.

Barry, K. (1979). *Female sexual slavery.* New York: Avon.

Barthel, J. (1981). *A death in California.* New York: Dell.

Bayes, M. (1981). Wife battering and the maintenance of gender roles: A socio-psychological perspective. In E. Howell & M. Bayes (Eds.), *Women and mental health.* New York: Basic Books.

Biderman, A. D. (1964). Captivity lore and behavior in captivity. In G. H. Grosser, H. Wechsler, & M. Greenblat (Eds.), *The threat of impending disaster.* Cambridge: MIT Press.

Brownmiller, S. (1975). *Against our will: Men, women and rape.* New York: Simon & Schuster.

Bugliosi, V., with Gentry, C. (1974). *Helter skelter: The true story of the Manson murders.* New York: Norton.

Dickey, C. (1985, October 11). Klinghoffer died in power play. *Cincinnati Enquirer*, pp. A-1, A-16.

Dortzbach, K., & Dortzbach, D. (1975). *Kidnapped.* New York: Harper & Row.

Dutton, D., & Painter, S. L. (1981). Traumatic bonding: The development of emotional attachments in battered women and other relationships of intermittent abuse. *Victimology, 6,* 139-155.

Dworkin, A. (1983). *Right-wing women.* New York: Perigee.

Elbrick, C. B. (1974, March). *The diplomatic kidnappings: A case study in international terrorism.* Proceedings of an intensive panel at the annual convention of the International Studies Association, St. Louis. Milwaukee: Institute of World Affairs, University of Wisconsin.

Ferraro, K. J. (1983). Rationalizing violence: How battered women stay. *Victimology, 8,* 203-212.

Finkelhor, D., & Yllö, K. (1985). *License to rape: Sexual abuse of wives.* New York: Holt, Rinehart & Winston.

Fly, C. (1973). *No hope but God.* New York: Hawthorn Books.

Gentemann, K. M. (1984). Wife beating: Attitudes of a non-clinical population. *Victimology, 9,* 109-119.

Hearst, P. C., with Moscow, A. (1982). *Every secret thing.* New York: Pinnacle.

Hilberman, E. (1980). Overview: The "wife-beater's wife" reconsidered. *American Journal of Psychiatry, 137,* 1336-1347.

Huston, K. (1984). Ethical decisions in treating battered women. *Professional Psychology: Research and Practice, 15,* 822-832.

Koob, M. (1982). *Guest of the revolution.* Nashville: Thomas Nelson.

Lang, D. (1974, November 25). A reporter at large: The bank drama. *New Yorker,* pp. 56-126.

Leidig, M. W. (1981). Violence against women: A feminist-psychological analysis. In S. Cox (Ed.), *Female psychology: The emerging self.* New York: St. Martin's.

Lovelace, L., with McGrady, M. (1980). *Ordeal.* New York: Berkley.

MacKinnon, C. A. (1983). Feminism, Marxism, method, and the state: Toward a feminist jurisprudence. *Signs, 8,* 635-658.

McClure, B. (1978). Hostage survival. *Conflict, 1,* 21-48.

McNulty, F. (1980). *The burning bed.* New York: Bantam.

Miller, J. B. (1976). *Toward a new psychology of women.* Boston: Beacon.

Ochberg, F. (1978). The victim of terrorism: Psychiatric considerations. *Terrorism, 1,* 147-168.

Pepper, C. B. (1978). *Kidnapped! 17 Days of Terror.* New York: Harmony.

Polk, B. B. (1981). Male power and the women's movement: Analysis for change. In S. Cox (Ed.), *Female psychology: The emerging self.* New York: St. Martin's.

Rich, A. (1980). Compulsory heterosexuality and lesbian existence. *Signs, 5,* 631-660.

Smith, S. (1984). The battered woman: A consequence of female development. *Women & Therapy, 3,* 3-9.

Smith, W. E. (1985, December 9). Massacre in Malta. *Time,* pp. 42-44.

Symonds, M. (1982). Victim's responses to terror: Understanding and treatment. In F. M. Ochberg and D. A. Soskis (Eds.), *Victims of terrorism.* Boulder, CO: Westview.

Walker, L. (1979). *The battered woman.* New York: Harper Colophon Brooks.

Walker, L.E.A. (1985). Feminist therapy with victim/survivors of inter-personal violence. In L. B. Rosewater and L.E.A. Walker (Eds.), *Handbook of feminist therapy: Women's issues in psycho-therapy.* New York: Springer.

Watson, R., with Nordland, R., Stanger, T., Walcott, J., Warner, M. G., & Kubic, M. J. (1985, July 8). The hard road to freedom. *Newsweek,* pp. 17-20.

11

Beyond the "Duty to Warn"

A Therapist's "Duty to Protect" Battered Women and Children

BARBARA HART

Therapists[1] offering services to men who have assaulted or abused their women partners or children have begun to recognize a "duty to warn" possible victims of the violence the therapists believe will be perpetrated by their clients. Activists assert that, despite the recognition of this professional duty to disclose danger, counselors and educators working with batterers rarely invoke the duty to warn, although it could safeguard battered women and children from the violence that may be inflicted on them by the batterer/clients.

Perhaps the absence of disclosure of the risk of danger stems from a belief, prevalent among therapists, that any duty to warn arises only when a client specifically sets forth a plan to assault or kill a particular victim. Advocates for battered women disagree with this conclusion and strongly encourage expanded disclosure of the dangers that battering clients present to victims. Feminists further challenge therapists working with batterers to assume a broader "duty to protect" potential victims. The scope of this duty to protect should go well beyond the traditional obligation of warning.

In this chapter, I will explore the current legal and ethical standards, applicable to therapeutic practice, that are related to warning intended victims of dangers presented by clients. Next, I will examine the rationale for a broad duty to protect. Finally, I will explore three specific protection strategies that should be exercised by therapists to enhance the safety and empowerment of battered women and children—to protect identified victims—whose abusers are receiving therapeutic and educational intervention services.

Duty to Warn

Common law on the issue of a therapist's duty to warn is little more than 10 years old. The landmark case of Tarasoff v. Regents of the University of California[2] directs that if a therapist concludes or should have concluded that his or her patient presents a serious danger of violence to a third party, he or she incurs a duty to use reasonable care to both warn the intended victim of such danger and to protect the victim and third parties from the danger presented by the patient.

Tarasoff is a California case. However, it is largely followed in other states even where there may be no common or statutory law setting forth any obligation of a therapist to give such warnings or to take actions to prevent the foreseeable danger posed by a patient.

Most appellate courts that have had the opportunity to review this issue, while failing to outline criteria for defining the limits of the duty to protect, have held that when a therapist determines that his or her patient presents a serious danger of violence to another person, he or she is obliged to use reasonable care to protect the intended victim against the danger. Further, to discharge the obligation, the therapist should warn the potential victim.[3]

Liability for damages sustained by a victim may be assigned when a therapist has failed to warn the intended victim, when a warning by the therapist might have averted the harm inflicted on the victim, and when the therapist, exercising a reasonable degree of skill, had or should have had knowledge and care pursuant to the standards of his or her profession, reached a determination that his or her patient was a serious danger to another person (Wolfe, 1984).

The case law suggests that the therapist exercising his duty to warn the potential victim should not just warn the battered woman or child, but should also give notice to persons likely to apprise the victim of the threatened or potential danger promptly—for example, the police, the battered women's program, the potential victim's immediate family, and so on.

The most unsettled issue in the emerging legal doctrine on the therapist's duty to warn is the question of which potential victims are owed warnings. Many jurisdictions have held that a warning is owed not just to the specific or identified victim, but also to the persons foreseeably endangered by the client's behavior.[4] Some courts have restricted the class of persons owed the duty to "readily identifiable victims."[5] Other courts have determined that there is no obligation to warn victims when the actual victims were no more likely to be victimized by the patient than was the general public.[6] There is a conflict about whether a potential victim is owed the duty to warn when the victim knows of the patient's dangerous propensities, history, and previous violent acts.[7] A number of appellate courts have established a rule that a mere warning, by itself, might not discharge the duty if the warning was "unspecific and inadequate under the circumstances."[8]

Professional associations, including the American Medical Association, the American Psychiatric Association, and the American Psychological Association, have adopted ethical standards of practice that detail the therapist's obligations to potential victims of clients. The Principles of Medical Ethics (1984) of the American Medical Association provides that "where a patient threatens to inflict serious bodily harm to another person and there is a reasonable probability that the patient may carry out the threat, the physician should take reasonable precautions for protection of the intended victim, including notification of law enforcement authorities." The language of the other professional ethical guidelines suggests that the therapist's apprehension of potential danger by a client, not actual threats, creates the ethical duty to protect victims.

Although research has demonstrated that few therapists breach the confidentiality of communications made within the therapeutic relationship in order to warn potential victims of threats or danger, those therapists who issue warnings to potential victims almost never simply warn the victim. They also initiate notification of others or seek hospitalization of the patient. Therapists participating in a NIMH study indicated that the most crucial factor in evaluating the risk of danger posed by clients was the client's history of violent behavior. The more informed the therapist was about the client's history of violent behavior, the more equipped the therapist was to assess whether the client's state of mind, menacing behaviors, and threatening statements warranted disclosure to potential victims.

Despite the common law and professional standards mandating warnings, many therapists are reserved about disclosure of communications made by clients or of conclusions drawn from therapeutic situations about the potential danger posed by clients. They often raise two concerns: (1) The confidentiality of therapeutic relationships must be absolute for the client to seek services and to share fully of himself so as to benefit from therapy. They argue that this fundamental principle of therapeutic intervention is defeated by disclosure. Trust is violated, and the client is likely to terminate therapy or begin to communicate selectively. (2) Other therapists point out that the therapeutic gains for a patient in discovering and reviewing his rage and violent fantasies in treatment—his honesty in disclosure—should be supported by preserving confidentiality.

Nonetheless, the courts and professional associations that have considered these serious concerns have concluded that the societal interest in the safety of third parties (and sometimes the safety of client) outweighs the client's interest in absolute therapeutic confidentiality.

Few psychoeducational or treatment programs for batterers have established internal policies to address the legal and ethical constraints on client confidentiality posed by the risk of violence presented by battering clients. RAVEN,[9] a counseling and educational program for men who batter in St. Louis, Missouri, has developed a formal procedure to fulfill the duty to warn. It specifically informs clients, as follows:

> SAFETY INITIATIVES: RAVEN staff will reach out when we have a concern for (client) safety, the safety of your partner or the safety of children. This may take the form of phone calls to agencies, family members or authorities as seen necessary. You will always be informed about a Safety Initiative. An effort will be made to talk with you before we take an initiative of this kind, although, because of time constraints this may not always be practical.

Like RAVEN, the Reduce Abuse Program (RAP)[10] of the Family Service Association of Philadelphia informs all clients that any information shared with the program will be held confidential with the exception "of threats to another person's physical safety and any reports of child abuse." RAP's internal memo to clinicians points out that only serious threats of a severe nature will give rise to the duty to warn. In exercising the obligation, two courses of action are suggested. The first is to notify the woman of the threat or danger and to advise her of her need for protection. The clinician also refers her to legal resources and to the local shelter. The second procedure is to warn the battered woman and advise her about the possibility of an emergency involuntary commitment for her husband. RAP volunteers to assist her in pursuing this mental health treatment for the batterer. The second procedure is employed less often than the first. The policy recognizes the importance of supporting victims in making safety plans but does not preclude clinicians from taking definitive action to ensure the victim's safety.

Other programs working with batterers require that applicants execute broad releases to permit therapists to warn potential victims of danger or threats apprehended by intervention staff. The release form is frequently similar to that below.

Consent to
Warning of Victim

(Must be signed before attendance at first treatment session.)

Should I threaten or demonstrate an intent to violently assault the woman I battered or anyone else during the course of my participation in this program, I hereby authorize _____ (name of organization) and/or its agents or representatives to disclose my threats or conduct to my intended victim(s), the police and anyone else they deem necessary to protect potential victims from violent assault by me. I am not entitled to prior notice of this disclosure or warning.

I consent to this disclosure and agree that it shall remain in effect from this date and for the duration of my association with the program.

DATE:_____ Signature_____
                                        Witness_____

Rationale for "Duty to Protect"

Feminists and profeminists agree that the ultimate goal of our work with battered women, children from violent homes, and batterers is to end the violence and terrorist control inflicted by the batterers. While working toward this end, activists recognize that an essential interim goal is to protect the victims of male violence.

To meet these goals in the context of batterer treatment programs, activists conclude that the interests of battered women and children in safety and freedom from terrorism must be weighed as heavily in therapeutic interactions as the interests of the batterer in rehabilitation. This is not to say that each batterer's desire to transcend his past practices of tyranny and violence is incidental to the therapeutic or educational process. It is only to say that the needs of the battering client cannot be paramount in batterers' treatment programs.

To assure that the interests of potential victims of violence are sufficiently addressed by the program for men who batter, all procedures and practices must be evaluated from the perspective of whether they advance or endanger the safety of battered women and children. Do interventions seek as much to protect battered women and children as to help batterers?

Thus the mere warning of victims upon a conclusion that a batterer represents a serious danger does not suffice in achieving the balance between victim protection and batterer rehabilitation. Instead, all batterers' program policies and practices must specifically advance the safety interests of battered women and children. Only recognition of a duty to protect will adequately address the countervailing needs of victims.

Other arguments in support of the broader duty to protect arise specifically from the predictable responses of batterers to therapy. Often the information gleaned by batterers in educational or treatment programs furnishes them with new knowledge that they can use to enhance their intimidation and nonviolent controls over battered women. Other batterers come into programs illprepared to deal with the directed facilitation and confrontation strategies used in these programs. Most batterers hold their partners responsible for placing them in the uncomfortable therapeutic situation and frequently harass their partners about resentments related to treatment. Sometimes they violently punish battered women. Other battering clients have organized collectively to support each other in manipulation and control of their partners.

We cannot ignore these unintended byproducts of men's counseling and educational programs. Feminists and profeminists insist that therapists must address the protection issues raised by treatment programs. Thus, activists posit that there is an ethical and professional duty to protect battered women and children when batterers are in men's treatment programs. This duty includes the duty to warn of acute, immediate, and present danger of violent acts that may result in serious danger to battered women and children. But the duty to protect goes beyond warning and includes protection strategies. Suggested protection strategies are outlined in the next section.

Protection Strategies

Assessing the
Lethality of Batterers

While some batterers accidentally kill or maim their partners, it appears that most killings of battered women are the result of intentional, life-threatening behavior by batterers. Many murders of battered women are not spontaneous, impulsive events, but rather are executed after deliberation, often associated with obsessive fantasizing about the merits of terminating life.

Although the lethality of a batterer cannot be predicted with any certainty, battered women are usually the best evaluators of the potential for lethal violence because they generally have more information about the batterer than anyone other than the batterer himself. Each battered woman also has a wealth of practice in recognizing how the batterer's life experiences, emotions, and behaviors interrelate. From this gestalt, she can often identify signs of enhanced danger. This is not to say that she can modify or reduce the risks of lethality; but that she can frequently recognize periods where violence or terrorism is likely to erupt.

However, when a batterer joins a men's counseling or educational program, the battered woman has virtually no knowledge about the information he receives, how he responds to it in the group, what he communicates in treatment, and how all of this will influence his pattern of violent and controlling behaviors.

For example, during the course of the treatment program the batterer may hear other men complain because their women partners are not congratulatory about the small changes they are making. Frequently, batterers are bitter that their efforts in treatment have not quickly produced harmony, trust, and loving relationships. Further, when battered women note the absence of change despite treatment, many leave their partners. The decision by a battered woman to leave is often met with escalated violence by the batterer. Other batterers in the group hear the bitterness and sometimes learn of the violent fantasies of the man whose partner is not grateful for change or who has decided to leave. These exchanges profoundly affect other batterers, who may choose to respond by escalating violence against their partners to prevent any contemplated defection. Treatment impinges on the complex thought processes and habits of batterers and may facilitate their choices to commit violent or lethal assaults.

Battered women are not privy to exchanges occurring in treatment and, therefore, cannot assess the potential impact on their partners regarding the risk of life-endangering assaults. Counselors and educators have more knowledge about the reaction of clients to the exchanges in groups, having the advantage of feedback from both verbal and body language from all batterers during treatment sessions. When a man's despair appears to be sharply strengthened by such interchanges; when he responds in a dramatically different fashion to a specific discussion; and when his reaction potentiates one or several of the risk factors described below, there is cause for concern. His battered partner will not have this information to integrate with all the other data she uses to evaluate the probability of violence. Absent this information, she cannot make a fully informed assessment of the current danger to herself or her children. Thus, it is incumbent upon therapists to evaluate carefully the risks of possible serious or lethal assaults posed by their clients. Should a therapist reach the conclusion that there is clear risk of danger to a battered woman or children, a warning and other protective strategies should be instituted.

The following factors should be considered when assessing lethality:

Threats of homicide or suicide. The batterer who has threatened to kill himself, his partner, the children, or her relatives must be considered extremely dangerous. Not all batterers who kill have threatened or attempted suicide previously. However, my experiential data suggests that most have done so.

The batterer who threatens suicide should be considered potentially homicidal. The coupling of homicide with suicide is a frequent occurrence with men who kill family members. Threats or attempts of homicide and suicide are strong indicators of potential lethality.

Fantasies of homicide or suicide. The more the batterer has developed a fantasy about who, how, when, and where to kill, the more dangerous he may be. A batterer may have fantasized events that would "trigger" him to commit homicide, suicide, or assault. One "trigger" may be the battered woman's leaving him. Men who have threatened to kill battered women, should they terminate the relationship or leave for safe shelter, have all too often attempted to follow through. The batterer who has previously acted out part of a homicide or suicidal fantasy may be more invested in killing as a viable "solution" to his problems.

One can never really know which batterer will attempt to kill a battered woman or her children. However, when certain indicators are clustered, the danger of homicide and life-endangering assault invariably increases. Thus the man who has made threats or attempted homicide or who fantasizes about killing his battered partner, himself, or their children may be lethal, particularly if any of the following factors are present:

Weapons. When a batterer possesses weapons and has used or threatened to use weapons in the past in his assaults on the battered woman, the children, or himself, the batterer's access to those weapons increases his potential lethality. When his instruments of aggression are removed, he may look for others or he may not. This does not mean that a man who is intent on homicide will not acquire other weapons; however, a man who might kill impulsively, rather than purposefully, may be less likely to proceed if his weapons are unavailable.

Obsessiveness about partner. A batterer who is obsessive about his battered partner—who either idolizes her and feels he cannot live without her or believes he somehow owns her because she is his wife—is likely to act more dangerously to keep his partner. The man who keeps telephoning a battered woman, who works hard to track her down, who stalks her, or who feels that if he cannot have her no one else will, may be potentially lethal.

Centrality of the battered woman. A slightly different factor is the central role the battered woman plays in the batterer's universe. The therapist should evaluate how isolated the batterer is. If he is cut off from family, friends, or a support system, he may turn toward thoughts of homicide or suicide, especially if the loss of the battered woman represents or precipitates a total loss of hope for a positive future.

Rage. An angry man can be exceedingly dangerous. The rage may be at her desertion. Anger may erupt because of circumstances in his life that are completely unrelated to the battered woman. An enraged batterer may make a decision to commit homicide or suicide.

Depression. The batterer who has been depressed for a substantial period of time may be a candidate for homicide or suicide. When a man is heavily in debt or is unable to obtain employment, or when the future looks bleak to him in many ways, these situational stresses coupled with depression might enhance the batterer's consideration of homicide and suicide.

Drug or alcohol consumption. Consumption of drugs or alcohol when in a state of despair or fury, or fantasizing the relief or revenge offered by terminating life, can also elevate the risk of lethality.

Access to the battered woman. Clearly, access to the battered woman is an important factor in predicting lethality. If the batterer cannot find her, he cannot kill her.

The clustering of several of the factors above gives a better picture of the potential for violence than looking at any single factor. Therapists cannot predict with certainty when a man will kill either himself or his family members. However, when the above factors suggest that a batterer is considering serious or lethal assaults, battered women must be warned and therapists must implement other protection strategies.

Information Dissemination to the Battered Woman

Information is power. Men who batter engage in information withholding, manipulation, creation, and distortion in order to control their battered partners. These disinformation practices render a battered woman less able to assess the danger her batterer poses for her life and well-being. One method by which therapists can assure that the safety interests of the battered partners of their clients are met is to assure that information about violence against women, services for battered women, and treatment for batterers is broadly disseminated.

For a battered woman to be able to develop strategies to safeguard herself and her children and to resist the controlling and coercive practices of batterers, she must be provided comprehensive information about legal remedies and protection, safe shelter facilities, government benefits, support systems for battered women, and educational opportunities for displaced homemakers, as well as information about the causes and effects of battering. All of this knowledge and the opportunity to explore its ramifications fully is readily available from battered women's service programs. Therapists should strongly encourage partners of battering clients to seek information from advocates for battered women.

Further, battered women must be adequately informed of matters related to treatment programs for batterers. Information about the philosophy and curriculum of the treatment program; the effectiveness of the program and how this is measured; the limitations or shortcomings of the program; logistics, such as the duration, location, hours, costs, and attendance requirements of the program; and the evaluation process and the battered woman's participation in it. Warning procedures, patterns of typical resistance by batterers to treatment, and methods of assessing lethality should be shared with each client's partner. Battered women should also have the opportunity to review audiovisual and written materials used in the treatment program.

Since no person can digest all of this information in one or two sessions, it is critical that the battered women's program offer several discussion sessions in which this information can be shared and applied to the respective experiences of each battered woman.

Disseminating information will enable battered women to anticipate and evaluate the risks and danger of physical assaults presented by their battering partners. Therapists facilitating this communication with battered women are surely employing a protection strategy consistent with their professional duty to protect the probable victims of the violent conduct of their clients.

Intervention Against
Male-Bonding Activities

The bonding of batterers in treatment creates significant risk of increased danger to battered women. Therefore, therapists seeking to fulfill their obligation to protect the likely victims of client violence have concluded that interruption of male-bonding activities is a helpful protection strategy.

Male-bonding is a positive, valued concept in the dominant culture. It speaks to networking and friendship-building among men. Male-bonding also describes the feelings of solidarity and camaraderie experienced by men in association with other men.

In sharp contrast, however, activists define male-bonding as solidarity in the oppression of women. Feminists assert that male-bonding can be a political act of maintaining power over women by forging and nurturing linkages between men. These linkages enable men to remain in positions of authority over women. Male-bonding imposes discipline in the ranks of men that enforces their sexism. Ritualized group conduct can facilitate men's belief in the rightness or correctness of gender oppression. Male-bonding can prevent the weaker links from deserting male privilege by the potent promise of humiliation and expulsion from the brotherhood.

Treatment programs for men who batter may serve to strengthen, rather than diminish, male-bonding. Perhaps the most typical vehicle for bonding in batterers' groups is the "bitch" session. Men "bitch" about their women. They complain about the awful partners they have. They are invariably offended by women's insubordination and resistance to control, and reflect on men's entitlement to the servitude and obedience of their women partners. In their tirades against women, batterers conclude that, rather than being victimizers, they are, in fact, the victims of women who control them. In the process of bitching, batterers engage in intense victim-blaming. Bitching helps batterers justify conduct directed at coercing compliance with their demands. Bonding legitimizes the batterer's strong assertion of male authority.

Male-bonding typically erects barriers to the reporting and exploration of acts of violence or abusive conduct by members. Men in unity and support of each other often trivialize or minimize violence and its effects. Mutual, positive regard permits batterers to tolerate the continued violence of group participants.

Too frequently, batterers share triumphant stories with their treatment group about victories they have achieved in circumventing court orders of protection or in evading criminal charges. They also commiserate over losses sustained in the legal system.

Battering clients also engage in male-bonding when they establish support systems outside of treatment that serve to persuade or coerce battered women not to act in their own best interests. Battering clients sometimes take concerted action to dissuade battered women from reporting acts of violence, separating from the abuser, moving out of personal isolation into her own support community, or insisting on adherence to the provisions of protection orders.

Most therapists are clear that the male-bonding activities outlined above critically interfere with the rehabilitative process of battering clients. Fewer recognize the danger that these acts of male-bonding may pose for battered women and children. Intervention must be initiated by therapists to avert male-bonding activities that subordinate or endanger battered women and other family members.

Male-bonding must be confronted in treatment sessions with men who batter. This does not mean merely that men are called to account when they disparage women or avoid honest examination of their own conduct. Confronting must go beyond stopping bonding behavior. Where therapists discern that members of a treatment group have engaged in bonding such as that described above, either within the treatment setting or outside it, notice of this bonding and its potential adverse ramifications must be given to battered women. When a therapist concludes that the male-bonding activities of clients present a danger of escalated violence, extraordinary action may be required by the therapist. Intervention might include: apprising the court that mandated clients are demonstrating coercive conduct outside of the group that is certain to interfere with the safety and autonomy of victims; terminating the entire treatment group with notice to relevant persons of the factors precipitating the termination; identifying other clients or former clients who will pursue intervention to interrupt bonding activities; or using the media to expose the manipulative or coercive practices that may be organized as an unintended by-product of batterer treatment.

The concepts of male networking and friendship-building without bonding must also be taught. Batterers cannot be expected to relinquish friendship and support, except where they inextricably include bonding—intentional or unintentional acts of solidarity in the oppression of women. Guideposts for assessing the differences between bonding and networking need to be made explicit in treatment programs.

For therapists not to intervene and interrupt male-bonding is to be complicit with batterers in their avoidance of accountability to the family members they victimize. Failure to intervene when male-bonding represents a clear and present danger to battered women surely will subject therapists to civil liability. As the law evolves, perhaps even criminal culpability will attach when therapists fail to intervene actively to stop such activities that clearly pose a risk of danger to battered women and children.

Conclusion

This chapter is intended to raise serious questions about the current, limited responsibility therapists of batterers feel toward their clients' partners. The duty to warn is now a legal and ethical standard. However, advocates for battered women see the need for stronger commitments. The duty to protect must become the new standard if battered women are to be safe.

NOTES

1. The word *therapist* is used in the generic sense. It is intended to mean physicians, psychiatrists, psychologists, social workers, marriage counselors, and lay persons who provide counseling or educational services to help modify violent and controlling behaviors of men who batter.

2. Tarasoff v. Regents of the University of California, 1529 P. 2d 553, 118 Cal. Rptr. 129 (1974), vacated, 17 Cal. 3d 425, 551 P. 2d 334, 131 Cal. Rptr. 14 (1976), 83 ALR 3d 1201. (See Givelber, Bowers, & Blitch, 1985.)

3. Peck v. the Counseling Service of Addison County, Inc., N.E. 2d, Vt. (Sup. Ct., June, 1985); Jablonski v. U.S., 712 F. 2d 391 (9th Cir. 1983); Hedlund v. Superior Court, 34 Cal. 3d 695, 669 P. 2d 41, 194 Cal. Rptr. 805, reh'g denied (1983); Brady v. Hopper, 570 F. Supp. 1333 (Colo., 1983); Mavroudis v. Superior Court of San Mateo County, 162 Cal. Rptr. 724 (1980); Lipari v. Sears Roebuck and Company, 497 F. Supp. 185 (Neb., 1980); McIntosh v. Milano, 403 A2d 500 (N.J. Super., 1979); Tarasoff v. Regents of University of California, supra.; Alberts v. Devine, 479 N.E. 2d 113 (Mass. Sup. Jud. Ct.). The court held, in part, that a patient can sue his psychiatrist for breach of confidentiality unless the psychiatrist did it to warn of serious danger to potential victims. (See Wolfe, 1984.)

4. 383 ALR 3d 1201; Jablonski, supra. This case is significant because the court imposed liability for failure to protect a potential victim even though the mentally ill patient made no actual threats against this individual; Hedlund, supra. Where the court found that psychologist owed a duty to protect and a duty to warn the child of the potentially violent patient's girlfriend because, although the patient had only made threats against the mother/girlfriend, the child was a foreseeable and identifiable victim of an assault upon his mother. The mother sustained severe internal and lower extremity injuries while the child suffered no physical injuries but did sustain emotional and psychological injuries. Even though the child was only two years old, the court held that there was a duty to warn the child as well as the mother/girlfriend.; Lipari, supra.; McIntosh, supra.; Tarasoff, supra. (See Small, 1985.)

5. Peck, supra.; Mavroudis, supra.; Leedy v. Hartnett, 510 F. Supp. 1125 (M.D. Pa., 1981). The court held that the psychiatrist was not liable for the release of a potentially dangerous mental patient nor for his failure to warn the persons with whom the patient was going to stay after discharge because the court reasoned that the potential victims were not a group of "readily identifiable persons," since the patient posed no more danger to them than to anybody else with whom he might come in contact.

6. Cairl v. State, 323, N.Y. 2d 20 (Minn., 1982); Leedy, supra.

7. For a case finding that there is no duty to warn, see Re Estate of Vottler, supra. For a case in which the court imposed liability because of the failure to warn, even though the victim had received warnings from a variety of sources, see Jablonski, supra., p. 398.

8. Jablonski, supra., p. 398. (See American Medical Association, 1984, para. 5.05, Current Opinion of the Judicial Council.)

9. RAVEN (Rape and Violence End Now), Safety Planning, P.O. Box 24159, St. Louis, MO 63130.

10. RAP (Reduce Abuse Program), Family Services of Philadelphia, South District Office, Suite 807, 311 Juniper St., Philadelphia, PA 19107.

REFERENCES

American Medical Association (1984). The principles of medical ethics. Author.

Givelber, D. J., Bowers, W. J., & Blitch, C. L. (1985, April). *The Tarasoff controversy: A summary of findings from an empirical study of legal, ethical and clinical issues* (pp. 16-19). Washington, DC: National Institute of Mental Health.

Small, L. B. (1985, Summer). Psychotherapists' duty to warn: 10 years after Tarasoff. *Golden Gate University Law Review, 15*(2).

Wolfe, S. A. (1984). The scope of a psychiatrist's duty to third persons: The protective privilege ends where the public peril begins. *Notre Dame Law Review,* pp. 770-790 .

12

Not-So-Benign Neglect

The Medical Response to Battering

DEMIE KURZ
EVAN STARK

This chapter explores the medical response to abused women, proceeding from the assumption that the emphasis on security, advocacy, and empowerment, which guides the battered women's shelter movement, is also the most appropriate for health care providers. We show that the current medical response to abuse alternates between a narrow clinical focus on physical injuries outside of the social context that makes them intelligible and an approach that stigmatizes abused women so that they appear responsible for the violence. To determine whether, and under what conditions, a feminist perspective can take hold in a medical setting, we consider the extent to which current responses are rooted in misinformation, sexist bias, or in the structure of medical knowledge and practice.

The question of how health professionals respond to abuse can be answered empirically. It is interesting that while the overall impact of battering on medical care is enormous, the medical response to abuse has been slow and sporadic. Battering has been equated with severe injury and consigned to emergency medicine. The vast majority of health visits by abused women involve complaints or problems that may have little organic basis, and reveal relatively minor injuries (Stark et al., 1981), which greatly complicates the encounter between the emergency clinician and the abused woman. For the woman, the assaultive relationship presents both a situational crisis and an ongoing social emergency, punctuated by physical attack. But to emergency clinicians trained to respond to life-threatening heart attacks, gun-shot wounds, or auto accidents, the abused women's sense of impending "emergency" seems inappropriate, and the complex psychosocial picture she presents seems more suited to psychiatric management than to medical care or social service.

We draw on two different studies of the emergency medical response to assess whether and to what extent clinicians or abused women are able to work through this dilemma to an intervention that can be reasonably expected to prevent—or at least reduce—ongoing battering. One set of questions concerns whether abusive injury and/or its multiple sequelae are identified, whether the potential consequences of abuse are appreciated, and the extent to which diagnosis, medication, referrals, or follow-up are consistent with the nature of the problem. Another set of questions concerns what clinicians think about battering, the relation between their perception and their treatment of abused women, and the ways in which they rationalize their response. A third set involves the potential for changing current response patterns. In combination, the studies provide a complementary picture of the formal and subjective dimensions of the medical response to battered women in emergency settings.

The New Haven Study

The New Haven study assessed the medical response over time toward battered and nonbattered women by mining written medical records. The data were examined to shed light on clinician-client encounters, the woman's relation to the hospital over time, how clinicians communicate with one another about abuse, and the potential impact of current interventions on the course of battering.

Sample Selection and Methods

The New Haven study targeted a sample of 3,676 patients randomly selected from among the women who presented to a hospital emergency service with injury or complaint of injury during a single year. Using the medical records of these women, each trauma episode after the age of 16 was critically assessed and assigned to one of the following groups based on the relative probability or risk that it resulted from assault by a social partner:

Positive: Record states patient's injury was inflicted by a male family member or male intimate.

Probable: Record states patient was hit, kicked, beaten, stabbed, and so on, but no personal etiology was indicated, and it was not, for instance, an anonymous street assault.

Suggestive: Alleged etiology did not appear to account for the type, location, or severity of the injury.

Negative: The pattern of injury was consistent with the recorded etiology. This category includes muggings or anonymous assaults.

Next, the trauma episodes in each woman's record were aggregated and the woman was assigned to a risk group based on the episode in her adult trauma history with the highest probability of being associated with abuse. On this basis, 18.7% of the women (n = 642) were classified as abused, 86% falling into the positive or probable categories. A second stage of randomization generated a control sample of 689 negatives. Information abstracted from the complete medical records included *medical data* on specific diagnoses, labels, medications, utilization patterns, and referrals at emergency and nonemergency sites.

Findings

The dimensions of the medical response reported here include identification, disposition, prescription of medications, and labeling.

Identification. "Assault by husband or boyfriend" was explicitly noted by a health provider in 9% of the 5,070 injury episodes ever presented by women in the sample. The 347 women who presented these injuries were rated as "positive" but only 15% of the 483 positive episodes were identified as "abuse" or "battering." By contrast, using the "trauma history" to determine risk, a total of 1,616 "abusive" injuries were identified among the battered women as well as an additional 2,101 injuries that occurred in the context of ongoing violence, but could not be directly traced to abuse. Clinicians correctly associate a mere 4.5% of abusive injuries with violence and a mere 1.8% of the total 3,717 trauma episodes ever presented by abused women with "abuse" or "battering." While 40% of all injuries presented by women occur in abusive relationships and 19% of female trauma patients are abused, abuse and battering are rarely identified.

Disposition. The majority of abusive episodes are not life-threatening. Still, 4% of positive episodes resulted in hospitalization, double the rate for any other injury category. Like most injury victims, abused women were typically sent home without additional medical or social service attention or follow-up. In 47% of abusive episodes and 57% of negative episodes, women simply returned home after emergency room visits. What is most remarkable is that fewer than 12% of the abusive episodes are triaged to appropriate social services. By contrast, 8% of the positive episodes, where violence by a social partner was noted, were triaged to psychiatry, a rare referral for all other types of injury. In fact, an abused woman is twice as likely to be referred to psychiatry rather than to social services, an indication of how medical and surgical staff view abusive injury.

Just as the research began, the hospital extended its "rape crisis team" procedure to abused women and instructed residents to identify and treat abused women, then refer them to the counselling team or shelter. How effective was this approach? Overall, of the 188 positive episodes presented during the sample year, 80% of the women who told their clinician they had been assaulted by a male intimate were *not* referred to the team the hospital itself had created. Overall, if a woman presented any abusive injury during the year, she had less than one chance in 10 of being referred appropriately. During the study, the local shelter also established ongoing liaison with hospital administration. Nevertheless, only 23 of 461 at-risk trauma episodes presented to the hospital during the year involved either treatment of shelter residents or the referral of abused women to the local shelter.

Drug prescriptions. Patterns of disposition are forms of administrative communication and management that operate largely among various levels of the medical complex. Patterns of drug prescription more directly measure the medical encounter and the management styles specific to this encounter. Data on prescribed medication were available for 5,070 injury episodes. In 16% of these instances, at least one drug was prescribed: 76% of such prescriptions involved pain medication; 10% involved minor tranquilizers or sedatives; and 14% involved a variety of agents such as sleeping medication, major tranquilizers, and antibiotics.

At-risk episodes were significantly more likely to result in the prescription of medication, specifically, in the prescription of pain medication and minor tranquilizers. The increased use of such medications is particularly serious because abusive episodes are more likely to involve injuries for which tranquilizers and pain medications are contraindicated, such as head or abdominal injuries or injury during pregnancy. Such drugs are also contraindicated for patients who abuse alcohol or who are at high risk for attempted suicide—both of which are often associated with abuse.

Labeling. Labeling is here specifically defined as the act of designating behaviors, complaints, or groups in ways that seem devoid of therapeutic intent, that are unsupported by hard evidence, and through which providers can relieve their frustration by punitively blaming women for their problems. Only 4% of the nonbattered women were labeled in their records, while one fifth of the battered woman had quasi-psychiatric designations such as "hysteric," "neurotic female," "well-known woman with vague complaints," "crock," "depressed, anxious lady" and "hypochondriac." While battered women were disproportionately labeled prior to the first recorded abusive episode, 83% of the labels were applied after the onset of abuse. Conversely, 86% of all women who carried labels were battered. Thus, far from being a general means of responding to unruly patients or unmanageable problems, the label seems to be a "flag" that frames and justifies a punitive response to abuse.

Suicide attempts. The psychosocial sequelae of abuse are virtually never recognized as such. Nevertheless, like unidentified abuse-related injuries, they elicit a distinct and punitive response from health providers. This is illustrated by the response to attempted suicide. Evidence from the trauma sample indicates that one-sixth of the battered women attempted suicide at least once and that fully half of the positive women who attempted suicide did so more than once. The risk of attempted suicide becomes almost five times greater for battered than for nonbattered women only after the onset of abusive injury.

These figures suggest that domestic violence may be the most significant precipitant of female suicide attempts yet identified. Abused women are clear about the cause of their suicide attempt. Where only 11% of the nonbattered women who attempted suicide reported a marital or lover's quarrel as a precipitating cause, 44% of the battered women mentioned such disputes. Yet, after initial medical treatment, battered women who attempted suicide were significantly more likely than nonbattered women to be sent home and/ or to receive no referral of any kind after a suicide attempt. While almost all the nonbattered suicide attempts (96%) were referred to mental health resources, 22% of the suicide attempts by battered women elicited no referral for mental health services of any kind.

Discussion of Results of
the New Haven Study

The medical response to battering appears to follow a sequence. Starting from symptomatic treatment of discrete injuries, medical care progresses to labeling and psychiatric referral as secondary psychosocial problems arise (Appleton, 1980). As the clinical profile becomes more complex—often including suicide attempts and child abuse—social service makes every effort to keep the family together as the best context in which to treat the woman's secondary problems. We speculate that this pattern of response may actually promote the evolution of battering (Reiker & Carmen, 1986). When abuse is treated symptomatically and a woman is simply sent home, "accidents" continue. Repeated help-seeking makes abused women "well-known" and their persistence is misread as a problem in "compliance." Meanwhile, the general complaints and minor psychosocial problems that accumulate in the context of ongoing violence give clinicians a handle with which to explain multiple "accidents" and, simultaneously, to rationalize limiting a woman's access to resources. As a sense of entrapment mounts, women's help-seeking may become more desperate, and problems may progress from alcohol and the abuse of medication to multiple suicide attempts or child abuse. But crisis intervention is punitive. Children are removed from the home, women are hospitalized with no evidence of psychiatric disease or, if a woman attempts suicide, she is simply "sent home, no follow-up." A variety of mental health interventions, ranging from family therapy to mental hospitalization, seem to emphasize "appropriate role behavior" and are designed to "stabilize" family situations in which ongoing violence is virtually inevitable (Schechter, 1982; Stark & Flitcraft, 1983, 1985).

The Philadelphia Study

Having looked at the collective response of clinicians to abuse, we turn next to specific encounters between emergency staff and abused women. Is a more complex process of rationalization involved that can help us explain the pattern of neglect, inappropriate medication, labeling and punitive referrals identified in New Haven? To what extent does it reflect actual clinical experience (and frustration) with abused women? To what extent are larger ideological predispositions and biases involved? And, perhaps most important, how does the medical response change when care is guided by a feminist rather than a strictly medical orientation? These are the questions to which the Philadelphia study responds.

Sample Selection
and Research Methods

The Philadelphia group studied battered women and the medical response in four hospital emergency services (ES). The emergency services were selected to reflect variation in ethnicity and class. When observers were introduced to staff, a short in-service on battering was presented, including a discussion of its social origins. In addition, staff in two of the services completed questionnaires about battering prior to the observation phase. Observers followed the cases of all female trauma patients seen by health care professionals during different shifts. A woman was considered battered if she reported to the observer or a staff member that she had been injured by her husband or boyfriend. Based on this definition, interactions between 98 battered women and ES staff were observed for a period of two to five months in each hospital. Observers followed directly as much of each interaction as possible. As soon as it was over, they interviewed staff about what had transpired, taking verbatim, detailed field notes. Questions included what was said and done, what physical diagnosis was made, whether the staff thought battering had occurred, and how the specific case compared to other cases of battering.

Results

Data are presented here that describe staff attitudes toward battering and staff views of battered women. Next, a brief case example is presented of the impact of a feminist hospital-based intervention with battered women.

Staff attitudes toward battering. Virtually all respondents to the questionnaire (90%) indicated that they believed ES staff should try to identify battered women and 82% considered it "part of their job." Staff respond to battered women in three distinct ways. In 11% of the cases, staff make a "positive" response. They take a woman's battering seriously and view it as legitimately deserving of their time and attention. In addition to giving her treatment, they note battering on the case record, speak to the woman about what happened, assess her safety, and attempt to provide some assistance or give her a card with hot-line numbers. Staff respond in this way because they see the women as "deserving." Staff believe these women have no discrediting attributes and are "true victims." Staff are especially sympathetic if they believe the women are taking some action to change their situation, or if the women are perceived to be in immediate physical danger.

In 49% of the cases staff make a "partial" response: They note a woman's battering and give it some attention, but it has a lower priority than other cases. Thus, the response may or may not be appropriate for that woman's condition. In 40% of the cases staff do not respond at all. Staff give two major reasons for these responses. First, staff say they are not responsive because they feel the women are "evasive." In 16% of all cases, staff describe the women as evasive, hiding something, or unwilling to talk. Staff become particularly irritated if they suspect a woman was battered, take the time to ask, and the woman fails to respond. Second, staff mention other stigmatizing traits. In 23% of the cases the women were believed to have "Alcohol on Breath (AOB)," and the remainder to be on drugs or to be acting in "bizarre" ways. Women in these categories were considered difficult to understand, uncoopera-tive, and therefore, a waste of time, although 40% became cooperative and willing to talk in the emergency service as the effects of alcohol wore off.

Staff views of battered women. Observers interviewed most ES staff about their views of battered women. An analysis of these interviews and also of informal conversations with staff demonstrates that two views of battered women predominate. First, although the majority of cases were not recognized despite patients' providing explicit informa-tion about their abuse, staff characterized all battered women as "evasive"—implying that the abuse was not a legitimate dimension of the case. The second view was that battered women are "repeaters," implying that a battered woman could easily change her situation if she wished. When she did not, she was viewed pejoratively.

Cardiologist: Why do anything for people who do not take responsibility for themselves? What good does it do when they won't come in and do something for themselves? Last night we had a battered woman. It took five hours for her to be convinced to come in by neighbors.

Male M.D.: It is ridiculous because the women go back. We see it all the time. They are in the examining room. The man has gouged out her eye or stabbed her or something like that and she is in the ER and gets mad because we won't let the guy in.

The cardiologist focuses on the woman's prior reluctance to seek help rather than the obvious courage she has mustered to finally come in. The male doctor fails to grasp the immediate danger to women who are accompanied by their assailants, and the survival function of evasiveness in these circumstances. None of the staff mention the obvious social and economic factors that make it difficult for women to leave their families.

Contrasting with the propensity for staff to stigmatize all battered women as "repeaters," data from one ES suggests that many women are interested in changing their situations. This ES had an advocate for abused women and two thirds of the battered women who discussed their situation spoke about changing it. While the validity of these statements cannot be established, the fact that so many women are seriously weighing their options challenges the "repeater" stereotype.

An Alternative Approach to
Battered Women: A Case Study

Staff developed a different approach in one ES where a physician assistant (PA) with a feminist perspective acted as an advocate for abused women. She believed that women battered by men were victims of sexist institutions and practices, that their problems were a legitimate medical concern, and that battered women could be helped to leave violent relationships. She also reinterpreted pejorative characteristics attributed to battered women by her colleagues as understandable behavior for women who had been deliberately assaulted by men.

The PA had an immediate impact on how seriously women's abuse was taken. She trained a variety of ES professionals to identify abuse and to talk supportively with battered women. The data indicates that a group of eight professionals allied with the physician assistant identified and sympathetically treated more battered women than other ES staff at this or any facility. As a result, in this ES 47% of the cases were in the "positive" category as opposed to 11% in the other ES; 21% were in the "partial" category as opposed to 49%; and 32% fell into the "no response" category as opposed to 40% in the other ES: The PA frequently had productive encounters with women considered "evasive," "AOB" or "troublemakers," resulting in their seeing a social worker and/or deciding to prosecute the batterer.

The PA also received permission to do half-hour training sessions with new residents on treating battered women. This had inconclusive results, however, and the majority of resident staff still seemed to take little interest in battering. In addition, she devised a card system to track battered women in the ES. This helped in referrals to the social worker and her responsiveness, in turn, increased the responsiveness and sense of accomplishment among the rest of the staff. Because the social worker followed battered women after they left the service, staff felt they had made a referral that had more meaning than just handing a woman a card with phone numbers of the relevant agencies.

Discussion of Results of
the Philadelphia Study

These findings provide further evidence of inappropriate medical responses and indicate how these responses are related to health providers' conceptions of battering and of battered women as patients (Kurz, 1987). In the majority of cases, battering is either denied or its importance is not acknowledged, although a majority of those questioned see identifying battering as part of their job. The possibility that this reflects misinformation was reduced by briefing staff about battering prior to the observational phase of the study. It seems clear that battering is neither a salient nor a high-priority issue for ES staff. Physicians believe that their true work is "saving endangered lives" and that all other work has less priority (Roth, 1972). While many abusive injuries are serious, they are rarely life-threatening and the woman's definition of her situation as a crisis is often not accepted.

However, this does not account for the overwhelming dismissal of abuse or the stigmatization of battered women as "evasive" and "repeaters." Here, it seems, staff generalize their experience from a minority of abused women to an entire class. Stereotypes, based on the trouble clinicians have with some battered women, are used to rationalize a desire to avoid dealing with a difficult issue. What begins as a way to manage a specific subgroup of patients is generalized to help staff manage the larger set of issues battering poses to emergency medical care.

But battered women are stigmatized for reasons that go beyond pragmatic considerations. Whether battered women are evasive, present "AOB," or are forthright about their predicament, many behave in ways clinicians regard as uncooperative, disrespectful, and "unfeminine." Beyond this, some staff are simply uncomfortable with the issue of violence against women, or else view an inquiry about battering as an invasion into "personal" affairs. As one neurosurgeon said, "It is none of my business who hit her. I am just here to treat her." Since it elicits perfunctory treatment, stigmatizing all battered women protects staff not only from potential troublemakers, but also from the larger set of issues battering creates for medicine as a system of authority, the expertise of which is limited to managing social problems at the individual level.

Regardless of intent, in using the term "evasive," staff shift the blame for the lack of an effective outcome to battered women themselves. The stereotype of "repeater" extends the view that it is the woman who will not take steps to change her situation. By blaming the victim, the stereotypes rationalize the lack of an appropriate clinical response and incorporate the woman's social predicament in traditional medical terms, as a problem she "is" rather than a problem created for her by the assailant. This is a maladaptive way of resolving the tension professionals experience between their professional norms, such as identifying abuse, and how they actually do their job. These stereotypes are particularly dangerous because they do not reflect the strengths and capacities of battered women. Reliable comparative studies of abused women suggest that they have a better sense of reality than their assailants have (Finn, 1985), and are more "social" and "sympathetic" than control groups are (Graff, 1980). While abused women in mental institutions have low self-esteem and may blame themselves for the violence (Carmen, Reiker, & Mills, 1984; Hilberman & Munson, 1977-78), this is not true for battered women generally.

Implications: Medical Reeducation and Feminist Strategy

This chapter has explored the medical response to battering as prototypical of the general service response. These studies demonstrate that clinicians fail to acknowledge abuse as a source of injury or other problems. Instead, they reinterpret women's experience in ways that are consistent with strictly medical views of behavior and disease. Although abuse is rarely recorded, abused women are treated differently as a group. The New Haven study documents a "battering syndrome" that includes a history of medical neglect, inappropriate medication, labeling, and punitive referrals and interventions that accompany the escalation of abusive injury and psychosocial problems. We speculate that clinicians make an "implicit diagnosis" of abuse in which psychosocial sequelae such as alcoholism or depression are viewed as its cause and where the woman—not her assailant or his violence—is seen as "sick." The Philadelphia study demonstrates how this process unfolds through individual encounters. Even though staff typically believe battering is a legitimate medical problem, they stigmatize abused women. Then, by generalizing their experience with an "uncooperative" minority, they are able to rationalize treating the majority of abused women as "deliberate deviants," as people who, because they refuse to change their situation, are causing their own problems, and so have no legitimate claim on medical resources. While nurses appear as threatened by abused women as are male physicians, a feminist PA is able to mobilize her colleagues for a more effective—if limited—response.

Explanations for the Medical Response

How can we understand the lack of appropriate and sensitive medical response to battered women? Is the problem simply a result of the lack of correct information, of sexist attitudes, or of structural and situational factors that constrain service and medical professionals? These possibilities will be examined in turn.

Misinformation

The most straightforward explanation for the medical response is that clinicians lack accurate technical knowledge about abuse. Like child abuse, battering was historically shut "behind closed doors." Now the "news" is out. Ideally, once health professionals are acquainted with the dimensions and causes of woman abuse and given the means and incentives to identify it, they will report the problem, respond sensitively to battered women, and refer them to appropriate sources of help, such as the battered women's shelter or self-help groups. This approach draws support from traditional sociological views that trace bad medical practice to problems (or problem patients) that fall outside the normative conceptions of illness (or illness behavior) established through professional training (Freidson, 1970; Parsons, 1951).

If misinformation is the problem, the solution involves heightening clinical awareness and broadening the definition of good professional practice to include more appropriate responses. The emphasis here is primarily on technical knowledge. As Nelson (1984) argues, child abuse reformers were successful because, by presenting the problem as a medical and psychiatric issue, they "depoliticized" the issue, simultaneously satisfying the welfare system's need to rescue children from desperate circumstances and placating fears that state interventions to protect children would disrupt traditional family structures. Similarly, by professionalizing the response to battering, reformers can legitimate the issue and elicit resources not readily available to programs labeled "feminist."

While our studies provide no definitive test of this perspective, they do suggest that technical education—and even the provision of resources—are unlikely to alter substantially the current medical response. In Philadelphia, clinicians already believed that identifying battering was good medical practice and had been introduced to theories of its social causation prior to the observations reported here. During the study in New Haven, residents received training in how to respond to abuse, a hospital-based counselling team was created, and local shelter services were available and publicized. This natural experiment produced no change in the medical response. Indeed, although Connecticut now requires that hospitals report aggregate data on battering, after almost a decade of public attention to abuse, the study hospital was able to identify only 47 cases for the six months ending in July, 1985. This represents only one case identified for every 8 actually presented in the emergency service alone and excludes the vast majority of health visits by battered women to primary care services.

Sexism

A second explanation comes from the women's health movement, which defines the problem as personal bias or "sexism" institutionalized as professional (i.e. male) dominance. Having replaced women as primary healers, men consolidated their authority in professional elites (such as organized medicine) and then extended their control over women's bodies by "medicalizing" a range of personal or social issues (Ehrenreich & English, 1973; Gordon, 1978).

The most compelling support for this explanation is the propensity for clinicians to label and stigmatize abused women according to classic female stereotypes and to regard their aggressive behavior or persistence in help-seeking as "unfeminine" and unworthy of attention. The presumption that abused women are "deliberate deviants" incorporates and conveys a similarly stereotypic conception of women's responsibility when "things go wrong at home." While gender does not appear to differentiate how clinicians respond to abuse, political orientation does, lending credibility to the argument that some clinicians will respond to feminist arguments, and that improved practice will result.

Women-run health clinics offer one alternative, although their emphasis on gynecological issues limits their current utility for abused women. More pertinent are reforms within the medical care system to give women a larger voice in determining their choices (empowerment); to shift authority in abuse cases from male doctors to nurses, physician associates, or social workers; and to introduce protocols in which battered women's shelters are central. Reforming professional education is also key. But here the emphasis is less on technical knowledge (such as learning to identify abuse) than on helping clinicians understand how gender influences women's health problems and current medical practice (Reiker & Carmen, 1984).

Structural Constraints

Sexism neither explains why clinicians respond differently to battered and nonbattered women nor why they provide only symptomatic medical treatment to injuries that have obvious social etiology. A third explanation of the medical response to battering is consistent with the feminist critique of medicalization and sexism (Stark, 1981). The medical approach reduces male violence—a social process rooted in gender inequality—to biological, individual, or situational factors, and focuses prevention on the individual level. This focus minimizes the historical and social dimensions of women's experiences that are so crucial to understanding and responding appropriately to wife battering. Clinicians learn to catalogue abuse alongside other "illnesses." Whether abused women are received like other patients requiring "treatment" or as "victims" requiring "rescue," medical interventions inevitably reproduce and extend female dependence.

This dovetails with a critique that views the entire service infrastructure as an ambivalent legacy because it eases individual suffering by "policing" daily life; legitimates the existing system of domination; and actually increases inequities in knowledge, resources, and authority, from which much suffering arises in the first place (Donzelot, 1977; Meyer, 1984). So, for instance, while feminist activists understood rape as a political symbol of a misogynist society, which required a political response, hospital-based rape-crisis groups "medicalized" the issue by assigning women the status of "victim" and consigning them to therapy for "rape trauma syndrome." The result is that a community-based political service has been coopted.

The medical model of disease and the health care system in general discount the political context of health problems in favor of individual, biological, or psychiatric causes. "Good medical practice" means prioritizing physical emergencies, adequately comprehending only the immediate and strictly medical dimensions of a problem, and calling on psychiatry and social services to manage "problem patients." These norms are reflected in how emergency staff use their scarce time and resources. By presenting their social situation as emergent, abused women directly challenge the medical model, and their persistent "accidents" threaten to expose the ineffectiveness of "good medical practice." The staff reconciles prevalent behavioral norms and values with growing external pressure to treat battered women as "part of my job" by denying the abuse, discounting its clinical significance, or by locating its origins in the woman's behavior.

From this perspective, it is not enough to concentrate on technical education, or sexist bias among health professionals, or on how medical care is delivered and by whom. Instead, the very structure and purpose of the health and social services bureaucracy must be called into question and its basic assumptions challenged, including the presumption that an expansion of individually oriented social services for battered women is an adequate response to problems rooted in inequality. While the emergency response to crisis situations should obviously be improved, the prevention of battering requires the redefinition of care.

The Limits of Feminist Reform

Given this analysis, what can be done to make the medical system more responsive to the needs of battered women? One answer is to identify and support in-house advocates or professionals who can provide feminist training with adequate technical assistance and political support. By redefining the status of abused women in political terms (e.g., converting problem patients into patients with problems), one physician assistant provided an alternative framework within which motivated colleagues could justify changing their priorities so that battered women received the time and resources their "social" emergency required.

But the credibility of feminist health staff depends on two factors these studies do not describe: the visibility of a community-based battered women's movement and the growing struggle against the situational constraints that confront all women working in the health care system. By confirming the abused woman's sense of reality through collective support and individual advocacy, the battered women's movement challenges the same behavioral and ideological norms that limit the routine effectiveness and self-expression of nurses and hospital social workers. Just as importantly, it offers the protection and liaison needed to make something other than "repeating" a real option for abused women. A growing feminist consciousness among nurses, social workers, and other health providers makes it possible for health staff to think about their job related grievances in relation to the generic situation of women. While outside challenges to organized medicine have traditionally elicited defensive attacks on activists as "unprofessional" or against advocacy as "counterproductive," feminist nurses have made the battering issue (which also affects female staff) part of their confrontation with the way medical care is defined and administered by a "male elite."

Another answer is to shift the emphasis away from battering defined as a physical crisis requiring an emergency medical response. The situational constraints in the emergency setting clearly aggravate the normal propensity of clinicians to stigmatize medical complaints with no organic basis and emergent social problems that are not typically life-threatening. In pragmatic terms, this implies targeting educational efforts to primary care clinics (including obstetrical services, community health facilities, and mental health centers). Not only are the situational constraints in these settings more amenable to change, but staff are more willing to understand battering as a sociopolitical process of victimization punctuated by violence, and to acknowledge its multiple psychological correlates. Parallel efforts are needed to pressure community-based women's clinics to go beyond their current emphasis on childbirth and gynecological problems and to encompass violence. "Training" should focus on identifying and working to build model programs with feminist health professionals, thus avoiding the dual pitfalls of browbeating and cooptation (which results when a community-based program is brought in-house and loses its political thrust). This approach permits us to retain our adversarial posture—thus providing a crucial service—while we make the alliances needed to overcome the underlying political inequality at the root of battering.

At bottom, however, the behavioral norms of the health care system are incompatible with our major task: enhancing women's control over resources so they can live a safe and independent life. As persons who attempt to straddle the worlds of theory and practice, we take little comfort in the complex and deeply rooted obstacles to feminism we have described. These limits highlight the importance of a dialogue between feminist theorists and researchers and those who express their feminist ideals through organizing and direct service to battered women. Theoretical discussions of violence against women have been few and far between (Breines & Gordon, 1984; Dobash & Dobash, 1979; Stark, Flitcraft, & Frazier, 1979). Sophisticated feminist critiques of social services are rarer still. Among the hundreds of monographs on abuse, many by researchers sympathetic to feminism, few show evidence of the theoretical or strategic sophistication the issue deserves (see Reiker & Carmen, 1984). It is almost as if we too have been swayed by the medical tendency to view a woman's predicament one-dimensionally, as a problem suited either to "help" or "politics" or action or analysis, but not both. It is this division that must be healed before we can say with conviction that not simply medical care but autonomy and independence hold the key to ending abuse.

REFERENCES

Appleton, W. (1980). The battered woman syndrome. *Annals of Emergency Medicine, 9,* 84-91.

Breines, W., & Gordon, L. (1984). The new scholarship on family violence. *Signs, 8,* 490-531.

Carmen (Hilberman), E., Ricker, P., & Mills, T. (1984). Victims of violence and psychiatric illness. *American Journal of Psychiatry, 141,* 378-383.

Dobash, R. E., & Dobash, R. (1979). *Violence against wives.* New York: Free Press.

Donzelot, J. (1977). *Policing the family.* Paris: Editions de Minuit.

Ehrenreich, R., & English, D. (1973). *Witches, midwives and nurses: A history of woman healers.* New York: Feminist.

Finn, J. (1985). The stresses and coping behavior of battered women. *Social Casework, 66,* 341-349.

Freidson, E. (1970). *Professional dominance: The social structure of medical care.* New York: Atherton.

Gordon, L. (1978). The politics of birth control, 1920-1940: The impact of professionals. In John Ehrenreich (Ed.), *The cultural crisis of modern medicine.* New York: Monthly Review Press.

Graff, T. T. (1980). Personality characteristics of battered women. *Dissertation Abstracts International, 40,* (7-B) 3395.

Hilberman, E., & Munson, K. (1977-78). Sixty battered women. *Victimology, 2,* 460-470.

Kurz, D. (1987). Responses to battered women: Resistance to medicalization. *Social Problems, 34*(1), 501-513.

Meyer, P. (1984). *The child and the state: The intervention of the state in family life.* Cambridge: Cambridge University Press.

Nelson, B. J. (1984). *Making an issue of child abuse: Political agenda setting for social problems.* Chicago: University of Chicago.

Parsons, T. (1951). *The social system.* New York: Free Press.

Reiker, P. P., & Carmen (Hilberman), E. (1984). *The gender gap in psycho-therapy: Social realities and psychological processes.* New York: Plenum.

Reiker, P. P., & Carmen (Hilberman), E. (1986). The victim-to-patient process: The disconfirmation and transformation of abuse. *American Journal of Orthopsychiatry, 56,* 360-371.

Roth, J. A. (1972). Some contingencies of the moral evaluation and control of clientele: The case of the hospital emergency service. *American Journal of Sociology, 77,* 838-855.

Schechter, S. (1982). *Women and male violence.* Boston: South End.

Stark, E. (1981). What is medicine? *Radical Science Journal, 12.*

Stark, E. (1984). The battering syndrome: Social knowledge, social therapy and the abuse of women. Unpublished doctoral dissertation. SUNY-Binghamton, Department of Sociology.

Stark, E., & Flitcraft, A. (1983). Social knowledge, social policy and the abuse of women. In D. Finkelhor et al. (Eds.), *The dark side of families.* Newbury Park, CA: Sage.

Stark, E., & Flitcraft, A. (1985). Woman-battering, child abuse and social heredity: What is the relationship? In N. Johnson (Ed.), *Marital violence.* Sociological Review Monograph, 31. London: Routledge & Kegan Paul.

Stark, E., Flitcraft, A., & Frazier, W. (1979). Medicine and patriarchal violence: The social construction of a "private" event. *International Journal of Health Services, 9,* 461-493.

Stark, E., Flitcraft, A., et al. (1981). *Wife abuse in the medical setting: An introduction for health personnel* (Monograph No. 7). Washington, DC: Office of Domestic Violence.

Telch, C. F., & Lindquist, C. U. (1984). Violent versus nonviolent couples: A comparison of patterns. *Psychotherapy, 21,* 242-248.

Walker, L. (1979). *The battered woman.* New York: Harper & Row.

Walker, L. (1983). The battered woman syndrome study. In D. Finkelhor et al. (Eds.), *The dark side of families.* Newbury Park, CA: Sage.

PART IV

Building Bridges:
Theory and Practice,
Academics and Activists

13

Collaborative Feminist Research and the Myth of Objectivity

LEE ANN HOFF

For years the need for unity among disadvantaged groups had been apparent to me and I had viewed myself as a bridge builder of sorts between various factions. So I was intrigued by the suspicion of feminist activists toward academics that I observed during the research project on which this chapter is based. Early in the study I was tempted to ask my activist sisters: "Can't you see that I am not the enemy?" Yet, as I proceeded, the roots of antagonism between those inside and outside of academia became clearer.

In this chapter, I explore the reasons why, with all my good intentions toward abused women and others, it was reasonable for feminist activists initially to regard my research with suspicion. Specifically, the chapter calls into question a hallmark of the scientific method: its claim of objectivity. Mainstream researchers hold dear the assumption that if one pays meticulous attention to details of design and data analysis, the problem of bias and subjectivity in research is sufficiently controlled so as to not invalidate the findings. Feminist analysis, critical theory, and reflexive sociology in complementary critiques, reveal serious flaws in these assumptions. Such traditional assumptions and the myth of neutrality in research were central to the conflict I observed between feminist academics and activists during a field study of violence against women.

Before I give specific illustrations of the problems and possibilities of collaborative feminist research, I will provide an overview of the study I conducted. Also, and most importantly, I will outline the method-

269

ological problems that hinder our efforts in developing a fuller understanding of wife abuse.

The Original Study

The study on which this chapter is based, "Violence Against Women: A Social-Cultural Network Analysis" (Hoff, 1984), concerns the influence of values and social support on battered women, as expressed through women's social networks. This issue was examined with nine battered women and 131 network members, using qualitative methods in a natural setting for approximately one year in a metropolitan area of New England. Values and network factors were examined for their influence on the women before, during, and after their experience of violence.

Theoretically, the study demonstrates links between individual battered women, their social networks, and the larger society. Victim-blaming and self-blame of battered women are traced to traditional values about women, marriage and the family and to interpretations of violence as a medical phenomenon or a "private" matter between the couple.

Analysis revealed that values associated with victim-blaming are supported by male dominated social and political structures that create a context in which violence against women flourishes with social approval. Further, the attempts of natural network members (family, friends, and neighbors) to help battered women were insufficient, underscoring the public aspects of this problem that go well beyond the individual or family. Yet, formal network support from those publicly and professionally charged to help (e.g., nurses, physicians, police, and so on) was gravely lacking.

The study underscores the importance of approaching a politically sensitive topic in a way that will not be damaging to those being studied, while at the same time not compromising the valid principles of social science research. The collaborative approach used in this study provides an alternative to the traditional dominant/submissive relationship between researchers and those researched.

Methodological Issues

While preparing for this research, several issues emerged that are pivotal to the problem of collaborative feminist research discussed later in this chapter. A central issue was the relationship between the researchers, the topic, methods of study, and the theory guiding the research. This issue influenced the context of the study, the feminist methods I chose, and the outcomes of the research. Applying my critical feminist perspective in the study of violence led me to the conclusion that certain methods of research, especially those claiming to be objective and value-free, are problematic and ethically questionable. These factors also led to my multiple-methods approach to the topic. Here I have extended Reinharz's (1979) notion of the relationship between the person, the problem, and the method. Reinharz and others (e.g., Gergen, 1982; Wallston, 1981; Watson-Frank, 1980) urge researchers to examine the extent to which their values influence a choice of research topics and methods.

In doing this research, I was prepared as a psychiatric nurse clinician as well as social scientist. Also, the feminism informing my clinical and academic work left me with deep concern about the gaps between feminist theory and practice and between mainstream and feminist research. The polarizations between these groups seemed to shortchange both sides. Success in my aim to bridge some of these gaps implied close attention to definition of the topic and choice of methods.

The division between feminist and mainstream researchers can be traced in part to differing theoretical orientations. Traditionally, explanations of violence against family members were cast largely from general violence and aggression theories in nonfamily settings (Goode, 1971; Wolfgang, 1958). In 1979, Gelles and Straus made the first attempt to develop a theoretical framework specific to the study of family violence. The theories they reviewed fall into three categories: intra-individual, social-psychological, and social-cultural. From the feminist perspective, sociocultural and political factors are *central* to an interpretation of violence that does not collude in victim-blaming by suggesting, for example, that victimization by violence can be traced to the psychological characteristics of the victim (see Breines & Gordon, 1983). And further, the feminist approach goes beyond general socio-cultural explanations to explicate the patriarchal nature of the social and cultural context of violence.

Gelles and Straus discuss the confusion of theoretical and ideological concerns around aggression and violence and attempt a way out with a "purely behavioral" definition: Violence is a physical act (of aggression) that must be separated from its social meaning (1979, pp. 554-555). In my research, *violence* is defined as a form of human social action *intended* to inflict physical harm on another person. To understand this form of social action, the *meaning* of physical acts of aggression cannot be separated from the act itself, as is suggested in mainstream social science research. It is interesting to note that Straus, Gelles, & Steinmetz, (1980) also define violence in terms of intention, yet they neglect to measure intention. Since meanings are as variable as the number of human beings capable of violent behavior, it is one thing to establish incidence of violent acts experienced by women; it is quite another to understand the processes and *context-specific meanings* of violent social interaction, including the relationship between verbal and physical aggression.

Accordingly, it became clear to me that an interpretive understanding of violence against women demanded a different method of research than a quantitative/causal analysis of violent acts between family members (Cicourel, 1964; Phillips, 1973; Reinharz, 1979). This conclusion was underscored by feminist critiques of mainstream social science research (e.g., Dobash & Dobash, 1979). Specifically, Oakley (1981) describes interviewing women in the traditional format as a methodological ideology that masks the superordinate/subordinate research situation in the guise of obtaining "objective" scientific data. The interviewer/interviewee relationship in mainstream social science thus appears to complement the dominant/submissive theme of traditional male/female relationships. In contrast, feminist interviewing implies a collaborative relationship between interviewer and interviewee, and an openness to what develops from being "inside the culture" of the person being interviewed (see Geertz, 1973; Oakley, 1981).

In grappling with these issues, I saw that researchers, practitioners, and clinicians who deal with violence are, like others, influenced by the purposes, values, and politics of the society in which they claim membership. However, when charges of ideological purposes are leveled at feminist research, an assumption of exemption from ideology is implied for mainstream studies. It is important to note here that feminists do not claim to be value-free. We assert, rather, that the values informing research be made explicit, regardless of one's theoretical orientation. This insistence is central to the argument about neutrality in research. Feminists (and increasingly mainstream researchers) claim that values are inherent in all research, whether or not these values are made explicit by the researchers.

Nevertheless, research demands an empirical basis for claims about violence, including the influence of sexism and patriarchy, if it is to be distinguished from a journalistic account of battered women's biographies. Unraveling the relationship between the personal and the political, and synthesizing the women's accounts with formal social analysis is a central challenge.

Basic to my research, then, is explicit recognition that the study of violence against women is not simply a matter of "objective scientific analysis." Several values are assumed in this research: (1) Women as persons are equal to men, though like people of certain color, class, and age, as a group they do not enjoy social equality with white males. Similarly, women, like men, are moral beings, not merely helpless victims. (2) Violence against women is not simply a "social fact" that can be measured and correlated statistically with other "social facts" and personal characteristics of victims, and with moral and legal ramifications. As such, one may either be held accountable for it or, under certain conditions, be excused. (3) The research enterprise itself is embedded in the values and knowledge system of western culture. (4) Knowledge from research should benefit those researched.

The Process of Collaborative Feminist Research

The Problem of Access

The chasm between feminist activists and academics, researchers, and professionals exacerbated my problems of access. The problem of access to this research population could not have been resolved through traditional methods (e.g., survey research or even single interviews). In fact, the problematic gap was so wide because traditional research methods had supplied such "evidence" as the "equality" of violence between women and men (Straus, Gelles, & Steinmetz, 1980) ("evidence" used to question the support and public funding of programs for battered women). In contrast, I developed a nonexploitative methodology and convinced the women participants and their radical feminist advocates of the ethical grounds of the research.

Having decided on a processual field approach to this study, the next step was to find a natural setting. This "step" turned out to be a rather major political process lasting several months, which took shape as the "problem of access." Analysis of this process supports my earlier contention about the inextricable relationship between the problem, theory, and method, and the person doing the research. It also reveals strikingly the political and ethical implications of researching a value-laden topic such as violence against women. Finally, it helps us to let go of the myth of neutrality.

I focused my efforts to gain access to the shelter in which I had trained as a volunteer. I got acquainted with this setting and the research possibilities through several avenues: weekly staffing of the hot line and residence; attendance of at least one meeting per week with other staff of the collective operating the shelter; and exploring my research ideas with a formerly battered woman involved in the original development of this shelter and a formerly battered woman who provided insights from her experience as a battered woman, her graduate study, and her involvement as a social activist among ethnic groups.

The next step was to develop a letter inviting women to participate in the study. Residents of the shelter provided feedback about the letter and the study as a whole; without exception they expressed interest in taking part in the project. The letter and the aims of the study were presented to the shelter collective's decision-making committee.

I encountered almost militant resistance among some members of the shelter collective. These women wanted to know in detail how I considered myself different from other researchers. They expended great efforts to protect the shelter residents from being "used." There was no general knowledge of university requirements such as consent forms, procedures for guaranteeing privacy, and so on. Paradoxically, I was asked to furnish details of my research, which were not yet formulated because of the participatory, processual approach I had envisioned. To have supplied such prestructured details would have meant engaging in the very impositional research I had so painstakingly tried to avoid. When I explained that my research was "different," the response was, "That's what they all say." Yet, three of the more experienced women in the collective seemed to sense intuitively that my approach was indeed different from the studies they had rejected before on grounds of being exploitative. The collective's precedent for refusing collaboration in research was weighed against the "different" proposal I presented. Throughout the entire discussion I felt intimidated and powerless, while at the same time convinced of the value of this project and the appropriateness of my method.

What is the meaning of the reluctance of these feminist activists to support my research? In historical perspective, this interaction between the researcher and members of the collective is understandable, because allegedly objective "scientific" studies sometimes omit the contextual elements of research findings and tend therefore to distort the subject (Roberts, 1981; Wardell, Gillespie, & Leffler, 1981). Members of the collective and other feminist activists struggling for a political stand on the issue focused on the national survey of "domestic" violence (Straus, Gelles, & Steinmetz, 1980) to support their argument regarding the exploitative uses of research. To the surprise of even the researchers, this survey revealed that women were equally as violent as men. This finding flew in the face of practically everyone's subjective knowledge of this topic. It also defied local county hospital statistics citing 70% of all assault victims as battered women, not men. When these surprising findings were analyzed further, however, it was found that, indeed, when merely counting physically violent acts (from pushing or a slap, to use of lethal force and weapons), women engage in violence just about as often as men, but their violence is usually in self-defense and is much less damaging physically than is true for men. By this time though, the damage had already been done as far as feminist activists were concerned. Various "professionals" had been heard quoting the survey findings out of context to support their argument of "equality" of violence between men and women.

So my status as academic researcher was problematic, yet my background as a mental health professional did not help either. In this collective, professional credentials were not sought and for the most part were ignored if the staff person did not qualify in the ways that counted there: "politically correct," empathy toward battered women, appreciation of violence as a possibility in the lives of all women. Indeed, my history as a rape victim was one of my most important credentials. While I did not deliberately hide my professional credentials, I was very careful not to flaunt them. Overtly, my professional preparation was a clear liability in establishing trust and rapport; covertly, it was an asset in helping me understand the dynamic process and regulate my behavior accordingly.

An antiprofessional view, similar to the antiacademic bias, was evident in the collective. It was, after all, well documented that mental health and social service professionals were, for the most part, part of the problem, not part of the solution for battered women (Dexter, 1958; Hilberman, 1980; Martin, 1976; Stark, Flitcraft, & Frazier, 1979). Therefore, without evidence based on more extensive experience with me, suspicion of me as an "infiltrating professional" was not surprising. The general attitude was something like this: After centuries of collusion by society's major institutions—including more recently, researchers and human service professionals—to define the issue of violence against women as a "private" matter, feminists nevertheless managed to bring the matter to public attention as a social/political problem. Now that the issue is exposed as something more complex than the individual psychology of battered women, professionals and academics want to jump on the bandwagon of a popular issue and exploit it for their personal gain or ideological purposes (Ahrens, 1980; Schechter, 1982).

At first glance such a defensive posture by the activists may appear unfounded. After all, many sincere and sympathetic persons—professional and lay—have helped advance our understanding of violence and contributed to programs sheltering battered women and their children (Schechter, 1982). Yet, what is remarkable about the caution of these feminists—based solely on their practical, political experience—is its correspondence with the academic critique of mainstream social science. That is, science, for all its claims of objectivity, has in fact often been used as a powerful tool to mask an ideological, political agenda (Wardell, Gillespie, & Leffler, 1981; Hoff, 1985).

The politicized women working in the women's movement in this urban U.S. setting seemed similar to citizens of politically awakened developing countries that had overthrown colonialism. They recognized at least some anthropologists as tools of colonial administrators, disguised in the purportedly "neutral" endeavor of science. Having embarked on a path of self-determination, people being researched now require researchers to pass a test based on the needs and values of those being researched (Adams 1981, pp. 155-160; duToit, 1980). The standard term *subjects of research* took on a different meaning: In this traditional mold, those being researched seemed more like "objects" who were "subject" to the predetermined designs of the researcher. Even the term *informants,* as used traditionally in anthropology, is inadequate to describe the new role in research demanded by politically sensitized members of society.

However, it is one thing to acknowledge and incorporate the needs of those being researched into the research design. It is quite another to accomplish this without compromising the knowledge goals of the researcher to the political objectives of the researched. In this research, my efforts to deal with this problem began as follows. I declared this assumption from the outset: Research with disempowered groups on a value-laden topic such as violence against women cannot be *only* a scientific endeavor; it also has ethical and political aspects. Clearly, at every specific step of the research project, this general resolution had to be put into practice through a difficult process of balancing differing needs. I see the failure to acknowledge these intertwined political/scientific aspects of the problem as a major factor in the continuing polarization between academics and social activists concerned with this problem.

Secondary Effects
of the Research Process

Distinguishing possible research effects from all other factors operating in the lives of the study participants was a significant part of the research process. It touched on the political aspect of studying this sensitive topic, the antagonism between some feminist activists and researchers, and the methodology used. Various measures were pursued throughout the months of research to document and clarify these interacting factors.

In the early phases of this study I had envisioned contacting former battered women through follow-up programs of shelters, only to find that such programs were practically nonexistent—at least in a formal sense. As it turned out, research itself served as an avenue for certain follow-up services to the women. While I took extraordinary care to avoid any interactions with the women that could be interpreted as exploitative, I also had to avoid doing too much for the women and thus creating possible unhealthy dependencies. This involved my conscious attention to distinguish between research, advocacy, therapeutic, and friendship relationships with the women.

This kind of thing is not new among field workers: The study participants do an essential part of the study by the information they contribute; without them there would be no study. The researcher typically offers to return favors in the form of goods and services, and relationships inevitably develop out of such extended involvement. While some researchers pay the participants, I decided not to do so. Instead, I assisted the women in the following ways: babysitting, transportation, cooking meals or bringing food or treats to their home, loaning my car, writing advocacy letters, being available on the phone, calling lawyers, going on outings, and so on. At the end of the information-gathering phase, I also promised the women that they would share in any book royalties if and when the study is published. The process of juggling several kinds of interaction with the women was sometimes helped and sometimes complicated by my commitment to a collaborative research relationship in which the usual hierarchical lines between researcher and participants were at least partially blurred.

Without exception, an unintended but welcomed side effect of the study was the beneficial outcome of the research process for the women participants. Throughout the project I noted periodically that the women found it very painful to recount their experiences associated with the battering.

> It was self-enlightening, but emotionally painful. Weighing the two, it's worth it, though the pain was positive. . . . It's been therapeutic but painful. It got things out that may never have been gotten out. What it dug up for me was the relationship of the battering with my *own* problems, what kept me in it, etc. I've told you things I've never told anyone.

When emotional pain became evident during interviewing or other interaction with the women, their decision to participate in the research was reassessed. None of the women withdrew once they became involved beyond a superficial level. At the end of the formal process of data-gathering, the women were asked explicitly to comment on the effects the research had on them and why they decided to take part in it.

> That (a lengthy research interview) was the most incredible experience I've been through. I took about five steps forward. It helped me so much. You were the first person I could really marathon with. I answered a lot of my own questions, but I didn't realize how little I thought of myself before we talked. I even started making meals for myself. I've come a long way, though still have a long way to go.

The women stated informally at various times that it was valuable for them to take part in the project in spite of the emotional and time investments demanded by it. Relationships and trust had developed to produce a context in which to continue exploring sensitive, painful experiences.

> I wanted to make a contribution more than I wanted to bury it. Maybe I could have both—make a contribution *and* bury it.

> A few things tied together. It has brought up topics I've never discussed with anyone. There's a therapeutic benefit in examining things. It could be a real burden if the interviewer made one feel more guilty. Interviewers have to be thoroughly screened in their expertise and values. [This woman

has some training in research methods.][Why did you take part?] It's hard to say no. It's a worthwhile cause. I'd like to be able to contribute to helping other women to get out of their situations, to get out sooner or not get into them at all.

I realize that a lot of women have gone through this...the understanding helped. You have truly listened to me and were objective. I don't talk to my family. I finally wanted to speak out about my situation.

Another woman affirmed the value of trying to help others through the research.

I thought if I could be honest and open maybe it could help someone. I've always wanted to share, so someone can draw strength from it. I didn't even know there was literature about this. I felt very isolated, like people with leprosy. Some people want to stay away from battered women, like they're going to catch that disease. I want people to know that I'm a human being, that I'm not a bad person and that I don't feel that I was *responsible* for the battering. I was responsible for letting myself get *involved* in something like that but maybe if I'd been more realistic about life and myself and had a higher self-esteem maybe I wouldn't have gotten battered, but he was responsible for hitting me. I just want people to know that just because they were battered life doesn't stop there...There's a chance for them.

The women's generally positive accounts of the research process can be interpreted in terms of the extent and stability of time spent with them, factors that are related to the collaborative methodology used for the study. In contrast to brief survey interviews, the time spent with the researcher extended over several months for all the research participants and over a year for some. Even though explicit attention was directed during the study to separate the research process from therapeutic intervention, the very fact that the women received sustained attention and interest for an extended period of time results in secondary therapeutic side effects of the research process, apart from the opportunity they saw in helping other women. Anthropologists have described such relationships and positive side effects for decades. They also account for a phenomenon called "going native," that is, the anthropologist becoming totally absorbed into the culture being researched.

Even if the researcher does not "go native," the problem of dependency on the relationship with the researcher must be dealt with. Generally, the study participants and I have maintained a collegial relationship, with mutual interests in follow-up research and other activities concerning battered women. From my perspective as the researcher, I sense the potential of long-term friendships with most of the women. As a result of the research process, my own life will never be the same. The women's accounts have left me with moral outrage at their unnecessary suffering, inspiration from their strength and courage, and a reaffirmation of my feminist vision for social change. In the case of the shelter collective, however, I continue to detect from some members distrust about my designs as a researcher. This suggests only partial success in my intent to bridge gaps between feminist activists and academics/researchers through this research.

Conclusions

This chapter examines some of the methodological issues that emerged during a one-year field study on violence against women. Analysis of the "problem of access" and "secondary effects of the research process" reveals the importance of making values explicit when embarking on the study of a sensitive topic with political and ethical ramifications for study participants. Evidence from this study helps to dislodge the myth of objectivity in research and supports the counterclaim that research is intervention.

REFERENCES

Adams, R. N. (1981, Summer). Ethical principles in anthropological research: One or many? *Human Organization: Journal of the Society for Applied Anthropology, 2,* 155-160.

Ahrens, L. (1980, May-June). Battered women's refuges: Feminist cooperatives vs. social service institutions. *Radical America, 14,* 41-47.

Breines, W., & Gordon, L. (1983, Spring). The new scholarship on family violence. *Signs: Journal of Women in Culture and Society, 8,* 490-531.

Cicourel, A. V. (1964). *Method and measurement in sociology.* New York: Free Press.

Dexter, L. A. (1958). A note on selective inattention in social science. *Social Problems, 6,* 176-182.

Dobash, R. P., & Dobash, R. E. (1979). *Violence against wives: A case against the patriarchy.* New York: Free Press.

duToit, B. M. (1980). Ethics, informed consent, and fieldwork. *Journal of Anthropological Research, 36,* 174-186.

Geertz, C. (1973). *The interpretation of cultures: Selected essays by Clifford Geertz.* New York: Basic Books.

Gelles, R. J., & Straus, M. A. (1979). Determinants of violence in the family: Toward a theoretical integration. In W. Burr et al. (Eds.), *Contemporary theories about the family* (Vol. II). New York: Free Press.

Gergen, K. J. (1982). *Toward transformation in social knowledge.* New York: Springer.

Goode, W. (1971). Force and violence in the family. *Journal of Marriage and the Family, 33,* 624-636.

Hilberman, E. (1980). Overview: The "wife beater's wife" reconsidered. *American Journal of Psychiatry, 137,* 1336-1347.

Hoff, L. A. (1984). *Violence against women: A social-cultural network analysis.* Unpublished doctoral dissertation, Boston University.

Hoff, L. A. (1985, January). Suicide and life-threatening behavior [review of C. Neuringer & D. Lettieri, *Suicidal women: Their thinking and feeling patterns.* New York: Gardner, 1982.]

Martin, D. (1976). *Battered wives.* San Francisco: Glide.

Oakley, A. (1981). Interviewing women: A contradiction in terms. In H. Roberts (Ed.), *Doing feminist research.* London: Routledge & Kegan Paul.

Phillips, D. L. (1973). *Abandoning method.* San Francisco: Jossey-Bass.

Reinharz, S. (1979). *On becoming a social scientist.* San Francisco: Jossey-Bass.

Roberts, H. (Ed.). (1981). *Doing feminist research.* London: Routledge & Kegan Paul.

Schechter, S. (1982). *Women and male violence.* Boston: South End.

Stark, E., Flitcraft, A., & Frazier, W. (1979). Medicine and patriarchal violence: The social construction of a "private" event. *International Journal of Health Services, 9,* 461-493.

Straus, M. A., Gelles, R. J., & Steinmetz, S. K. (1980). *Behind closed doors: Violence in the American family.* New York: Anchor.

Wallston, B. S. (1981, Summer). What are the questions in psychology of women? A feminist approach to research. *Psychology of Women Quarterly,* 597-617.

Wardell, L., Gillespie, D. L., & Leffler, A. (1981). *Science and violence against wives.* Paper presented at the National Conference for Family Violence Researchers, Durham, NH.

Watson-Franke, M. R. (1980). Bias, male and female. *Man, 15,* 377-379.

Wolfgang, M. (1958). *Patterns in criminal homicide.* Philadelphia: University of Pennsylvania Press.

14

Integrating Feminist Theory and Practice

The Challenge of the Battered Women's Movement

ELLEN PENCE
MELANIE SHEPARD

The long tradition in Minnesota of socially responsive government and corporate foundations, as well as social activism at the grass roots level, has created a supportive atmosphere in which to work on the issue of violence against women. This climate has provided the state's battered women's movement with the opportunity to put into practice much of the theory and vision articulated by feminists across the country who are committed to stopping violence against women. This chapter describes the efforts of one program, the Domestic Abuse Intervention Project (DAIP), to work toward institutional change in the criminal justice system, and examines several philosophical issues that have emerged from its development.

In Minnesota, as in most other states, the formative years of the movement focused on providing safe housing and advocacy for battered women by establishing shelters. While the need for institutional change was recognized by the growing number of grass roots organizations, scarce resources and limited people power forced them to concentrate on helping women in immediate danger to find safety.

Women's Advocates, one of the oldest surviving shelters in the country, opened in Minnesota in 1974 and provided an incredible source of information, guidance, and strength for the ever-increasing number of programs. Between 1976 and 1979, 14 other shelters opened, with each region of the state having a fully funded shelter, and the metropolitan area of Minneapolis/St. Paul having five. Nonresidential programs started forming to meet the need for geographic or specialized services that could not be met by the shelters. By 1980, 30 operating programs were members of the Minnesota state coalition.

With only a few exceptions, the newly developed programs attempted to create grass roots organizations that would give real power and true credence to the leadership of battered women. Borrowing language from each other's proposals, mission statements, brochures, and articles of incorporation, programs formally and informally networked, created philosophy, identified problems, found solutions, and celebrated successes.

While programs for battered women continued to expand and develop, workers in the field often faced the question: "What about the men; what are you doing for them?" In response to this concern, the State Task Force for Battered Women, which advised the state of Minnesota on the distribution of some $2 million, decided in 1979 to fund a two year pilot project for violent partners. Such a project was appealing to funders and legislators because it seemed to get at the "root" of the problem. Over a two-year period, three programs were provided $250,000 in funds to focus on the batterer.

The first three projects all had a similar orientation of providing counseling and advocacy, but each proposed working with different populations. All three programs worked with court mandated clients, and to differing degrees, attempted to affect changes in the referral and enforcement process used by the courts. Two of the programs proposed focusing much of their work with men of color and their partners.

The following year, activists in the shelter movement began discussing the need for an approach that was geared more toward the use of community institutions to intervene actively with assailants and impose legal sanctions against those who batter. The first such program to be developed, and later replicated in over 20 Minnesota communities, was the Domestic Abuse Intervention Project (DAIP) in Duluth.

Models of Intervention

Currently, there is debate on the appropriateness of various approaches for working with men who batter, which reflects the different theoretical perspectives of service providers and activists. These approaches can be grouped according to three basic levels of analysis: the intraindividual, socio-psychological, and sociocultural (Gelles & Straus, 1979). Efforts to stop individuals from battering have concentrated in two areas: criminal justice reform and treatment. With few exceptions, most of the literature has focused on treatment models. In the literature describing different treatment approaches, emphasis may be given to eliminating individual skill deficits, improving interpersonal relationships, changing behavioral and cognitive patterns, and/or providing education about sexism and the use of violence to control and dominate women.

While much of the practice literature discusses the importance of social and cultural factors, the focus of treatment has often been on the personality or skill deficits of the batterer, although there is no empirical evidence of a personality profile that can be attributed to all batterers. Yet characterizations of batterers that describe them as lacking self esteem and the ability to express feelings appropriately, and being overly dependent, impulsive, and controlling, have led many practitioners to conclude that a supportive environment—one that allows for the sharing of feelings and for teaching interpersonal skills—is an important element of treatment (Brisson, 1982; Currie, 1983; Deschner, 1984; Ganley, 1981; Purdy & Nickel, 1981; Star, 1983).

At a social-psychological level of analysis, many practitioners have adopted a social-learning perspective, whereby battering is seen as a learned behavior, which is often a response to stress (Ganley, 1981; Purdy & Nickel, 1981). Cognitive behavioral treatment methods derived from social learning theory are being applied in programs for batterers (Deschner, 1984; Edelson, 1984; Purdy & Nickel, 1981; Saunders, 1984). Family systems theory is also being used by practitioners, whereby violence is seen as a relationship issue and is viewed in terms of interaction between the couple (Cook & Frantz-Cook, 1984; Geller, 1982; Neidig & Freidman, 1984). From this perspective, intervention focuses on changing relationship patterns that maintain violence.

From the sociocultural perspective, programs often attempt to restructure rigid sex role expectations that are believed to contribute to domestic violence (Feazell, Mayers, & Deschner, 1984). Some programs, including the Domestic Abuse Intervention Project, draw from feminist theory to address issues of sexism in more depth by focusing on the social acceptance of male violence and the use of violence to control and dominate women (Adams & McCormick, 1982; Currie, 1983; Pence & Paymar, 1985). The emphasis is on changing the attitudes of group

participants, typically through the use of an educati
peer support groups. Criminal justice intervention i
component of many of these programs.

The Domestic Abuse Intervention Project chall
emphasize abnormalities within the batterer, the relationship, or the
victim because these "promote treatment strategies which do not alter
the power system which creates the foundation of battering behavior"
(Pence, 1985, p. 2). An emphasis on personal skill deficits, stress, and/or
relationship issues, shifts attention away from the use of violence as a
means of control and domination, which is the basis for battering
behavior. Instead, wife beating is viewed as a crime, which must be
responded to in an effective manner by the police and the courts imposing increasingly harsh penalties and restrictions on the abuser. Although
counseling and education are viewed as an individual response to a
social problem, rehabilitation services are desired by both the courts and
victims and provide an opportunity to challenge the batterer's belief that
he has a right to control his partner's behavior. While the model of
intervention developed by the Domestic Abuse Intervention Project has
been altered, and in many ways has been improved by other communities, a description of the DAIP represents a fairly accurate picture
of what a feminist intervention project was designed to accomplish.

Program Description

From its inception, the Domestic Abuse Intervention Project sought
to influence the way the criminal justice system and human service
organizations responded to domestic violence. The result has been a
shift in both policy and practice at each stage of the criminal justice
process, as well as in the treatment provided by local counseling
agencies. The project coordinates the intervention of law enforcement,
criminal justice, and human service and battered women's advocacy
programs to provide comprehensive community intervention to assailants in domestic assault cases. The project was also designed to reduce
cultural supports for battering by shifting the responsibility for holding
batterers accountable for their use of violence from the victim to
community agencies of social control.

The goal of the Domestic Abuse Intervention Project is to protect
battered women by bringing an end to the violence. Four objectives of
the intervention process were implemented to achieve this goal:

   (1) to bring cases into the courts for resolution and to reduce the screening out of cases by police, prosecutors, judges, and other court personnel

   (2) to impose and enforce legal sanctions and to provide rehabilitation services to the assailant to deter him from committing further acts of violence

   (3) to provide safe emergency housing, education, and legal advocacy for women who are assaulted

   (4) to prevent assailants from either getting lost in or manipulating the judicial system by coordinating interagency information flow and monitoring each agency's adherence to agreed-upon policies and procedures

In order to achieve these objectives, policy changes were implemented in every aspect of the criminal justice and human services system in the city, and a small autonomous monitoring agency, the DAIP, was organized.

Intervention with the Assailant

One of the first steps taken was to encourage the police department to limit officer discretion in handling domestic assault cases. In 1982, after much testing, a mandatory arrest policy was adopted by the Duluth police department. The policy required that an arrest be made when the responding officers could establish probable cause to believe that an assault had occurred within the past four hours and there were signs of injury to the victim. Later the policy was expanded to require arrest when officers established that a civil protection order was violated. This policy applied in all cases in which the assailant and victim were currently or had formerly been residing together. It resulted in an increase in arrests from 22 in 1980, to 175 in the 12 months after its first fully operational year in 1983 (Pence, 1985). Under state law, and in accordance with the written policy, police officers were required to file reports on all calls involving a complaint of an assault. Shelter advocates were then allowed to review all police reports three times a week in order to provide follow-up advocacy to women in situations in which arrests were not made. In cases in which arrests were made, the jailor, after incarcerating the assailant, contacted the shelter, providing the name of the victim, her address, and phone number. The shelter, within a two-hour period, dispatched an on-call advocate to meet with the victim to discuss protective procedures, the court process, and resources available to her in the community. Assailants arrested were typically held overnight in jail, allowing time for shelter advocates to contact women to offer assistance.

Prosecution guidelines were adopted by the city attorney's office, which discouraged the dismissal of charges and linked battered women with advocates at the onset of the criminal justice process. Central to all negotiating meetings was the principle that a battered woman would not be forced to participate in a prosecution process that she was opposed to. Prosecution guidelines gave victims more input and control in the use of plea-bargaining and charging. Conviction rates were increased from an estimated 20% in 1980 to 87% in 1983 (Pence, 1985). A key reason for such a high prosecution rate was the increased use of the civil protection order by women unsure of their desire to involve the criminal prosecution process.

County court judges agreed to allow for input regarding sentencing from victims and project staff by ordering presentence investigations prior to imposing sentences and by agreeing to suggested guidelines that would be followed by probation officers when making sentencing recommendations. While the court did not agree to limit its autonomy in imposing sentences, it did generally agree to impose stayed jail sentences on first time misdemeanors without aggravating circumstances and to order participation in six months of education or counseling groups and chemical dependency treatment, if appropriate. Sentencing guidelines suggested a 20- to 90-day jail sentence for second offenses, in addition to appropriate counseling or treatment. The court also agreed to obtain input through the project staff and the probation officers regarding the special safety needs of victims during the probationary period, such as restricted or limited contact with the assailant. Finally, the court agreed to enforce its orders vigorously and to support the monitoring by DAIP staff of court orders and assailants' compliance with probation agreements.

About half of the domestic abuse cases handled by the courts in the city of Duluth are civil protection orders. The DAIP has worked to formalize civil court proceedings so that a determination is made that abuse does or does not exist. This is in sharp contrast to the previous practice of holding a brief and informal hearing in which the court typically asked if anyone had objections to the issuance of an order, and if not, proceeded to issue an order without ever determining whether or not abuse existed. These procedures led to the failure of the court system to enforce its order vigorously because it had never adequately established the need for the order at the initial hearing. Under current practices where domestic abuse is established by a reasonable preponderance of the evidence by the court, the abuser is typically ordered to limit or cease contact with the victim, to participate in the DAIP counseling and educational program, and in some cases, to limit or cease contact with the children.

Another change in the handling of civil protection orders was the court's reversal in its policy of not issuing orders in which the respondent and the petitioner were living together and wished to continue living together. Under the existing procedures of the court, once a person has begun the counseling or education program, and at the request of the petitioner, the respondent may return to the home after a hearing to determine what safety precautions are necessary.

Whether the assailant is ordered by the criminal or civil courts to participate in the counseling/education program, the rules of their participation are the same. Seven open-ended men's groups and one women's group are required to accommodate the number of court ordered clients. The DAIP contracts with the participants for a 26-week program that includes two orientation sessions provided by the DAIP. Some 80% of the participants are required to attend 12 weeks of a group counseling offered by community counseling agencies and 12 weeks of DAIP-sponsored educational classes. The other 20% of the participants are required to attend 24 educational classes sponsored by the DAIP. More than two unexcused absences from counseling or educational groups in a three-month period typically results in a DAIP request for a revocation of probation hearing or a court review of the civil protection order.

Involving local agencies in providing group counseling not only expanded the services available in the community, but also resulted in a shift in the treatment methods being used in working with batterers. Prior to the project, counseling agencies were using couples counseling in domestic violence cases, which has been criticized for failing to place responsibility for the violence with the batterer. With the initiation of the project, counselors from three agencies (Lutheran Social Services, Human Development Center, and Family Service of Duluth) were trained by Dr. Anne Ganley in a psychoeducational model. The model stresses client accountability, a clear and consistent treatment goal, use of confrontation techniques, a structured group format, and a directive counselor role (Ganley, 1981).

The counseling groups focus on anger management by concentrating on specific ways of dealing with anger, stress, and conflict. Two tools used by the counselors in the program, as well as by many others in the field, are the "time-out" procedures and the "anger log" (Ganley, 1981; Sonkin & Durphy, 1981). In the "time-out" procedure, men are instructed to leave situations where they are becoming angry and to engage in stress-reducing physical and mental exercises. The "anger log" is used to facilitate self observation and to analyze and change thinking patterns (or cognitive restructuring). It is a written homework assignment in which the men describe an event that triggered their anger, rate their anger level, record their "self talk" or internal dialogue that escalated the anger and the "self talk" that they could have used to reduce it, as well as identify other feelings they were having at the time. Group discussion of the logs facilitates the identification of behavioral patterns and alternatives.

During the counseling groups, the concepts of control and dominance are introduced as the purpose and function of battering. The education groups emphasize this further by focusing on the use of abuse as a means of controlling the thoughts, feelings, and actions of the victim, and challenges the assailant's belief system. A range of abusive behaviors such as isolating the victim from contact with others, abusing her emotionally through repeated criticisms and degradations, using intimidation to threaten and frighten her, demanding compliance or subservience because of male privilege or entitlement, restricting access to finances, and using physical and sexual abuse, are identified as controlling behaviors used to impose one's will on the victim. The curriculum includes a series of taped vignettes that illustrate these controlling behaviors. Group participants analyze these tapes, as well as their own behavior, through the use of "control logs" that include a description of the situation; the intent of the behavior; identification of feelings; the effect of the actions taken on those involved; the impact of the previous violence on the immediate situation; and alternative noncontrolling, nonabusive courses of action.

The counseling and education groups approach the problem of domestic violence from different and, in some ways, contradictory perspectives. Drawing from cognitive behavioral methods, the counselors focus on changing specific behaviors and on teaching skills for handling conflict and managing anger. While this approach addresses the violence, it fails to address the nature of the relationship, which is one of dominance over the victim. Psychologically abusive behaviors may continue to be used to maintain this position of dominance. The educators, on the other hand, are challenging deeply held cultural and societal beliefs about the role of women in relation to men. Participants are taught that it is not their anger that leads them to be violent, but rather their belief that they have a right to control and dominate women. The educators encourage men to examine the destructive nature of the tactics they believe they can use to assure their victim's compliance with their perception of what her role should be.

Intervention with the Victim

Since the first battered women's programs, started in the early 1970s, there has been debate over many strategies within the movement, including: the value of organizing for change in the criminal justice system, what policy and procedural changes are needed, the need for developing programs for abusers, and even the value of starting shelters as opposed to direct political action. Perhaps the only strategy that has been widely agreed upon is that organizing battered women's groups that provide information, education, and support is a critical component of our work.

The women's advocacy component that is implemented by the shelter is a crucial aspect of the coordinated approach adopted in Duluth. Four full-time staff work with over 500 women who never reside at the shelter. The intervention advocates help in every aspect of legal and welfare advocacy, and organize and facilitate four neighborhood-based educational groups. Many women identify the educational groups as the most significant factor in their struggle to end the violence being used against them. Perhaps the best description of the women's education groups can be found in this quote from one of the shelter advocates.

> Twelve—eighteen—twenty-five women crawled into a smoky room, listening to someone talking about the "dynamics of battering" or "psychological abuse." And as she listens, she sees other women nodding, hears other women talking, realizes that all these women have also been assaulted by their partners. She talks to the women sitting next to her. She makes connections. She's not so alone. She has information about why she is being battered. She knows that there are people out there that care, people she can call. She has a place she can go and talk. There are a lot more doors open now. And should she decide to leave her abuser, to get a court order for protection, to file assault charges, she knows that an advocate will be there to help her with the paperwork, to sit the long hours on the bench in the courthouse. (Pence & Burns, 1985, p. 3)

Women's groups are designed to create a place where batterers and their coconspirators in the system cannot control the discussion; they cannot interpret the facts; they cannot silence women's minds nor keep women from speaking. The purpose of the group is for women to rename their experiences. To look not at what defect within them made

their partners hit them, but how men are able to take control o
lives so completely. And finally, the groups are designed to cre
space for women to find their personal power to join with other women
to take back control of their lives. The best police and court systems will
be ineffective without building in such a support system for women.

Advocates teach women how to use the courts, how to gather much of
the evidence needed for the trial, how to work with the prosecutor in a
case. Women have begun in unprecedented numbers to use the court
both because they now understand how to use it and because the court is
willing to take measures to protect them. The educational groups focus
on teaching women about all forms of battering, its impact on them and
their children, and the importance of consistently holding the abuser
accountable for his behavior. As women begin to name and explore the
abusive and violent ways they have been controlled and the impact those
controls have had on them, on their relationships, and on their children,
the abusers' ability to use their partners to shield themselves from the
courts is diminished.

The role of the shelter and the advocate cannot be underestimated.
With few exceptions, battered women become increasingly isolated
from family, friends, and their communities. This isolation is inten-
tionally imposed by the abuser to cut her off from a potential support
system he may view as threatening. When a man is physically abusing his
partner or child, almost all contact with outside influences becomes a
threat. Friends, family, church members, neighbors, and professionals
in the community often increase her isolation by "not noticing" the
abuse. When outsiders do get involved, too frequently they begin to
pressure her to do something about his violence, thus failing to
understand the inability of victims to stop their partner's violence
without a tremendous amount of support and a force more powerful
than he (i.e., the courts).

The intervention process must always keep the victim's safety as its
first consideration and resist tendencies to minimize the danger in these
cases. Outside intervention may result in a more forceful attempt by
abusers to isolate their victims. Some abusers will attack their victims
regardless of any threat of jail or punishment. Without the ability to
provide women safe shelter, intervention can increase the danger to
some women.

Program Evaluation

Two studies conducted to evaluate the program indicated significant
reductions in rates of abuse, particularly during the first three months of

the intervention process (Novak & Galaway, 1983; Shepard, 1987). Shepard (1987) found that approximately 70% of the victims reported no recent physical abuse at a one-year follow-up. While significantly less psychological abuse was reported, 60% of the women did report having experienced some form of psychological abuse. The extent to which different program components contributed to outcomes is unclear. Novak and Galaway (1983) did find that fewer victims reported experiencing violence from DAIP court mandated participants than from those who were not mandated.

In 1984, the DAIP embarked on a participatory research project by asking 11 formerly battered women to design a victim survey that would be used to determine the need for changes in policies or procedures in the various agencies involved in the project. A majority of the 60 victims who responded to the questionnaire reported that they had had favorable experiences with the police, shelter, and civil court processes. They reported less favorable experiences with probation officers and prosecutors. All of the victims felt that the assailant should have been ordered to attend counseling and education groups and a majority (60%) felt safer when the assailant was participating in the groups, which is also documented in the studies cited earlier. A total of 80% of the victims reported that the combined response of the police, courts, DAIP, and shelter had been helpful or very helpful.

Although the survey was anonymous, participants were invited to an open forum to discuss the results of the survey and to help the DAIP and shelter staff interpret the data. Attending the forum were 30 respondents, in addition to 25 women who were currently participating in women's groups. A total of 31 recommendations were made for altering procedures or policies. Some 42 women volunteered to serve on our committees that were formed to follow up on the implementation of the recommendations. Eventually, 23 of the recommendations were implemented.

This evaluation process did more than provide DAIP with an agenda for further work. It pointed out the importance of battered women organizing on their own behalf. The women's recommendations and their efforts to implement these recommendations brought the project back to its grass roots, where the battered women's movement began.

Putting Feminist Theory into Practice

In implementing this program, project staff attempted to put a feminist theory of battering into practice. Community agencies were called upon to impose legal sanctions against batterers, and rehabilitation services were developed that emphasized the use of violence as a means to control and dominate the victims. Program evaluation is an ongoing process that must take place within the context of a feminist analysis of battering. At each step, it is necessary to examine whether practice matches theory. In this final section, several issues that have emerged from this process are examined.

The Process of Empowerment

In every phase of organizing the DAIP, careful attention was given to obtaining input from formerly battered women. This was done in many ways, including hiring formerly battered women for the program staff, seeing that all members of the governing policy board were either formerly battered or had lived in a violent home as a child, going to women's groups three or four times a year to seek input for policies and procedures, involving shelter staff in all the decisions about policy and procedures, and continually assessing the effectiveness of the program through anonymous interviews with battered women whose partners came into the system. However, it was not until the participatory research project took place that it became apparent that the project lacked a grass roots foundation in its approach to social reform.

The lack of grass roots foundation was evidenced in the process used in the past for changing policies and procedures in the local criminal justice system, which had excluded the participation of battered women. Typically, criminal justice officials had met to discuss policies with a representative from the shelter, DAIP and, perhaps, a sympathetic judge or probation officer, who would provide support and a bit of gentle, political arm twisting. During the forum where women met to interpret data from the surveys, it became evident that the women wanted to follow through on recommendations by meeting directly with law enforcement and court officials. Two meetings were set up and were attended by dozens of women who had been involved in criminal justice cases during the past two years. At these meetings, police administrators and chief prosecutors were, for the first time, put in the position of being directly accountable to battered women instead of to only a small group of people negotiating on their behalf.

The process of directly involving battered women in negotiations resulted in two realizations on the part of DAIP staff. First, it became clear that, in the past, staff had been empowered through their participation in the project, but battered women had not. Organizing strategies for implementing project reforms had ignored the importance of empowering battered women by integrating them into the process. Second, the need for broad-based support and participation from battered women became apparent. The agenda developed by women during the forum was more comprehensive and meaningful than that which could have been developed by staff in consultation with battered women.

The Pitfalls of Models

The DAIP has learned from the forum, as well as from countless other experiences, that it must be open to revision and change, particularly because it has served as a model program. Just as the first shelter in Minnesota, Women's Advocates, became the model for all shelters in the state that opened from 1976 to 1983, so did the Domestic Abuse Intervention Project in Duluth become the model for over 20 intervention projects that started between 1982 and 1986. Throughout the past three years, literally hundreds of people have come from Minnesota and other states to observe protection order hearings, trials, women's groups, and men's groups; to interview policy administrators, judges, prosecutors, shelter workers; and to ask the question, "How did you get it to work?"

In comparing notes with these many visitors, it became apparent that it was often difficult to draw parallels between our communities. Obstacles that seemed almost insurmountable to those of us organizing in Duluth, presented no problems in other communities. Therefore, it was important for each community that sought to use the written materials and the experiences of those who had worked in the Duluth project to filter that experience through the political, social, and cultural realities of their own communities.

The major pitfall encountered, however, was not the need to adapt the model to different communities. Rather, it was the need for each community to experience its own learning process, from which would emerge a theory and philosophy upon which to base its intervention. Paulo Friere, in *Pedagogy In Process* (1983), recommends caution when bringing radical/transforming concepts in the form of knowledge and experience to new communities. He states, "If the dichotomy between teaching and learning results in the refusal of the one who teaches to learn from the one being taught, it grows out of an ideology of domination. Those who are called to teach must first learn how to continue learning when they begin to teach. . . . Experiments cannot be transplanted; they must be reinvented" (p. 10).

While it is not necessary continually to reinvent the wheel, we must be mindful that the process of discovery is fundamental to the acquisition of meaningful knowledge. The many hours of discussion, debate, testing, thinking, and rethinking that went into the development of the first shelters and the first intervention projects in Minnesota produced more than a product. It created a consciousness within the group of organizers and the community that kept those projects in motion. As new people join these projects or as new communities replicate them, the process of creating must be continued. Too often there is a gradual bureaucratization of model programs when organizers leave and new staff and volunteers move in to maintain the model. Likewise, communities that have not gone through the process of discovery may be able to implement the model mechanically, but not its spirit. This process separates practice from theory and causes stagnation.

Any model must be recognized for both its strengths and weaknesses. The Domestic Abuse Intervention Project has opened doors for advocacy programs to institute criminal justice reforms across the country. However, just as the DAIP formed a small group of negotiators to go into the system to negotiate policy changes and procedures without authentic participation of battered women, so did the dozens of other projects that organized using that model as a base. Both the mistakes and the successes of the project are being replicated.

What About the Men?

This question brings us back full circle. What does the battered women's movement or the women's movement at large have to do with men or men's lives? Almost every issue these days is discussed in terms of some imaginary continuum from one extreme position to another. In answering this question, one end of the continuum would hold that the women's movement has nothing to do with men, save those activities that restrict men's ability to control women. The other end of the continuum would hold that both men and women are victims of this culture and the women's movement should care for both the battering man and the battered women.

Both ends of the continuum seem equally misguided. On the one hand, the DAIP rejects the notion of men as victims of sexism. Any system that gives one group power over another group dehumanizes both those with too much power and those without enough power. However, that does not make those who abuse their access to power innocent victims of the system. Ultimately, each of us must be held accountable for the choices we make. This project challenges men to see their use of violence as a choice; not an uncontrolled reaction to their past, their anger, or their lack of skills, but a choice.

On the other hand, the energy and resources it takes to place restrictions on the hundreds of thousands of men who physically attack their partners is staggering. The successful implementation of the DAIP makes us painfully aware of how limited such a strategy is in our ultimate goal of ending battering. While all of our data suggests that victims are more satisfied with the system's response to their need for protection, there is no evidence to suggest that such a community intervention model will eventually lead to less battering.

Conclusion

If our practice is rooted in feminist theory, then the realization that this model will not eradicate battering should neither surprise nor discourage us. Battering is rooted in a culture of domination, a culture that does not celebrate our differences in race, age, sexual preference, physical and mental abilities, and gender, but instead uses these differences to exploit and dehumanize. Surely we cannot expect that sending out the police to pluck batterers from their homes, using the courts to make all sorts of nasty threats of doom, and rounding up counselors and teachers to convince men to stop beating their partners will end violence against women.

It is only when we put this and similar projects into perspective that we can come to an understanding of its place in the women's movement. This work can and does make individual women safer. It can and does save women's lives. It can make it easier for women to be about their real business, the work of transforming the culture that violates every part of their being and spirit. Projects like these are not about changing men, but about creating safe space for women to live in and participating in their communities in order to create a more sane society.

There is a difference between reforming institutions and transforming society. Much of that difference lies in the process by which reforms are achieved. While the DAIP has achieved institutional reform, the process used to achieve this reform could have been far more empowering to battered women. The growing trend in the movement to negotiate for change on behalf of women, rather than to organize women to affect change on their own behalf, is nowhere better modeled than in the design and implementation of the DAIP. This trend, if unaltered, is likely to lead to a continued distancing of programs from a feminist analysis, and will cause stagnation in our collective creative ability to change and transform this society.

It is the challenge of continually basing our practice in feminist theory that provides the most exciting opportunities for those of us who work in this movement. When we abandon or modify theory or philosophy, in the interest of practicality, we move away from our strength (Vazquez, 1977). It is the constant interaction of theory and practice that keeps a movement dynamic, growing, changing, and most importantly, moving.

REFERENCES

Adams, D. C., & McCormick, A. J. (1982). Men unlearning violence: A group approach based on the collective model. In M. Roy (Ed.), *The abusive partner*. New York: Van Nostrand Reinhold.

Brisson, N. (1982). Helping men who batter women. *Public Welfare, 40*, 29-35.

Cook, D. R., & Frantz-Cook, A. (1984). A systematic treatment approach to wife battering. *Journal of Marriage and Family Therapy, 10*, 83-93.

Currie, David D. (1983). A Toronto model. *Social Work With Groups, 6*, 179-188.

Deschner, J. P. (1984). *The hitting habit*. New York: Free Press.

Edelsen, J. L. (1984). Working with men who batter. *Social Work, 29*, 237-242.

Feazell, C. S., Mayers, R. S., & Deschner, J. (1984). Services for men who batter: Implications for programs and policies. *Family Relations, 33*, 217-223.

Freire, P. (1983). *Pedagogy in process*. New York: Continuum.

Ganley, A. L. (1981). *Court mandated counseling for men who batter: A three-day workshop for mental health professionals*. Washington, D. C.: Center for Women Policy Studies.

Geller, J. (1982). Conjoint therapy: Staff training and treatment of the abuser and abused. In M. Roy (Ed.), *The abusive partner*. New York: Van Nostrand Reinhold.

Gelles, R., & Straus, M. (1979). Determinants of violence in the family: Toward a theoretical integration. In W. R. Burr, R. Hill, F. I. Nye, & I. L. Reiss (Eds.), *Contemporary theories about the family* (Vol. 1). New York: Free Press.

Neidig, P., & Freidman, D. H. (1984). *Spouse abuse: A treatment program for couples*. Champaign, IL: Research Press.

Novak, S., & Galaway, B. (1983). Domestic Abuse Intervention Project—Final report. Unpublished manuscript.

Pence, E. (1985). *Criminal justice response to domestic assault cases: A guide for policy development*. Duluth, MN: Domestic Abuse Intervention Project.

Pence, E., & Burns, N. (1985). *In our best interest*. Duluth, MN: Women's Coalition and the Domestic Abuse Intervention Project.

Pence, E., & Paymar, M. (1985). *Power and control: Tactics of men who batter.* (Facilitators guide to educational curriculum.) Duluth, MN: Domestic Abuse Intervention Project.

Purdy, F., & Nickel, N. (1981). Practice principles for working with groups of men who batter. *Social Work with Groups, 4,* 111-112.

Saunders, D. G. (1984, June). Helping husbands who batter. *Social Casework,* 347-353.

Shepard, M. (1987). *Intervention with men who batter: Evaluation of a Domestic Abuse Program.* Paper presented at the Third National Family Violence Research Conference, Durham, NH.

Sonkin, D. J., & Durphy, M. (1981). *Learning to live without violence: A book for men.* San Francisco: Volcano.

Star, B. (1983). *Helping the abuser.* New York: Family Services Association of America.

Vazquez, A. S. (1977). *The philosophy of praxis.* New York: Humanities Press.

15

Building Bridges
Between Activists,
Professionals, and Researchers

SUSAN SCHECHTER

Before the growth of shelters, many people viewed battered women as passive, dependent, or aberrant. The battered women's movement caused us all to see abused women in a new light. Shelters offered the supportive framework through which women turned "personal" problems into political ones, relieved themselves of self-blame, and called attention to the sexism that left millions violently victimized. Temporarily freed from threats of retaliation and danger, battered women in shelters could display their long-ignored energy, rage, and coping abilities and reveal their similarity to all women. Any theory of violence against women that failed to account for the extraordinary personal transformations that occur in shelters would distort the truth about battered women.

Over the last several years, researchers, government officials, and professionals have appreciated the importance of services for battered women, yet at the same time, they have transformed the issues that feminists and grass roots women painstakingly raised. For example, by 1977 activists had forced the words "battered women" into public consciousness. However, funders, researchers, and professionals began

AUTHOR'S NOTE: All but the last section of this chapter are drawn from my book *Women and Male Violence*. My thanks to the South End Press for publication permission.

to proclaim a "spouse abuse problem"; in their false notion of equality, men were the victims of violence as frequently as women were. This change from battered woman to battered spouse masked the insights about male domination and abuse that feminists had forged.

Although women hit men, the experience of violence is usually not the same for the two sexes. Although men may be injured, battered women are left terrified. They may be subject to constant harassment, threats of death, and degrading sexual abuse. Feminists were the first to see that battering is not a gender-neutral experience. Rather, battering is a pattern of coercive control over women that uses diverse methods, and leaves women questioning their self worth and perceptions of reality. Obviously, when one human being is frightened of another with whom she lives, the two are not equals, nor can they negotiate with each other freely. In other words, a relationship of domination exists. This is not the social reality that men usually experience. Battering deprives women of their dignity and control over their lives and is, therefore, an integral part of female oppression.

Some 10 years ago activists created new, empowering services grounded in the belief that any woman could be beaten and that alternatives to domination could be found. Abused women were not the "clients" they are in some programs today, but rather participants in a joint struggle. The feminist movement had played a central role by providing new theoretical insights about women, an ideology of sisterhood, and the inspiration and support that led thousands of women to work ceaselessly, often for no money.

In a very brief time span, activists built a practice that offered battered women meaningful help for the first time. They also started and maintained institutions, negotiated with the state, changed laws, and accrued resources. They tried to maintain their visions, politics, and sanity as they dealt with constant crises, violence, and poverty in battered women's lives, and sometimes in their own.

Today feminist activists are worried about the future of services for abused women. Will shelters continue to receive funding and community support? Will mental health professionals and researchers continue to challenge feminist insights and deny the significance of gender as they study and treat family violence? Will yet another social and political issue be turned into a mental health or criminal justice problem to be solved by sending women to psychotherapy and men to jail or treatment? What will happen to battered women if a grass roots and feminist movement is undermined and professionalized?

This chapter offers professionals and researchers a bridge into the battered women's movement, an opportunity to learn the history and hear the concerns of those committed to creating feminist services and forging radical social change on behalf of women. It explores the distrust and caution that grass roots activists have been forced to maintain toward professionals and researchers, and offers suggestions about more respectful ways to approach battered women and grass roots service providers.

The Emergence of the Battered Women's Movement: Grass Roots Activism

In the early 1970s, it sometimes seemed as if battered women came out of nowhere. Suddenly feminist lawyers, therapists, and women's crisis and antirape workers were reporting hundreds of calls and visits from abused women desperately in need of housing and legal assistance. No mere accident, this groundswell was the result of the changing political consciousness and organizing activity of women. The emerging feminist movement painstakingly detailed the conditions of daily life that would allow women to call themselves battered. A fundamental assertion of the movement, women's right to control their bodies and lives, and one of its practical applications, women's hot lines and crisis centers, provided a context for battered women to speak out and ask for help. These courageous first steps by battered women and activists led to the formation of shelters—houses of refuge where battered women and their children could stay. Later, larger informal feminist networks and state and national meetings, like the 1976 International Women's Year Conference in Houston, provided the settings in which women found one another, and created a national battered women's movement.

That the battered women's movement is part of the women's liberation movement is illustrated concretely in hundreds of shelters and women's crisis centers in the United States. In St. Paul, Minnesota, Women's Advocates, one of the oldest shelters solely for battered women, began as a consciousness raising group in 1971. Later, wanting to move beyond their own small group experience, these women dreamed of opening a house for themselves and for any woman who needed a place to go. This house was to be a liberating, utopian community. Their early vision of a home never encompassed a battered women's shelter, although this is what it would become.

The first Boston shelter, Transition House, was also influenced by women's liberation ideas. Although the two women who started the shelter were former battered women, they were soon joined by two former members of Cell 16, one of Boston's earliest radical feminist groups. Women using the house were encouraged to explore their personal lives, learning the political parameters of "private" problems. For the activists at Transition House, physical abuse was not an isolated fact of daily existence. Battering was an integral part of women's oppression; women's liberation its solution.

Professionals within the battered women's movement sometimes had a different perspective. Although some professionals within the movement saw the cause of violence against women residing in family pathology, and others viewed it as a result of female oppression, those most professionally identified tended to emphasize providing traditional, "quality" services to women based on a separation between helper and client.

Generalizing about professionals is dangerous, however. Early in the movement, before government funding began, the primary motivation of most professionally trained women was a political or personal commitment to help battered women. Many professionals within the movement were feminists who worked as dedicated organizers for the first battered women's programs and later helped create legislative and social change in most states. Feminist attorneys and therapists often brought needed grant writing, lobbying, and group facilitation skills to the movement along with contacts for money within funding agencies. Or as some professionally identified women report, simply working with battered women and movement activists radicalized their views and changed their commitments.

As the movement grew, shelters with diverse philosophies and goals faced some common tasks and problems. Local groups had to convince sometimes skeptical communities and funding agencies that their shelter legitimately represented battered women. Success was never solely dependent on the women involved and their skills, nor were choices necessarily rooted in philosophical ideals. One shelter reported:

Our strongest support has to come from conservative organizations in our community—the Baptist Church, the Y, the United Way. Public funds aren't available in our town except for the police and fire departments and small services. We simply had to become part of the local Y to survive. We had to call the problem family violence, not battered women. Program development consists of taking what you can get and going with it. We don't have the luxury to choose our resources.

Publicizing the experiences of battered women as victims of male violence and social indifference was the most commonly chosen form of legitimating the need for a shelter. As one woman stated, "No one is in favor of domestic violence."

Throughout the country, women's groups tell animated stories about efforts to legitimate their activities. Some groups moved into buildings, declared their need, and squeaked by for months on courage, hard work, and the intense energy they generated. Their efforts moved people to respond. Others, the majority, spent years lobbying, testifying, and writing grants. Almost all relied heavily on educational forums, public hearings, radio, and television to reconceptualize the issue and explain its parameters, stressing that woman abuse was a community responsibility rather than an interpersonal "problem." Often, months or years were spent gathering allies among legislators, agency directors, and foundation staff, and convincing them that a problem and a constituency existed. Elected officials and the many state and local commissions on the status of women held hearings that legitimated the issues. Battered women came forward along with activists and professionals to testify repeatedly about the desperate need that mandated shelter funding. In many cities, women's clubs, the Junior League, or the National Council of Jewish Women responded as needed allies during hearings, and supplied small grants or volunteers.

For change to occur, strategies had to be matched by persistence, skill, and unpredictable luck. In one state, feminists spent three years lobbying their Public Welfare Department for funding with no results; the next year, a supportive woman became director, and substantial funding was granted immediately to programs statewide. In another state it took tragedy to create change. As legislators debated the first domestic violence bill, and women lobbied around the clock, two battered women were murdered by their husbands. Legislation was enacted rapidly. As one activist recalls, "Our local Junior League had a member whose husband killed her right after she had complained about him at a Junior League meeting. They became immediate supporters of the shelter, helping us enormously."

Because women's groups established services long before other organizations offered any help to battered women, many funding agencies and community institutions were moved, sometimes grudgingly, to trust them and use their programs. In huge numbers, battered women also turned to these new organizations, which, unlike other agencies, provided the concrete assistance they needed. The fact that most shelters stayed full from the first day they opened spoke most eloquently in the search for legitimacy and funding that continues to this day.

Acquiring and transmitting skills at a breathtaking rate, shelters moved to gain as much as possible for battered women from sometimes recalcitrant, endlessly delaying bureaucracies. Persistence and hard work were crucial as were patience and self-control in the face of condescension and sexist jokes about abused women and the cute "girls" helping them.

In addition to providing room and board for victims of abuse, shelters worked to protect battered women's rights, a more difficult and elusive task than it would seem. Advocates were forced to know more than the local welfare or police bureaucrats, who often ran circles around uninformed clients, denying them their legal rights through technicalities. Any shelter resident might find herself in family, criminal, or divorce court; she might need welfare benefits or have to sign up on a waiting list for a low-cost apartment from the housing authority. At any moment, if criminal charges were pressed or injuries noted, the police, the bureau of child welfare, and a hospital might also become involved. Staff and volunteers were extensively trained in advocacy and spent a substantial amount of time accompanying battered women through court or welfare centers, writing letters for them, or making phone calls. As one advocate said, "You have to do a million things to get one woman help."

The Expansion of Shelter Services: Transforming the Grass Roots

After subsisting on minimal amounts of money for 6 to 18 months, most shelters concluded that government funding was imperative. Monthly pledges and foundation grants could not pay bills based on expanding staff, programs, and the larger facilities sought as shelters. New funding, though never adequate, brought many advantages to battered women's shelters. Some women could be paid regularly for their work, and staff and volunteers could be trained more effectively. Problems could be met with consistent and systematic responses. Most importantly, the shelter received external support and validation. Police, judges, and welfare workers were forced to listen more carefully because shelters now asserted a reinforced claim as legitimate community institutions. It no longer seemed that doors would close at any moment. Survival carried with it the hope of building institutions that could respond credibly to the myriad of problems battered women presented.

Money, however, was not the unmixed blessing it originally seemed. A larger funding base sometimes undermined important movement principles. Shelters that chose to expand often saw themselves transformed in unpredictable, unwanted ways.

> I've seen this house go through many changes. The staff was originally all volunteer, deeply committed, and collective. At the beginning there was no money. As we got a little, I always knew how the house was run and how decisions were made.
>
> Then a director was hired who was here during the day. Lots of volunteers dropped out and now only work at night and on the weekends. We have more staff. I don't feel in control of the whole at all. I worry we are becoming another social service agency. We have debts for rehabilitation and we're tied to needing money.

This advocate details changes in the division of labor and in resident-staff interactions that are repeated throughout the United States in those programs that have expanded.

> There is a split between administrative and service work. We all have separate offices, which we never had before, and work specializations.
>
> We have communication meetings for staff to deal with their feelings about their work, once a week. This is a positive development, but you also worry about forming a "professional" skills attitude. You have to remember where you came from—battering could happen to me. Now we have formalized case reviews. In some ways it is useful, because you pay attention to individual women and staff perceptions of each woman are examined. It's good because personal feelings get involved all the time. All of us are racist, judge other people, and sometimes treat them poorly. A more formal process can control gossip and help you understand yourself. But it can also create distance between you and the residents.

Increased specialization transformed more than organizational structure.

In approaching funders and community groups, activists encountered charitable and professional values that emphasized helping the "needy" and often unwittingly assigned to women the permanent status of helpless "victim." The pervasive influence of psychological explanations for social problems was seen as funding agency after funding agency defined battered women as a mental health issue.

As funding increased, even the most politically sophisticated programs noted subtle changes in their treatment of women residents. For example, when individual shelters fought for and won welfare or Title XX reimbursements, they also had to fill out forms and account for "units of client services." Many of these "units" are credited according to the individual counseling and advocacy sessions provided. As a result, worker after worker has commented that she slowly and unconsciously started to call battered women "clients." Greater attention was paid to the individual woman's counseling needs and less to group sharing, peer support, and teaching battered women to advocate for one another.

The Expansion of Shelter Services: The Effects of Professionalization

The possibility of government funding encouraged many traditional social service agencies to start programs for battered women. In shelters controlled by these agencies, feminism plays no stated part, although its influence is felt programmatically and through individual feminists who may join the staff. Battered women's plight is recognized as serious, even if "clients" are defined solely as recipients of services. The need for advocacy and social change, especially to facilitate women's leaving or ending violent relationships, is acknowledged, although sometimes minimized. Women's weaknesses, as well as their strengths, are carefully scrutinized. These shelters often provide decent counseling, advocacy, and group supports, but place heavy emphasis on the need for individual therapy with professional counselors. Frequently, male responsibility for violence is relegated to secondary importance while a woman's personality takes center stage as the desired focus for change.

Feminist and grass roots activists have offered persistent criticism of professionals. At the start of the movement, professional arrogance and indifference toward battered women helped mold the antiprofessional biases still operating in some programs. Feminists were the first to analyze violence against women as part of the power dynamic operating between men and women in a sexist society. By their persistence, feminist and grass roots activists forced the words "battered women" into public consciousness and created new institutions. Professionals then moved in to claim violence as a mental health or criminal justice problem. The political analysis disappeared, changed, or was considered beyond the scope of professional concern.

While professionals ignored or refuted a feminist political analysis, they depended heavily on feminists' skills and information. Feminist activists had come to understand what battered women needed, and sometimes professionals used that information to start programs and gain funding without ever acknowledging its source. As professionals established "family violence" as their realm of expertise, their feminist colleagues were discredited as "not professional enough" and labeled irrelevant.

The emphasis on professionalism has created several simultaneous, contradictory tasks for the feminist battered women's movement. Shelters had to lay their claims to expertise in order to ward off competition from more traditional agencies, and obtain funding. This expertise, however, had to be defined as nonprofessional if shelters wanted to avoid having standards placed upon them that would alter egalitarian relationships with battered women and destroy a democratic movement for social change. Adding more difficulties, funding agencies, boards, and some staff advocated or demanded the hiring of professional directors or counseling staff in order to acquire the expertise needed to survive and help battered women. To provide services, staff needed to accrue and teach advocacy, counseling, and legal skills. As time went on, the directors of most battered women's programs were hired from the ranks of the legal and social work professions, and movement leadership became increasingly professional. Sometimes, imperceptibly, staff lost their connection to a movement in the process of learning their complicated jobs and becoming experts.

Within the feminist movement, there is disagreement over the role of professionals. Some worry, realistically, that without professionally degreed staff, their agencies will suffer in grant competition. On a personal level, professional status can provide dignity to the worker as well as a sense of mastery and specialized skills. Although some middle class feminists rebuff the hierarchical privileges and higher salaries attached to professionalism, working class women often want and need the skills, money, and control over their work that professional status can offer. For these women, middle class ambivalence toward professionalism is confusing. In third world neighborhoods, some professionals have played a protective role, bringing to the community urgently needed information. Yet professional status permits and encourages domination, just as it allows those who reject such privileges to share skills within an oppressed group.

Although shelters themselves testify and contribute to political and material changes in women's lives, many feminist activists want more than the service projects professionals hope to create. Grass roots activists assert that a movement is necessary to end violence against women, to keep the energy and anger of shelters alive, and to remind the government and men that a collective power is watching. Shelters that define themselves as part of a movement, however, lament that they have spent most of their time providing services and maintaining buildings and organizations. The need to make more demands on the system disappears, evaporating in the daily grind. However, the vision and the movement, defined as women helping women and organizing to stop violence, remain emotionally and politically primary for many shelters.

Those who prefer not to identify with a movement say that "quality" service should be the only goal. Helping means giving the best possible care to each woman using the shelter, and bears no connection to building a women's movement. As one professional said,

> Politics are messy and unnecessary. In fact, they might hurt us as we try to reach our goals. We might unite to share skills, find more resources, and reform institutions and laws to enhance the quality of battered women's lives, but we are not part of a women's liberation movement.

The need for a radical challenge to the current structured power relations between the sexes, races, or classes is usually minimized.

Those who want to build a movement see the necessity of challenging the status quo and reordering a society in which women currently lack power and control over their lives. Shelters that want to build a movement define themselves:

> We as women all face a common oppression. Millions of women are beaten, and we must keep organizing to help them; our shelter only holds thirty people at once; it is not enough. The only way to change the system is to build a strong women's movement that will organize and demand change. Battered women only exist today as a social category because

women united. We must continue this work or we will lose wh
won. Caring services are part of our vision, but providing less aı
women organize themselves is the most effective long-range cha
women's social subordination.

These differences between professionals and feminist activists continue today. In fact, they grow increasingly complicated as more
professionally trained women join the movement at the same time that
more battered women try to assume power within it. The struggles inside
the shelter movement also mirror the changes in the political climate.
During the 1980s, a more reactionary federal government has been
intent on restoring the traditional, male-dominated family, slashing
social welfare programs, and redistributing wealth upwardly. The
backlash against women, evident in this agenda, has again emboldened
those eager to attack feminist organizing and political programs. The
outcome is still unclear.

Many feminists and professionals who oppose this conservative
agenda have united to demand more for battered women and their
children. This includes greater funding for shelters and services,
increased welfare grants, jobs, more social services, and day care.
Feminists and professionals have lobbied for laws that have extended
police and judicial powers to protect abused women and stop the
assailants' violence.

Political disagreements have been effectively put aside so that
battered women can gain the resources and rights they are entitled to.
These effective coalition-building efforts should continue. At the same
time, feminists, battered women, and professionals need to begin a
dialogue that answers critical questions: How can professionals within
institutions like hospitals and mental health centers act to empower
battered women? What social policies and practices do battered women,
as a group, want? What interventions do they define as dangerous or
harmful?

Around the country, battered women are uniting in task forces,
frequently connected to statewide battered women's coalitions. These
task forces give abused women a structure through which they gain
support and the courage to make demands upon shelters and community
institutions. By uniting, battered women can no longer be tokenized;
they are reaching for power with which to transform their lives
individually and collectively. Their organized presence suggests that
they will demand accountability from shelters and community organiza-

tions that now claim to speak for battered women. It is the task of professionals and feminists alike to listen to those voices, share power, and place battered women's services in the hands of battered women.

Research on Wife Abuse: Growth of Academic Analysis

In the last several years, the backlash against feminism has also produced a resurgence of social theories that blame battered women for the abuse they endure or assert that gender is irrelevant to the study of family violence and to the design of intervention strategies. In 1986, at the same time that Drs. Straus and Gelles reported the findings from their newest survey announcing women to be as violent as men, a committee of the American Psychiatric Association attempted to classify battered women as masochistic personalities. In many recent publications, like Jeanne Deschner's *The Hitting Habit: Anger Control for Battering Couples* (1984), there are no clear-cut victims and assailants, only violent couples in need of psychotherapeutic transformation.

Battered women's closest ally, the shelter movement, is finding it very difficult to counter these arguments. Although shelters call upon their extensive experience to support battered women, they produce and can rely upon little research that challenges theories of victim passivity and provocation. The shelter movement has never had the time or money to conduct its own research, documenting how battered women are active on their own behalf, how they creatively avoid and survive the violence, and the conditions under which they ultimately leave. Few researchers have documented the complex steps through which women pass as they make positive changes in their lives. Nor do we know enough about those interventions that stop assailants and those that prevent further violence. The shelter movement has found most academic researchers in the field of family violence to be indifferent, if not hostile, to its posing these questions.

Researchers frequently fall into the trap of counting up the number of times that he hits her and she hits him and then assert that they have an analysis. When they do this, they hide the power relationship that battering reveals. Despite, or perhaps because of, their "sophisticated" methods, researchers rarely tap feminist practice for the insights it brings.

Differences over research priorities and ideology are only two troubling areas that researchers and battered women's activists must explore together. Ethics is a third. Reports from around the country leave many grass roots activists reluctant to cooperate with researchers. According to interviews with movement activists, promises of confidentiality and guarantees of safety have been broken by researchers conducting interviews with abused women. Too often, interview subjects have not been paid for their participation in studies even when payment was promised. Commitments to share or review findings have not materialized. Research studies with potentially significant impact on police and court practice have begun without any discussion with battered women's advocates who have been negotiating for social change with these systems for years.

In spite of these serious difficulties, many activists are eager to cooperate with researchers. The staff of shelters want to know about the effects of their work upon battered women and their children. Service providers care deeply about stopping and preventing violence and they want to evaluate the strategies they have been using to assist individuals and change institutions.

Shelters can help researchers formulate sophisticated and intellectually rich questions. Researchers, however, must be willing to acknowledge that battered women and their advocates are experts about violence. This can occur in many ways: research proposals can be shared and discussed in their formative stages; they can be evaluated with battered women to ensure subject confidentiality and safety and to explore the potential impact of the findings. Researchers can hold themselves accountable to battered women and shelters by developing clear statements about the purpose of their work and delineating the ways in which they will disseminate and use their findings. They can list, in writing, the review processes through which they will engage in dialogue with the battered women's movement about the interpretation of their data. They can include and defer to activists in any public hearings in which research findings are turned into social policy recommendations. They can strategize with activists long in advance of any of these meetings and agree to withhold or revise recommendations activists define as harmful or premature.

Researchers and grass roots activists have much to offer each other if trust can be built between them. Those researchers who have already won the confidence of the battered women's movement can help their colleagues by detailing the history of their efforts. The National

Coalition Against Domestic Violence and state coalitions of battered-women's services can also aid this endeavor by developing model contracts that their members or individual battered women use with local researchers. Battered women's organizations can also set up committees that review and monitor all requests from researchers.

These recommendations are offered in an attempt to move beyond the outworn accusations that activists are all anti-intellectual and researchers all opportunists. Neither is true, but both groups must search for means to minimize the power that researchers and writers wield over activists. It is clear that a great deal has been accomplished in the last decade by activists, professionals, and researchers. But, a great deal is not enough, given the magnitude of the problem. We must build bridges based on mutual trust and respect so that battered women, and all women, can be empowered.

REFERENCES

Deschner, J. (1984). *The hitting habit: Anger control for battering couples*. New York: Free Press.

Schechter, S. (1982). *Women and male violence: The visions and struggles of the battered women's movement*. Boston: South End.

Straus, M. A., & Gelles, R. J. (1986). Societal change and change in family violence from 1975 to 1985 as revealed by two national surveys. *Journal of Marriage and the Family*, *48*(3), 465-479.

About the Contributors

David Adams, M.Ed., is currently completing a doctoral degree in counseling psychology at Northwestern University. He is cofounder and clinical director of EMERGE: A Men's Counseling Service on Domestic Violence, in Boston—one of the first programs in the nation to provide specialized counseling and education to violent husbands. He has provided consultation and training on domestic violence interventions to many other agencies around the country, has been a featured speaker at many conferences, and has published articles about counseling the battering man.

Michelle Arbitell is currently working on a Doctor of Psychology (Psy.D) in clinical psychology at Indiana University of Pennsylvania and is a predoctoral intern at Geisinger Medical Center in Danville, Pennsylvania. Her interest in spouse abuse is an outgrowth of her clinical experiences in working with women who have relationships with emotionally and physically abusive partners.

Michele Bograd, coeditor of this volume, received her Ph.D. in human development from the University of Chicago in 1983. Her dissertation explored how abusive men, battered women, and nonviolent men and women perceived, defined, and evaluated acts of physical force between intimate partners. She is a psychologist in private practice in Cambridge, Massachusetts; a faculty member and research associate at the Kantor Family Institute; and a faculty member at the Family Institute of Cambridge. After providing an analysis of the efficacy of family therapy theory and interventions with battered women and their partners, she has broadened her focus to examine the relationship of gender and family therapy. She has published many articles and presented at numerous local and national conferences on gender, violence, and family therapy.

Lee H. Bowker is currently provost and vice president of Augustana College in Sioux Falls, South Dakota. He received his Ph.D. in Sociology from Washington State University, has served on the faculties of Whitman College, University of Wisconsin-Milwaukee, and was Dean of the Graduate School at Indiana University of Pennsylvania. He has published dozens of articles and numerous books in a wide range of fields. His recent contributions to the study of wife abuse are two books entitled *Ending the Violence* (Learning Publications) and *Beating Wife-Beating* (D.C. Heath).

Rebecca Emerson Dobash and **Russell P. Dobash** are members of the Department of Sociology at the University of Stirling in Scotland. They have conducted extensive research on violence against women and have published widely on various aspects of the problem. Their major publication is *Violence Against Wives: A Case Against the Patriarchy* (Free Press). They are completing *Women, Violence and Social Change in Britain and the United States* (Routledge & Kegan Paul), a cross-national comparison of the battered-women's movement and the state response to violence against women. Also, they are currently working with Scottish Women's Aid on a reeducation program for men who assault their partners. Other research interests include the imprisonment of women and men, financial consequences of divorce, and young people and the criminal justice system. *The Imprisonment of Women,* with Sue Gutteridge (Basil Blackwell), is their latest book.

Dee L. R. Graham, is Associate Professor of Psychology and a member of the Women's Studies' faculty at the University of Cincinnati, Cincinnati, Ohio. She received her Ph.D. in developmental psycho-biology at the George Peabody College for Teachers in Nashville, Tennessee. Recently, she has explored the usefulness of psychological dynamics underlying the Stockholm Syndrome in order to aid in her understanding of why battered women bond with their abusers, and why women bond with men generally.

Barbara Hart is an activist, organizer, and lawyer who works with the Pennsylvania Coalition Against Domestic Violence and the Leadership Institute for Women. She is the author of a recent book on designing and evaluating treatment programs for men who batter, *Safety for Women: Monitoring Batterers Programs.* She is currently promoting greater collaboration between activists and academics in conducting research on behalf of battered women. She is also working with activists and lawyers advocating for battered women who have killed their batterers or who have been coerced into committing crimes by their assailants. She is a consultant with the National Coalition Against Domestic Violence on issues of public policy.

Lee Ann Hoff holds a Ph.D. in anthropology and medical sociology from Boston University and a master's degree in psychiatric mental health nursing. In addition to her research with battered women, she is the author of the award-winning book *People in Crisis: Understanding and Helping,* and *Programs for People in Crisis: A Guide for Educators, Administrators, and Clinical Trainers* (1987), and related publications. She is an Associate Professor at Northeastern University in Boston, where she directs a Life Crisis Institute and does research and teaches in the areas of life crises, victimology, and women's health. She also works as a volunteer in victim programs and is active in women's health and peace movements.

Liz Kelly is a feminist researcher and activist. She was a cofounder of a refuge for battered women, rape crisis group and women's center, and has been active in a number of national campaigns and networks around sexual violence in Britain. She is currently working to effect policy changes that reflect women's needs and experience. She is developing a prevention curriculum for schools concerning forms of sexual violence. A book based on her doctoral research, *Surviving Sexual Violence,* will be published by Polity Press. She is employed as a part-time Lecturer in Sociology at Essex University and also teaches adult education women's studies classes.

Demie Kurz is a sociologist who does research at the Philadelphia Health Management Corp., a nonprofit health related policy institute, teaches the sociology of gender at the University of Pennsylvania and has codirected several research and training projects in woman abuse. She and her colleagues, along with the advisory board of the Battered Women's Training Project, are currently developing strategies for institutionalizing advocacy programs for battered women in the health care system.

J. Richard McFerron is Director of Academic Computing Services at Indiana University of Pennsylvania. He holds undergraduate degrees in mathematics and education and an MBA from Indiana University of Pennsylvania. His publications on family violence are based primarily on data acquired from the state of Texas reporting shelter intake questionnaires and include a recent article in *Victimology* titled "The Helpseeking Behavior of Battered Women: A Preliminary Analysis of 6000 Shelter Intake Interviews."

Ellen Pence is a feminist activist who has been involved in a range of programs on battering. She is currently Training and Special Projects Coordinator with Minnesota Program Development, Inc. She was also Director of State Programs for Battered Women with the Minnesota Department of Corrections. She has written several articles and numerous handbooks on responses to domestic violence. She has also produced a number of films and educational slide shows on battered women.

James Ptacek has worked with EMERGE, Boston men's counseling service on domestic violence, since 1981. He received his master's degree in sociology from the University of New Hampshire and is now completing a doctorate in sociology at Brandeis University, with a focus on the family, social psychology, and social theory. His current research concerns the effects of institutional interventions on men who batter, and the limitations of the "addiction" model when applied to explanations of violence against women.

Edna Rawlings is Professor of Psychology and a senior staff member of the Psychological Services Center of the University of Cincinnati, Cincinnati, Ohio. She received her Ph.D. in clinical psychology from the University of Wisconsin—Madison. She is a feminist therapist and coauthor of *Psychotherapy for Women—Treatment Toward Equality.*

Nelly Rimini was born in the U.S.S.R., raised in Israel, and received a master's degree in counseling/development psychology from Ohio State University. Currently, she is Counseling Coordinator at Women Helping Women—Hamilton County Women's Crisis Center in Cincinnati, Ohio. She is an active member of the Ohio Coalition on Sexual Assault, the Ohio Victim Witness Association, and the Ohio Coalition on Domestic Violence (ACTION). On the local level, she is involved with the Domestic Violence Coalition, the Hamilton County Network for Prevention of Child Sexual Abuse, and the Sexual Assault Care Network. Previously, she coordinated therapeutic intervention at a battered-women's shelter.

Lynne Bravo Rosewater, Ph.D., is a licensed psychologist in private practice in Cleveland, Ohio. She is one of the founding members and currently chairs the National Feminist Therapy Institute. As a national expert on both domestic violence and the Minnesota Multiphasic Personality Inventory (MMPI) profile for battered women, she prepares personality assessments of battered women who have killed their batterers for use in court. She is the author of *Changing Through Therapy,* coeditor of *Handbook of Feminist Therapy: Women's Issues in Psychotherapy,* and has contributed numerous chapters for other books on feminist therapy and test interpretation.

Daniel G. Saunders is Assistant Scientist, University of Wisconsin—Madison, Department of Psychiatry, and Program Evaluator of the Program to Prevent Woman Abuse, Family Service, in Madison. He began his work in the area of domestic violence in the mid 1970s as a counselor and activist, and during that time helped to develop services for and counseled battered women and their partners. He was a postdoctoral research fellow at the Family Violence Research Program of the University of New Hampshire and has published a number of articles on the treatment of men who batter, studies on the police response to battered women, and the development of a measure of attitudes about woman abuse.

Susan Schechter is the author of *Women and Male Violence: The Visions and Struggles of the Battered Women's Movement.* She is currently a consultant to the Massachusetts Coalition of Battered Women Service Groups, and to the AWAKE (Advocacy for Women and Kids) Project at Children's Hospital in Boston. She lectures at domestic violence conferences around the country and consults with battered women's shelters and coalitions. She is also a program associate at the Stone Center, Wellesley College. She has just completed a handbook for the National Coalition Against Domestic Violence entitled Guidelines for Mental Health Practitioners in Domestic Violence Cases. She is a former associate of the Leadership Institute for Women and former director of the Women's Education Institute.

Melanie Shepard is an Assistant Professor of Social Work at the University of Minnesota, Duluth. She completed her Ph.D. at the University of Minnesota, Minneapolis, and a master's degree in social work at the University of Wisconsin, Madison. She has conducted research and been a facilitator for men's education groups at the Domestic Abuse Intervention Project. She has practiced as a social worker in mental health and child welfare settings.

Elizabeth A. Stanko is Associate Professor of Sociology at Clark University in Worcester, Massachusetts. She is a feminist activist and has brought this perspective to bear on the field of criminology. She has published numerous articles and two books: *Judge, Lawyer, Victim, Thief: Women, Gender Roles, and Criminal Justice* (with N.H. Rafter, Northeastern University Press) and *Intimate Intrusions: Women's Experience of Male Violence* (Routledge & Kegan Paul).

Evan Stark received his Ph.D. from SUNY—Binghamton. He is currently a Henry Rutgers Research Fellow in the Graduate Department of Public Administration and Department of Sociology at Rutgers University, New Brunswick, New Jersey. He has written extensively on the issue of battering and institutional response. He is the author of *Women Battering: Survivors and Their Assailants—A Source Book,* to be published by Garland Press.

Kersti Yllö, coeditor of this volume, is currently Associate Professor of Sociology and Coordinator of the Gender-Balanced Curriculum Project at Wheaton College, Norton, Massachusetts. She received her Ph.D. in sociology from the University of New Hampshire, where she also held a postdoctoral fellowship at the Family Violence Research Program. She has published articles on cohabitation, the status of women and wife abuse, and is coauthor, with D. Finkelhor, of *License to Rape: Sexual Abuse of Wives* (Free Press).